AF644315

Death, Time and the Other

Ethics at the Limit of Metaphysics

Death, Time and the Other

Ethics at the Limit of Metaphysics

Saitya Brata Das

AAKAR

DEATH, TIME AND THE OTHER:
Ethics at the Limit of Metaphysics
Saitya Brata Das

First Published 2017

ISBN 978-93-5002-495-9 (Pb)

The publication of this book financially benefits from the University Grants Commission under the Special Assistance Programme (SAP) that is granted to the Centre for English Studies, Jawaharlal Nehru University.

Published by
AAKAR BOOKS
28 E Pocket IV, Mayur Vihar Phase I, Delhi 110 091
Phones : 011 2279 5505, 2279 5641
aakarbooks@gmail.com; www.aakarbooks.com

Designed by
Limited Colors, Delhi 110 092

Printed at
Saurabh Printers Pvt. Ltd., Greater Noida

For Franson Manjali

Contents

Acknowledgements

This work is the revised doctoral thesis submitted at Jawaharlal Nehru University in 2004. Written more than one and half a decades ago, it bears the mark of its time, as does everything else of human creation. There are a few things I said there that I now disagree with, and some I will have to modify in order for me to be able to say the same. This is why I have not made any substantial modifications. What I have done is nothing more than making some "corrections", largely "grammatical".

An earlier draft of "The Experience of the Limit-II" was published as "The Experience of the Limit: Nietzsche's Abyssal Experience of the Eternal Return", in Franson Manjali, ed. *Nietzsche: Philologist, Philosopher and Cultural Critic* (New Delhi: Allied Publishers, 2006), pp. 71-81. I would like to thank the publisher for permitting me to republish the essay. I acknowledge a generous grant received under the "Special Assistant Programme" of The United Grants Commission which made publication of this thesis possible. As always, "thanks" goes to Franson Manjali of Jawaharlal Nehru University for guiding this work, and to Gerard Bensussan of Strasbourg University, France, for extremely valuable suggestions and comments.

Preface

It was indeed a daring moment for a young student of English literature to embark on a research project in philosophy nearly 15 years ago. Saitya Brata Das was one of a bright batch of students who finished their Master's in the first semester of the year 2000. By a happy conjunction, I had returned after a stint as a Research Fellow at Indian Institute of Advanced Study, Shimla, with a rather heavy baggage of (mainly photocopied) books on contemporary themes in continental philosophy. Saitya virtually grabbed them all, read most of the books cover-to-cover, sentence by highlighted sentence, to acquire a philosophical formation in a short period of time. By the time he had embarked on writing his doctoral thesis, he was holding tightly to his chest, works by a number of great philosophers, Nietzsche, Heidegger, Lévinas, Blanchot, Benjamin and Derrida, etc. He had imbibed much of their precious thoughts, and even began speaking and writing like them.

This was indeed a welcome event for many of us in the University: the dawn of philosophy movement that began to expand outside the confines of the philosophy department, which in any case was quite nascent. Initially, it was the literary, and strictly poetic themes that seemed have attracted Saitya, still only a budding philosopher. Hölderlin, Nietzsche and Benjamin stood out in his order of preferences.

Death, Time and the Other are concerns around which Saitya's research has revolved in the last 15years. Of course, we know that each philosopher mentioned here has a different position on death. While Nietzsche was a philosopher of life, it was Heidegger who brought death to the philosophical centre-stage in our times. The former abhorred any mortification of life, whether it is religious-spiritual, scientific or philosophical. For the latter, death was like a sort of fulcrum on which turns the possibility of authentic existential and therefore implicitly political future. He takes it for granted that death is forbidding for every adult human, and therefore the possibility or the fear of encounter with death is potentially purifying for the self. It is as if life can remain somehow insulated from death, both before and after the retreat towards an existential authenticity.

It is this insularity of life of self as well as the existence of life that Lévinas and Blanchot questioned and rejected with regard to Heidegger. Nazism, to which Heidegger was a known accomplice, even if only temporarily, has exploded this insularity of life in relation to death. Against Heidegger, in the aftermath of the racism and the bloody Second World War that Europe witnessed, it was asserted that the boundary line between life and death cannot be determined in an essential and facile way. And therefore, between the existence of the self and that of the Other. Life merges into death, just as self can only pass into the Other. Being of the self or of anything else cannot exist as a totality, insulated from the Other, from the Otherwise than being, in any comprehensible way. Totality or totalization is possible only when insulating boundaries are created, whether in space, or even more, in time. That is, only by the human ruse, or perhaps the cunning of selfish reason. It is when the boundedness of space or time, or of language is created, that there comes into existence, totality or totalitarianism. Lévinas and Blanchot sought to see existence beyond the chronic closure. It is this exit from chronic existence to the diachronic time or the time of the other that Lévinas identifies as ethics, and ethics therefore pre-exists existence that Heidegger valorizes in his ontological-temporal investigation. Blanchot on the other hand, chooses to call (what is for him) the even more fundamental pre-existential language, writing or literature. The task of literature or writing is not to create significance in language, but to reach on to the space that is both anterior and exterior to the language that has already been formed in any specific milieu, local or global. And, this is also the task of philosophy.

Saitya was quick to discover these fine and subtle points and to deftly advance further. That is what lead him discover eventually political theology, especially in and through the work of the German philosopher Schelling. He discovered, and his more recent publication on Schelling attests to this, that no act can be as political as the exiting from a given God or the closure or religion as is the case with Christianity in its modern realizations. In this discovery, it is not Nietzsche alone that he is informed by, but rather the theologically-rooted writings of Kierkegaard, Rosenzweig, Benjamin, Derrida and others in a constellation of political theology. But that's where his unrelenting and indomitable spirit of philosophical enquiry has kept him going...

Franson Manjali

Introduction

The task of thinking at the limit of philosophy

What is it to think at the limit of philosophy? What thought of ethics, understood as infinite responsibility to the other, is possible beyond the closure of any discourses that claim totality, whether in the name of Being, or Subject? Such questions concern us in this work. We attempt to interrogate the philosophical discourse that claims to be a total discourse, or absolute philosophy; in a more specific manner, it is a certain relation to Hegelian dialectical-historical philosophy that is at stake here, so as to open up such philosophical thinking of totality to a wholly other thinking that cannot be thought *within* such a philosophical discourse of totality. We shall argue that such ethical responsibility to the other cannot be thought (or, is rather fore-closed) in dialectical-historical philosophy of immanence. While interrogating such a discourse of immanence, the task of thinking is to open up to the ethical transcendence of the Other. In a certain Lévinasian manner, we shall examine Hegelian philosophy of dialectical-historical, its pre-suppositions and assumptions, the conclusions it attempts to reach, its 'blind spots' or fault-lines, its caesura or interval, or its outside so that an ethical thought can rouse such a philosophical discourse from its dream of unconditional truth.

If such a philosophical discourse aspires for totality in the name of Being or Subject, it thinks—for Hegelian philosophy is also a philosophy of thinking the other—the other only to bring the other back into its fold of self-consciousness so as to constitute the totality in the name of the Subject. This Subject that realizes the absolute via its very othering is always determined in the dominant Western metaphysics from Plato to Hegel as presence, as Sense or signification. Variously named as speculative ontology or ontology of presence, this 'metaphysics of presence' has come to an end, exhausted itself, and at the limit of its possibility it has come to confront its impossibility to form the totality of signification. We shall examine in what sense such a philosophy of totality has exhausted itself in its utmost possibility, and in what sense thereby is it opened up to the ethical responsibility to the Other. This is to argue that this ethics of transcendence, which is also an 'ethics of finitude'—and we shall see in what sense it is so—can't be considered only as a moment of a totality, and therefore, the Other can't be incorporated so as to be subsumed within the totality of the Absolute self-presence of the Subject. The limit of this metaphysics is the end of this philosophical discourse of totality; the limit is, thus, also the manifestation par excellence of its radical finitude where it confronts its inexhaustible aporias.

It is our philosophical task at the end of such metaphysics of presence—that legitimizes itself while grounding itself in its Being—to think the other of philosophy. This study attempts to examine how the thought of this other is an ethical thought par excellence, and how the thought of difference in-itself is to be thought as irreducible to the *representation* of difference. Such a philosophical task requires an *unworking* of the *metaphysics of presence* (which we understand as speculative ontology of presence or even as philosophy of subject), to reveal in a rigorous manner the *blind spot* that eludes furtively from the sovereign gaze of a speculative eye to expose it to the very limit of its self-enclosure which it is unable to think. Such an *unworking* should be able to reveal not only how such a philosophy of subject constitutes itself its own grounding but also unworks what it traces out thereby, and reveals the limit of what it traces out, the limit that surreptitiously, furtively escapes the self-presence of the Subject. In other words, this *unworking* is a strategy of traversal, a limit-thinking that disrupts the very self-presence of Being; such unworking shows that the philosophy of the Subject cannot reach its totality of significations precisely because of its desire for totality. It thereby brings to manifestation what it cannot ground itself, and thereby bringing out what it cannot think: the differential thought of unthought, the difference–in-itself as the thought of the Other. The ethical thought of the Other is this differential thought of/at the limit of philosophy. The question of the ethical arises at the limit of philosophy when all our aspirations to ground every decision ontologically, whether in Being or meaning, are shattered, when we can no longer have any metaphysical grounding in God that hitherto has given meaning to existence. In a poem, Hölderlin names this absence of grounding as the abyss that the mortals have to reach into:

> The heavenly powers
> Cannot do all things. It is the mortals
> Who reach into the abyss? So the turn is
> With these. Long is
> The time, but the true comes into
> Its own. (Quoted by Heidegger 1975: 92)

Our post-metaphysical world can be understood as this destitute time when the old Gods have disappeared from the world, and the new Gods has not yet taken the place of the old: a time of nightfall and oblivion. Is it not that without Gods, it is the responsibility of the mortals who would have to 'reach sooner into the abyss' in order to take a turn, to understand the ethical possibilities in a Godless world when we no longer appeal to a transcendental world as the *real world* (as against a world that is an apparent one) or to *transcendental unity of apperception* as an ontological grounding of Being. Nietzsche's saying of 'the death of God' evokes such a time God's absence when we no longer appeal to *a priori* metaphysical foundation that would guarantee an infinite return of the same: there is no longer any guarantee that despite this unendurable crisis, it would bring back again into its fold the self-recovery of the self-same ground; rather, what the death of God implies precisely is the impossibility of the return of the same. It thus leaves us with an exigency—which should be considered as responsibility for the mortals—to respond all the time, with a tragic resonance which is at once liberating, to this *inexhaustible death of God*, to that emptiness which the death of God leaves us with. It is neither in order to fill this emptiness once and for all by another God, or by a human subject (for the death of God did not leave his killer intact either), nor is neither to be content to invoke, in a nostalgic manner, a time when this abyss was filled with all possible divine significations (from which the world, our all too human world, derived its significations): with the abolition of the metaphysical world, which is determined as the real world, we are not left with the apparent world either. With the abolition of the real world, the apparent world is too abolished. Nietzsche calls this sixth and last stage in his genealogy of *how the real world at last became a myth,* as the time of briefest shadow and midday (Nietzsche 1968: 40). Thus, with the abolition of the real world (from which the apparent world derived its signification), signification loses its derivative mode; without the referentiality to the real world, significations (based on a transcendental paradigm in which what is to be signified must be transcendental to what signifies) are let loose in a world which cannot be grounded either (therefore with the abolition of the real world, we abolish the apparent world too). What this implies is this: with the death of God, not only has the real world and along with it the apparent world lost its ontological grounding, but with their abolitions, even the modes of signification which somehow acts as transition between the two worlds (between the *intelligible* and *sensible*, *noumenal* and *phenomenal* world, *sign* is a strange transition whose characteristic mode of transition is understood in terms of *adaequatio* or *homoiosis*), loses its logical grounding. The death of God would, then, be at once the crisis of signification of a representational mode (based on the transcendental model), and a liberation as well (being no longer to be subsumed to the givenness of a constitutive identity through representation) of a sense 'yet to come'. Whether we still call this 'yet to come' as *signification* at all or call by another name, it is a question of an exigency, an urgency which is ethical. What the death of God leaves us with, and never ceases to leave us all the time, is this responsibility to turn again and again towards the abyss, to affirm this inexhaustible emptiness all the time. If we call this responsibility *tragic*, it is not because it's a pathos which is to be redeemed by a *cathartic recognition* but because we are given over to make ethical decisions, without God or any metaphysical foundation, when there is only undecidability: it is because what makes one ethically responsible for the Other is not (a responsibility to the Other even to the point of dying for the Other) because we all derive our significations from a common transcendental signifier (whether God or Idea), but because without any metaphysical signification that would have grounded our common world, we are left bare and naked. The Other is this bare, destitute being for whom "my" heart tears asunder. If any signification is possible which the death of God implies, it will perhaps be something like the following: responsibility to the destitute Other without any metaphysical comfort, a responsibility that is affirmed again and again by the death of God, and which the death of God affirms. But this ethical responsibility is possible only by traversing through our tragic destiny that we share together: our time of briefest shadows and mid-day: only he who has been abandoned by everything and left alone with the infinite, knows this profundity of life. As Schelling said once,

> Only he who one day has abandoned everything and has been abandoned by everything, for whom everything has capsized and who sees himself alone with the infinite, has come to the very bottom of himself and recognized all the profundities of life. This is a great step, which Plato compared to death (Quoted by Blanchot 1995: 99).

What Plato compared to death is, what Heidegger calls 'the abandonment of being by Being'. Bereft of God or any metaphysical comforts, he alone is left to recognize the profundities of life: disaster that shattered our Being, leaving only the stammering words that we share: fragments, ruins, shattering voices. These voices of disaster are our tragic thoughts: they are tragic because they expose us to a crisis, revealing thereby the finitude of human reason and the absence of any transcendental Being that would have brought redemption to the world shattered by disasters and ruins; they are tragic to the extent that they reveal to us the nature of things, exposing us to the Other whom I cannot master over by bringing back to the Subject to form a totality from which absolute significations produce themselves. This tragic exposure to the failure of a unifying, total possible significations (of the sovereign spirit), at once opens this exposed being to an infinite Other to whom one responds only in a language when all significations are shattered. Shattered are the significations that hitherto have promised us 'community', 'world' or 'meaning' and 'shared existence' ; shattered are those self-assuring mythic identities that has hitherto promised the identity of Being and thought—a promise that the Hegelian speculative logic has desired to fulfil by aspiring the closure of significations. This desire for the totality of significations, which despite their promises has proved to be despotic and cruel, reveals thereby, at the very heart of reason and unreason. What we witness in recent years—holocaust is only an empirical example—is the revelation of the work of disaster that this unreason of reason trails behind, revealing the terror of this desire for totality. Therefore, Nietzsche's saying of 'the death of God' has profound signification for us. It exposes, on the one hand, the finitude of a reason, the impossibility of grounding any significations in the name of Being, thought or the world; on the other hand, it leaves us with the task of exposing this limit itself, to think at this limit, to think the limit. Death of God is not a nihilistic thought, thought that is drowned into its own abyss from which it cannot recover itself(being lost to an infinite vicious circle) which would now affirm itself with an excessive indulgence like romantic unhappy consciousness. It is rather a thought, which implies that only by confronting nothingness of nihilism, we can go beyond nihilism. Henceforth, philosophy is left to put itself into question, to confront its limit and finitude; henceforth, thinking would confront its own limit, its abyss and groundlessness; henceforth, all concepts of identity would (that guaranteed hitherto) confront its aporias that will ceaselessly bind them to a vertigo which we sometimes call by the name, following Nietzsche, "madness". Henceforth our saying will be the saying of disaster; when everything has been said, what remains to be said is disaster itself: "Ruins of words, demise writing, faintness faintly murmuring: what remains without remains (the fragmentary)" (Ibid: 33).

Disaster is the unthought that puts philosophy into question. In what sense, so we ask, philosophy puts itself into question; in other words, what concerns the grounding of philosophy is a philosophical question par excellence, a philosophical question that reveals philosophy's own limit and finitude? Henceforth, the philosophical question will be the question of the end of philosophy. In other words, the question concerning the ethical responsibilities to the Other is the question concerning the ground of philosophy, its impossibility and its finitude. The question of ethics is the question of this limit of philosophy which philosophy itself cannot completely assimilate without an irreducible remainder. This is the task of the thinking at the limit of philosophy.

Difference and Time

Introduction

This strange discourse called 'philosophy'—that never rests on the existence of objects of thinking on the assumption of a given consciousness but rather constitutes itself as its own grounding—determines its thinking itself as its very subject of thinking, and hence, thinking its own other thereby. In other words, the subject of philosophy is none other than philosophy itself and its other. To think is to think its own limit—limit, which is other to itself, and yet, since to think this limit is to supersede this limit, hence, is thinking of itself.

To think is to think its limit. To think is to think the limit of thinking. Philosophy is nothing but this: thinking at the limit, thinking the limit. In thinking at this limit as the limit-thinking, philosophy aspires to think even the other of thinking: it's other, non-philosophy or other than philosophy. Limit is at once the barrier of thinking, the loss of the subject that thinks, the negation of itself that thinks, and yet, in thinking this negation, philosophy reinstates nothing other than itself. Philosophy is a discourse that thinks itself even in thinking its other; it maintains itself thereby even in the loss of its being, and even unto its death. To think is not only to know how to die but also, in this death, to maintain itself. Instead of an infinite death, which is a wrong infinity, philosophy is rather to think this death that reinstates itself in this death as life that is resurrected. As Hegel says,

> The self-knowing Spirit knows not only itself but also the negative of itself or its limit: to know one's limit is to know how to sacrifice oneself. This sacrifice is the externalization in which Spirit displays

> the process of its becoming Spirit in the form of free contingent happening, intuiting its pure Self as Time outside if it, and equally its Being as Space. The last becoming of Spirit, Nature, is its living immediate Becoming; Nature, the externalized Spirit, is in its existence nothing but this eternal externalization of its continuing existence and the movement which reinstates the Subject (Hegel 1998: 492).

Thinking is thinking at the limit: philosophy constitutes itself at this limit. Thinking of this limit (of thinking) thus, is the question concerning the very constitution of philosophy; it is the beginning and ground of philosophy. To use a phrase heavily loaded with metaphysical significance, it is a question concerning the genesis and structure of philosophy. Philosophy thinks at the limit, thinks this limit itself, and at this limit, grounds itself ontologically, constitutes its ground as thinking. Thinking at the limit of thinking involves thinking the other of thinking, its death and difference but yet—if thinking this limit is nothing other than maintenance of thinking itself even in its other, the maintenance of life even in death, maintenance of itself even in its sacrifice, then—thinking at this limit is nothing but thinking of its identity to itself and the maintenance of it. Thinking of difference would then be nothing but a moment of this identity; death would only be a necessary diremption of a resurrecting spirit; and the other would be a reification of the Being that thinks. The question concerning the ground of philosophy as the limit thinking is the question of this identity and difference, of Being and otherwise than Being, of essence and appearance. Philosophy grounds itself ontologically in this representative thinking of identity as the subject of philosophy whose necessary moments of difference are annulled to reify this very Subject as subject (not merely as 'substance'). Limit is the necessary thought of its own negation (or, death, or differential, or multiplicity) where the Spirit appears: Hegel's *Phenomenology of Spirit* is the story of phenomenalization of the Spirit, as to how the Spirit phenomenalizes itself. But to think this limit is to cross over this limit, and to supersede this death: the Spirit, thus, appears as finite only to be infinite! In this infinite identity of Being and thought, difference is a necessary but subsumed modality of finitude. To *think* the limit is already not to be limited; to *think* difference is already to bring difference to its infinite identity. In this identity of thinking and Being, philosophy grounds itself, constitutes itself *as such*: it constitutes itself by subsuming the other in the name of Being; it grounds itself as identity of identity and its difference; it forms a totality of significations by subsuming the differential modalities of finitude as its necessary moments; it thinks its limit only to cross over it so that the totality of system is possible.

We are, then, led to ask: can we not think difference-in-itself other than the way it is thought as the subject of philosophy, or, as the constitutive ground of philosophy in the philosophy of subject? Can we not think the limit of philosophy in such a way that it will not be a mere limit to be superseded by the thinking that thinks that limit in a representational manner, but, rather *always already* is the excess of it, or, *always already* is too destitute so that the subject that thinks cannot recuperate the other in its re-installation? Can we not think of the differential modalities of finitude appearing in a manner other than the way it has been thought in the history of metaphysics so that this finitude would not be thought any more as departure towards an infinite identity of Being and nothingness but rather as the departure towards an infinite difference of asymmetrical Being and as otherwise than Being? Can we not think the negativity in such a way so that it doesn't have to yield to the discursive knowledge of it, which ontologically grounds the very discourse of nothingness, but rather that infinitely ungrounds itself so that the totality of significations (which system aspires to constitute) infinitely remains open to the Other?

These are the questions that will be discussed in this chapter: the relevance of the question of limit as a question of identity and difference, or even better, as the question concerning the ground of philosophy. Taking Hegel's philosophy as reference wherein the history of Western Metaphysics, as Hegel himself saw it, as the history of Being reaches its highest point of gathering and its utmost possibility of accomplishment, we would like the pose the problem of closure of metaphysics itself. We would ask: in what way Hegel's Speculative ontology concerns itself with the question of identity (and difference) as the ground of the onto-theo-logical constitution of metaphysics (as history of Being)? What is the relevance of the question of limit in Hegel's speculative ontology? Does the thought of the limit is thought in Hegel's philosophy in such a way so that, instead of reinstating the representative subject that brings back into its fold the other to subsume it, rather limits the very possibility of such a philosophy of totality so that the other be thought as an ethical other par excellence, so that it remains open to what is unthought in metaphysics (namely, the difference-in-itself)? If that were so, the problem of temporality can no longer be thought as intentional thought of a phenomenological consciousness, but as transcendence to an infinite other (which, as we see, is an ethical question per-excellence!). Does in Hegel's philosophy temporality appear in such a way so that (instead of representing temporality as necessary negativity, or, as sublated mode of difference, which would secure the ontological ground of Metaphysics) it introduces the diachronic rupture to the very self-constitution of the speculative ontology? In what way can the question of time and death be thought of in such a way so that (instead of being seen as negativity of difference that would be annulled to conform to the self-identity of beyond-the-temporal Being) it would bring differential modalities of asynthetic temporalities as excess to the totality of signification? In all these questions we would deal with three themes: 1. identity, 2.difference (the question of ground is the question of identity and difference) and 3. temporality. Understood this way, this chapter should be guided by the following questions:

1. What relates the themes of temporality (death or negativity), identity and difference (as question of ground of philosophy) to each other?
2. How can these themes be thought of in such manner so that, instead of reifying a philosophy of totality that subsumes the other, it remains open to an ethical other?
3. This question of ethics (as opening to an Other) is a question of the limit of philosophy as such. We would like to ask: how the question of temporality, identity and difference is a question concerning the ground of philosophy (and its limit)? Or, to put in another way, in what way can the themes of temporality, difference and identity may be thought that, instead of grounding ontologically a philosophical discourse of totality, limits the very possibility of such grounding?

We would attempt an exposition of Hegel's speculative ontology to understand how Hegel responded to the questions of identity, difference and temporality, the questions concerning the ground of philosophy and its limits, the questions of ethical responsibilities at the limit of the philosophy of totality. We would also examine how Heidegger's reading of Hegel at once shows us the possibility of thinking beyond the Hegelian metaphysics; and we will examine how at the same time, it makes demands on us to think beyond Heidegger's thought of unthought itself.

Philosophy and non-philosophy

This philosophical question is the very constitutive of the philosophical discourse itself: the question of genesis and structure of itself that aspires to ground its possibility on an immanent ground. The question of the beginning of philosophy, thus, becomes a question for a philosophy of beginning. Philosophy that seeks to ground itself ontologically must ask itself: where lies the beginning of philosophy? In this very questioning, the possibility of its beginning is already implied. The question of the beginning of philosophy becomes a question of the ground of philosophy, its limit and its structure. Therefore one asks the question of the beginning of philosophy in this way: what concerns the ground of philosophy, or, how philosophy constitutes its own grounding in such a way that therein lies its beginning? Whether it is Kant's manner of asking the possibility of metaphysics (what is the *condition of possibility of knowledge*, or, to express it in another way: how *synthetic a priori principle* is possible?) or Descartes' meditations on first philosophy, or Parmenides' doctrine of the identity of Being and Thought, philosophy always asks the possible beginning of a philosophical discourse that has immanent grounding on an ontological principle. Here I would argue, with special reference to Hegel's speculative ontology, that Western metaphysics as a discourse of Being from Plato to Hegel via Descartes, determines its genesis and structure, its ground and limit on an ontological principle of the identity of Being and Thought where this identity principle is thought in terms of *presence*. Thus, the question of the genesis and structure of a first philosophy—in other words, the determination of its ground and limit on an ontological principle—is a question of identity and difference: of Being and nothingness, Being and its other. The immanent constitution of such discourse of Being on an ontological principle is seen in that it constitutes/grounds itself as ontology while the principle that grounds the synthetic relation between Being and its nothingness is not exterior to what the principle relates.

The identity between Being and Thought: the genesis and ground of philosophy is this ontological principle of identity. It is this principle which constitutes the very possibility of philosophy as such. Its very possibility lies in the very nature of identity as *possibility*: difference is determined *ad-privatum* as what *is not*, is not possible. The possibility of the ground of philosophy lies in determining the principle of identity as *possibility* where difference is something either to be excluded, or, is included as an immanent moment of identity. Though difference is seen as impossible in classical philosophy—because difference cannot ground itself ontologically—the recognition of the unavoidability of aporia that any ontologically grounded philosophy of identity carries within itself (the aporias of difference as the negativity of any possible philosophy) leads such ontological discourse, as in the case of Hegel, to the representation of difference as conceptual difference rather than *difference-in-itself*. Difference needs to be accounted (this is what Hegel's philosophy recognized for the first time, in an explicit manner) but this cognition of difference reduces *difference as difference* to the representation of difference as contradiction (difference as negativity) in such a way that identity would pass into difference that again would be recuperated or sublated: this means that difference would be conceived only *in sight of* a recuperable identity. The whole force of Gilles Deleuze's attempt to think *difference as difference* (which is irreducible to any representation of difference) lays in its opening of an excess that eludes any grasp of the philosophy of identity. Therein lies the limit of philosophy, its impossibility to constitute its beginning and its ground once and forever on an ontological principle of identity, its impossibility to achieve the full satisfaction of forming a totality of signification in the name of presence. Understood this way, this chapter should be able to show that the philosophical discourse of totality cannot avoid the aporias that unrepresentable difference brings into it, and therefore never achieves its totality. In other words, the philosophy of identity cannot think difference-in-itself without reducing difference to the self-presence of the same. This is what we would like to call *the limit of philosophy*. But this idea of limit is to be understood in a different way than what Hegel meant by limit as the recuperable limit of the negative.

Thus, we see that from Descartes to Hegel, or even back to Parmenides, the grounding of philosophy is always thought as the thought of identity, thought as identity in grounding itself. Thought grounds itself as identity—in presenting itself to itself—and in this presenting its presence, presenting itself as presence, it conceives as grounding that which is to be grounded. In other words, in grounding, the ground shows itself as presence. But in thinking this self-presence of ground as identity, philosophy runs against its own grain, because it inevitably comes against the question that needs to be accounted: is it not that what is to be grounded has to be other than what is grounding? In other words, philosophy that thinks its ground in the name of the principle of identity (of what is to be grounded and what ground itself is) needs, in a necessary order to account for its grounding, to account what is other than identity, that that is: difference. But the paradox is that—paradox that philosophy cannot remedy without recalling the infinity of difference—this exigency of difference, or, the other that should be able to reinstate its identity, threatens, at the very moment of its possibility of accounting (thus possible re-instatement of its ground) its *ground* as possible or ground as *possible,* for that matter would ceaselessly turn back against itself: grounding would unground itself since difference infinitely brings its *differance* between what is to be grounded and the ground itself, bringing thereby rupture or a delay of temporality into the thought of identity. There already would have been involved delay of temporality, or, difference of interruption between what is to be grounded *and* the ground itself (because identity thinking needs difference to be accounted so as to be what it *is*, identity itself as this *is*) and thereby making impossible thinking to be adequate to its thinking: ground becomes impossible to be adequate to itself! Therefore, philosophy of identity would come against this question: what if, what is to be grounded has to be different from what is grounding in order to be grounding at all (at the same time, precisely because of this exigency of difference, what is to be grounded will forever other than what is grounding, the excess of grounding)? This is the problem which is defined as problem-at-hand to be resolved when the question of grounding is being posed, to respond all the time, to that excess of philosophy which—we shall call this excess by various names: non-philosophy or philosophy's other—ruins the very project of total signification; it prevents the *adaequatio* of subject and object (inasmuch as it is seen as the project of philosophy) because the exigency of difference (that vertigo of the madness of reason, that excess non-being) makes impossible to achieve the closure of signification once and for all. Whatever desires the closure of signification, and to achieve the full satisfaction of its desire, nevertheless remains unsatisfied. The Hegelian philosophy can be seen as responding to remedy this aporia mentioned above: how to think difference in such a way so that difference would reinstate identity of ground and to be grounded rather than bringing forever unbridgeable rupture? How to think time that, instead of introducing interruption or delay between what is to be thought and thought that is thinking, precisely because of this interruption, would bring together thought to be thought and thought thinking itself? How to think the other than itself in such a way that would account not only this other but also, precisely because of the accounting this other, would bring itself to itself, and thus, securing its ground? Could Hegel's philosophy succeed thinking *difference as difference* thereby (thus thinking other as other, more infinitely otherwise than Being or Essence)? Possibly not! It is precisely because Hegel couldn't not think difference otherwise than in relation to ground which is already determined as identity: difference would remain unthought even in Hegelian philosophy.

This also means that philosophy cannot avoid its repeated contact with philosophy's other, or non-philosophy, precisely because of the very difference: because of this exigency of difference, philosophy carries within itself the traces of difference itself: that element of sensuousness and materiality which cannot be totally sublated into its universality, that very event of splitting that remains un-sublated; this so, not because beyond its Being a non-being would constitute its own speculative categories of Being, but because it cannot maintain itself as such. Therefore, saying always carries within itself what is unsaid (which yet does not belong to it) infinitely postponing the identity of

Being and Thought thereby, and engendering unaccountable difference, non-negative, unsublatable excess of Being.

This chapter attempts to show how difference-in-itself remains unaccountable in the philosophy of the same. Reading Hegel's *Logic,* I would argue that in Hegel's philosophy the demand for accounting difference led him to determine and represent difference-in-itself as contradiction so that difference in its sublated form can be conformed to make *possible* the identity of Being and Thought. What eluded, thereby, is difference-in-itself: what is supposed to make possible the achievement of absolute knowledge, makes its satisfaction forever inadequate to its desire (*eros*) so that absolute knowledge remains, because of the unaccountable remnant, more or less than absolute knowledge but never identical with itself. The incessant demand for philosophy to account its other or its difference to achieve a totality of signification is also the same incessant demand to account for the very temporality which constitutes difference-in-itself and wherein the Absolute appears. The demand for accounting difference is the demand to account for the very process, the very movement, the very time of accounting difference because absolute knowledge, to be absolute, not only has to know difference but also the knowing of its very movement of accounting difference as possible simultaneity of various moments of time. But this *ad-infinitum* of knowing, the very knowing followed by other possible knowing which again needs to be accounted, is something that makes it impossible to reach absolute knowledge once and for all. The totality of knowing difference remains to be accounted always because of the very movement and the very time that constitutes that knowing. Therefore, the question of difference, identity and ground is inseparable from the question of time. Hegel tried to solve the problem of reconciliation of Being and other, Thought and Being, identity and difference by substituting the atemporal *unity of apperception* of Kant's *a priori* principle by the movement of time wherein knowing takes place, yet thereby showing dialectically that it is in pointing beyond this time that the absolute knowledge achieves its labour of total reconciliation. But this very time or movement that Hegel substituted to make possible absolute knowledge makes impossible that Absolute knowledge itself. Time difference other needs to be accounted to make possible Absolute knowledge (time cannot be accounted by philosophy of identity without determining as presence), but this accounting itself leaves something remainder to be accounted in such a way that a system like Hegel remains open all the time despite its desire for closure. This constitutes the limit of philosophy in general and speculative ontology in particular. The relationship of difference, other and time in relation to the question of beginning and constitution of philosophy, its ex-scription and its limit, is beautifully captured by Michel Foucault,

> If [philosophy] is in repeated contact with non-philosophy, where then lies the beginning of philosophy? Is it already there, secretly present in that which is not philosophy, beginning to formulate itself half under its breath amid the murmuring of things? But, perhaps, from that point on, philosophy has no *raison d'être*, or, may be, philosophy must begin on a foundation that is simultaneously arbitrary and absolute. We thus see the theme of the foundation of philosophical discourse and the theme of its formal structure substituting itself for the Hegelian theme of the movement proper to immediacy (Foucault 1972: 236).

How does the theme of the foundation of philosophy and the theme of its formal structure substitute itself for the theme of movement (proper to immediacy) in Hegelian ontology? Does it thereby resolve the problems which carry along when the theme of foundation is posed? How can one understand the movement itself that is substituted for the theme of foundation of philosophy? The following points are to be noted here:

1. That philosophy is in repeated contact with non-philosophy, philosophy's other and that precisely for the sake of this contact, any consideration concerning the grounding of philosophy must take into account that it begins on a foundation at once absolute and arbitrary. What it conceives to be absolute cannot but simultaneously be arbitrary: this aporia lies at the very heart of a philosophical discourse that poses the question concerning its ground, aporia that ruins any attempt to conceive its foundation on a notion of difference without contamination. The limit of philosophy is the unaccountable aporia that demands to account what is other, what is difference-in-itself; the very beginning

of philosophy carries within itself this inexhaustible aporia to secure a foundation at once absolute yet arbitrary.

2. What is introduced by Hegel—transforming the transcendental anthropomorphic reason of Kant into the immanent principles of becoming, emerging in and through human experience, at the same time pointing beyond itself and towards the absolute—is *movement* into thought and thereby transforming difference into contaminating, essential difference. Therefore, Hegel believes that whatever Heraclitus (Hegel 1975: 132) says about becoming, he already incorporated into his determination of the essence of history as the essence of Being (essence that appears, and yet points beyond appearance), or, introducing the notion of *becoming* as the third, synthesizing principle of negation of dialectical reason. But it—this is what Foucault means by 'substituting the formal structure with the theme of movement'—did not solve the problem that Hegel hoped. Instead of making possible an absolute knowledge in the knowing *process* itself, the movement constitutive of this knowing infinitely *defers* and *differs* the very process of knowing absolutely. This unaccountability without a remnant de-constitutes this very process of constitutive-knowing process. The limit of philosophy is the impossibility to achieve the closure of signification in the name of the ontological principle of the identity of Being and thought; it is the impossibility of recounting the remnant that it forever leaves behind: the forever impossibility of sublating the absolute 'here' and 'now'.

Yet Hegel's speculative ontology constitutes such a desire for closure and which, precisely because of this desire for closure, cannot achieve the closure but infinitely *defers* and *differs* from such a possibility, and hence remains open all the time. Since for Hegel the historical movement of philosophical discourse of Being itself is seen as the dialectical synthesis of content and form that constitutes the actualization of the ontological principle of Being and Thought, we will begin with a discussion of how Hegel understood his own speculative ontology in relation to the progressive rationalization of real in history, as the actualization of what he identifies to be the fundamental problem and philosophical task: the actualizing of the ontological principle of the identity of Being and Thought as the problem of grounding and beginning of philosophy. In this way we can understand not only how Hegel saw his speculative ontology as responding to the task-at-hand—to the question of the ground and genesis of philosophy—we would also understand how Hegel saw the whole history of Western metaphysics itself as responding to the same task-at-hand in relation to which he saw his own philosophy as the gathering of thoughts of Western metaphysics to its utmost possibility. The importance of taking Hegel's philosophy lies precisely in this: in Hegel's philosophy not only the Western metaphysics reaches its utmost gathering point, but also in that it points beyond that gathering possibility itself to the thought of unthought, to what is other than itself. What is unthought in the Western metaphysics as the history of Being is the very thought of *difference-in-itself* which philosophy cannot think without reducing it to representation. If the philosophical task of our time is to think the non-philosophy or the other of philosophy, or, to determine the possibility and task of thinking at the limit of philosophy, then, Hegel is indispensable reading: that is, to read Hegel against Hegel himself. The *almost* impossible task of escaping from such an absolute totality of a philosophical discourse, to determine the limit and the margin of such a discourse requires a sustained ex-posing of Hegel himself to the aporia which Hegel's absolute seeing could not see: the "blind spot" of the absolute seeing, the vertigo in which reason loses itself by pushing itself to its utmost labour of possibility. It requires the task of thinking exceeding the absolute thinking, for absolute is always either more or less than absolute; it is either too late or too early for its absolute knowledge. We should be able to determine to what extent, allowing us to escape from Hegel, it is nothing but a trick played on us by the cunning spirit of reason. Referring to Jean Hyppolite's reading of Hegel, Michel Foucault says:

> But truly to escape Hegel involves an exact appreciation of the price we have to pay to detach ourselves from him. It assumes that we are aware of the extent to which Hegel, insidiously perhaps, is close to us; it implies knowledge, in that which permits us to think against Hegel, of that which remains Hegelian. We have to determine the extent to which our anti-Hegelianism is possibly one of his tricks directed against us, at the end of which he stand, motionless, waiting for us.

> If, then, more than any one of us is indebted to Jean Hyppolite, it is because he has tirelessly explored, for us, and ahead of us, the path along which we may escape from Hegel (Foucault 1972: 235).

To think against Hegel that remains Hegelian: in these words, Foucault has brought to our notice the difficult task of formulating a 'critique' of Hegelian philosophy without us being Hegelian in turn. Possibly we have to determine to what extent Hegel's philosophy itself brings itself to the point of splitting apart which it cannot reconcile once and for all but rather, precisely in the process of reconciliation, opens itself to what is other to itself; possibly we have to determine to what extent this fissure is at the very heart of speculative ontology itself: this caesura of thought is the very limiting of speculative knowledge. Beyond the Hegel of the speculative philosophy of identity whose absolute totality suppresses what is difference, there is another Hegel who engenders the possibility of the thought of difference-in-itself, the unthought, precisely in its desire of closure. This study examines such a possibility of thinking the unthought thought, the fissure at the very heart of the absolute, its excess or its remnant.

Identity, difference, and ground

Speculative ontology, as Hegel determines his own philosophy, is the gathering to the utmost possibility of what the destiny of metaphysics as the history of Being offers itself. It could not have been otherwise possibly. This interpretation—that in Hegel's speculative ontology reaches its utmost gathering possibility of metaphysics—is not the interpretation that we impose upon Hegel; it is Hegel himself who saw his own philosophy in like manner in relation to the history of philosophy. This metaphysics, of which Speculative ontology is seen to be highest accomplishment, determines its ground in the name of the identity of Being and Thought; this identity in turn is determined as subject-object identity. 'Overcoming metaphysics' means to show how this determination the identity of Being and Thought as subject-object *adaequatio*, forgets what Metaphysics itself presupposes: namely, the very meaning of Being as *presencing* or disclosing itself: what remained unthought in this history of Being is the ontological difference between

Being and beings. The need for rethinking the thought of *identity* and *difference* in its relationship to the question of Being is what the overcoming of metaphysics demands.

This is what Heidegger understood by his overcoming metaphysics: to show the limit of Western metaphysics that aspires to ground on an ontological principle which forgets its own presupposition: the difference of Being and beings. Overcoming metaphysics means exposing that metaphysics itself in such way that it discloses itself, brings out to view its own structures and formations, and despite its desire for closure, bringing out what is its unthought thereby, namely, the *difference* itself. The thought of overcoming of metaphysics is, thus, a relationship to the history of metaphysics itself; it is a sustained philosophical reading strategy of traversal and reversal. We would begin here with Heidegger's discussion of Hegel's relationship to the tradition, which should be able to help us to think unthought of difference other than Hegelian difference. And yet, in a double reading, we would need to go beyond Heideggerian unthought too, because, Heidegger's unthought is also guided by the same light of Being that illumines Western ontology, the light from the very Greek-Roman source from which both Hegel and Heidegger constitutes their philosophies where a far more profound thought of Other still remained unthought.

This part examines Hegel's speculative ontology in relation to the history of philosophy, as Hegel understood himself. The history of philosophy, for him, is not a connection of external events or a chain of opinions but a necessary unfolding of the possibility of the grounding of philosophy itself. For Hegel's speculative ontology, philosophy ultimately rests its grounding on Being; it is because in it the ground of philosophy realizes its utmost possibility as the subject-object identity in Absolute knowledge. Hegel does not understand the history of philosophy historiographically, as necessary sequence of events, but as the very self-engendering and self-unfolding movement of the absolute spirit. What unfolds in this movement of absolute spirit is the movement itself, the becoming of that absolute in its self-contradictory and yet the maintenance of its self-sameness even in its own negation, eternal recoil by negating its own negation, by annulling what itself posits as its other. The story/history of philosophy is the story of the immanent movement of self-unfolding spirit that progressively, by negating itself and negating its own negation, finds its home as return to itself; it thus recuperates the limit which it itself posits as its limit, by bringing back into its immanent fold what is difference, the other, its negativity. The story of the history of philosophy is the story of philosophy itself: it is the narrative of *auto-affection*, or self-constitution in its immanence; it is the story of the beginning of philosophy and its historical actualization as accomplishment; is it the story of the possibility of absolute grounding of itself by bringing its difference to its identity of Being and Thought. Hegel saw in Greek philosophy—in Parmenides' thought of the identity of Being and Thought—the beginning of philosophy, which, reaches its accomplishment in Hegel's own speculative identity of Being and Thought through dialectical synthesis of thesis and antithesis. Throughout the narrative of this philosophy's movement, the identity of Being and Thought runs its course through self-diremption, and in this course of narration, philosophy is seen to constitute its genesis and structure, its ground and its limit. Since for Hegel, the history of philosophy itself is this history of grounding of identity and difference, we will examine how Hegel himself saw his relationship to the history of philosophy itself.

For the purpose of examination we take up the following three lectures by Heidegger: *Hegel and the Greeks* (1998: 323-33), and two other lectures, *The Principle of Identity* and *The Onto-Theo-Logical Constitution of Metaphysics*, published together as *Identity and Difference* (1969). Apart from examining how Hegel saw his philosophy in relationship to the history of philosophy, we will examine how Heidegger's attempt of overcoming metaphysics has to go through, yet, beyond Hegel's speculative ontology. In these lectures, Heidegger reads Hegel's speculative ontology as responding to the task of grounding of philosophy on the principle of Identity. This has led Heidegger to examine the principle of *Identity* anew in his lecture called *The Principle of Identity* and the problem of ontological difference of Being and beings which, according to Heidegger, remains the unthought in Hegel's onto-theo-logical metaphysics. The second problem—the problem of unthought in history of metaphysics—is inseparable from the question of identity. In this way, Heidegger attempts to think difference itself as unthought without subsuming it to the demand of metaphysical representation of difference in absolute concept. In these lectures, Heidegger carefully distinguishes his thought of identity and difference as an attempt to *step back* from metaphysics. Hegel thinks identity and difference metaphysically, namely, in the name of grounding itself on Being where the grounding is conceived as subject-object identity through a mediating synthesis (thus forming a totality of significations). While in Hegel's onto-theo-logy, the subject of philosophy becomes philosophy of subject itself (when Being as the ground is determined as Absolute subject), Heidegger, on the other hand, attempts to disclose the unthought at the instance of the overcoming of metaphysics. If our philosophical task is to show the limit of philosophy itself, or, overcoming of it, then we have to examine to what extent Heidegger's overcoming of metaphysics, his thought of difference as unthought and his re-examination of the principle of identity, would help us think difference other than Hegelian way, and more importantly, to understand what determines our philosophical task for our time: unthought as overcoming of metaphysics itself. Heidegger's attempt to think identity and difference anew –no longer as a matter of grounding in Being in traditional metaphysical manner but as *step back* from metaphysics to think unthought itself—should be examined so that we can pose for ourselves how far Heidegger's overcoming of metaphysics helps us to think the limit of philosophy. If we would like to leave Heidegger's atmosphere of thinking through Heidegger's help, existence, then, would no longer be a matter of an ontological decision of ' to be' or 'not to be', nor can it any longer be determined as Being–toward-death but as an impossible ethical exigency toward the exterior other to whom 'I' is responsible. But such questions to Heideggerian thinking can only be formulated by taking into account his attempt to think difference itself in a non-metaphysical manner. For Heidegger and for us too, Hegel is not an individual philosopher against/ with whom we have to think but is a singular name in which the whole tradition of metaphysics thinks itself and discloses itself in the form of the question of identity and difference. 'Hegel' is the name in which the destiny of metaphysics exhausts its possibilities altogether. Heidegger reading Hegel to think difference itself, to think difference as difference rather than as representation of difference, is to think identity in a manner other than Hegelian way, that is, other than as absolute Subject.

In the lecture entitled *Hegel and the Greeks* Heidegger takes up Hegel's Berlin lectures on the history of philosophy for discussion. Here Heidegger argues that in Hegel's speculative understanding of the history of philosophy as the history of Being which determines the synthesis of the object-subject as thesis-antithesis, forgets in that determination of synthesis as identity, (of object-subject as thesis-antithesis leading to always already existing mediative synthesis) what is at stake concerning Being: the very ontological difference of Being and beings, the unthought thought of Metaphysics as the history of Being. In Hegel's speculative determination of being as positing subject, the very meaning of Being (in Parmenides' saying of the identity of Being and Thought wherein Hegel himself sees the beginning of philosophy) as coming into presence, as disclosure *(Aletheia)* remains unthought. Thus Heidegger asks, whether in that onto-theo-logical constitution of metaphysics where in Being is conceived as the ground of beings and identity is conceived as unity of the manifold representations (that makes thinkable the totality of meaning as absolute concept), thereby forgets the very meaning of Being itself—namely, as presencing and disclosing? It leads us to inquire how in Hegel's speculative philosophy Being itself came to be thought as absolute concept or as absolute subject and how identity as unity appears in speculative ontology as mediating synthesis of subject–object so that Being in its original meaning as presencing-disclosing is forgotten? How is it that Being came to be determined in Hegel's ontology in such a way that Being came to be seen as posited subject whose unity is the mediating synthesis of subject-object or even better, how Being itself came to be thought in such a manner so that the very oblivion of the meaning of Being as presencing–disclosing constitutes its metaphysics and so that the ontological difference of Being and beings remains concealed as unthought in the history of philosophy? How is it that in Hegel's philosophy of identity, the principle of identity has come to be conceived, in the manner of metaphysics, as subject-object synthesis so that identity is understood as unity of the manifold, conceiving thereby the *Onto-Theo-Logical* constitution of metaphysics thinkable at all, by making it possible to think Being as the ground of beings which constitutes metaphysics?

We have seen that metaphysics constitutes itself by determining Being as the ground of beings: here identity becomes a characteristic of Being itself. In Hegel, this identity is thought metaphysically as the unity of manifold representations. Identity thought speculatively as unity, makes it possible to conceive itself as absolute concept for Hegel; and Being, determined as having this identity becomes absolute knowledge as absolute unity of the subject-object. In this way, in Hegel's speculative philosophy, Being is reduced to the unity of representations, and the principle of identity is reduced to the metaphysical determinations of subject-object synthesis. What thereby escapes, so Heidegger argues, is the very meaning of Being which any metaphysical determination presupposes and yet, forgets: Being as *presencing* and *clearing* (*Lichtung*). We can now put this question in this way: how Hegel understands the history of philosophy speculatively in such a way that Being came to be interpreted as Absolute posited-positing subject? How Hegel comes to represent identity as unity or synthesis of the manifold representations (thereby forgetting the very meaning of Being whose subject matter is speculative ontology itself)? This demands on us to understand Hegel's determination of the history of philosophy itself and the very meaning of the 'speculative' in its metaphysical significance.

We have mentioned above that for Hegel the history of philosophy is the self-unfolding movement of the absolute in which the object-subject contradiction is determined speculatively (that means contradiction in dialectic is a posited one); and synthesis in which the contradiction is resolved, is the very self-engendering movement of the absolute producing itself as Subject. Thus, (1) Being in Hegel is determined as *Subject,* (2) a *producing and produced* one, as *work* of the negativity and (3) this production of Subject is the synthesizing of *posited object-subject contradiction as thesis-antithesis.* It is the very meaning of the 'speculative', which Hegel gives to it, determines Being as subject, subject as *production* and *work* and, subject-object contradiction as *posited.*

In his "Logic" of *Encyclopaedia*, Hegel understands the meaning of *Speculative* as that "apprehends the unity of terms in their oppositions—the affirmative, which is involved in their disintegration and in their transition" (1975a: 119). Commenting on Hegel, Heidegger says:

> This requires apprehending the shining of opposites against one another and in one another, which is the manner in which antithesis reigns as it is presented in the "Logic of Essence" (i.e., the logic of reflection). From its self-reflecting shining, or mirroring, *speculari* (*speculum:* mirror) receives its conclusive determination. Considered this way, speculative is the positive whole of that which "dialectic" is meant to signify here...the mirroring and uniting of opposites as the process of the production of spirit itself (1998: 326).

Understanding Hegel's determination of the meaning of 'speculative' as self-mirroring and as posited self-reproduction of subjectivity, the history of philosophy (here speculative dialectic is the method for Hegel that determines the event of thought as processual) can be thought as self-unfolding of posited producing-productive subjectivity that comes into its own absolute self-consciousness (that means, by sublating the opposites by shining onto each other, like the work of the mirror) in which reflection opposites pass into the other, becomes its other yet, negating this other again to maintain its self-sameness (that means, reflecting: reflection here means thought and *auto-reproduction*, or better, *auto-reproducing* of thought). One can see how Hegel here both preserves the Platonic *mimesis* while making immanent of its transcendent movement. Instead of a *transcendental* determination of Platonic oppositions in terms of *mimesis* that unifies, here Hegel determines *mimesis* speculatively, that means *immanently* that unifies the dialectical opposition by reducing Platonic alterity to contradiction (see Hyppolite 1997).

Thus, Hegel determines the history of philosophy *speculatively*, that means *in sight of* the absolute production of subjectivity and this production of subjectivity is the work of light:

> Western philosophy, as philosophy of Being, always has been the philosophy of light: the light of Being that illumines itself and produces itself in its own light. Hegel's speculative ontology is the utmost possibility of the work of light: light that is presence itself, presents to itself. Light is presence, Being's presence as light, Being's intelligibility to itself. Everything is determined in ontology in the name of this light: reason, non-being, other, difference, truth etc. We would ask whether Heidegger's very overcoming of metaphysics

> too, which we are concerned here, is also permeated by the same light of presence, the very philosophy of light that Heidegger is trying to overcome.

And this production of the Subject is produced dialectically, that means as unifying thesis and antithesis in synthesis. This synthesis, the third term, is what Hegel determines as the infinite negativity; it is the absolute subjectivity as absolute concept. The labour of the concept as the work of the negativity works in service of producing subjectivity: the Absolute subject as self-mirroring. Therefore, the history of philosophy (understood speculatively) cannot be separated from its possible *Aufhebung* (sublation) in view. For Hegel the character of conversation with the history of philosophy is *Aufhebung*: sublation that is the self-presence of the absolute Subject that recuperates even what is the other side of the light: the night! This history of philosophy, seen speculatively, is the production of subjectivity that has its stages of unfolding that are determined dialectically: this means, in its thesis, antithesis and the last stage of synthesis. Thus Hegel presents the Greek stage as the first stage of thesis wherein the beginning of philosophy takes place; the second stage of anti-thesis takes place with Descartes' and Hegel's speculative philosophy is the highest stage of synthesis wherein the Absolute Subject is the consummated concept. In this way, the whole history of philosophy is determined as the history of producing Subjectivity: the entire system of speculative philosophy is built upon in this sight of producing Absolute Subjectivity; Hegel sees the history of philosophy as a totality or a system for the sake of *Aufhebung*, of producing subjectivity. We will discuss here only what Hegel conceives as the first stage of thesis—that is, the stage concerning the question of the beginning of philosophy, a question posed for any philosophy of beginning.

The first stage, the stage of thesis where the question of the beginning of philosophy is announced in Parmenides' principle of identity—this principle of identity of Being and Thought is interpreted speculatively, that means as the mediated self-sameness of the reflective subjectivity. This determination of the ancient philosopher's thought of Being and the principle of identity forgets, according to Heidegger, the original meaning of Being as *presencing*, and the original meaning of the principle of identity as Parmenides thought is forgotten too. Being becomes a synthesis of epistemological subject-object subjectivity that is auto-producing and autogenetic. Metaphysics investigates beings in their totality by grounding itself on Being. In Hegelian speculative metaphysics, this totality becomes the historicity of beings. This speculative-dialectical determination of Being as productive subjectivity is constituted *in sight of* this totality. In the following part, we will discuss how Heidegger reads in Hegelian thought of *Aufhebung* the oblivion of Being. In his *Hegel and the Greeks,* Heidegger reads Hegel by presenting four words in respect to four Greek philosophers who speak the name of Being. The four words are the following:

1. [All] is the word of Parmenides.
2. [Reason] is the word of Heraclitus.
3. [Concept] is the word of Plato.
4. [Actuality] is the word of Aristotle. (Heidegger 1998: 328)

1. 'All': Hegel finds the beginning of philosophy in Parmenides' saying of the Oneness (All) of Being and Thought. 'Being' that is 'thought' here is the immediate: presence to Being in its indetermination as an object to itself. Here pure thought is an object for absolute Being (thought that is 'seized and made an object'): already in this determination Hegel sees a point towards Descartes who explicitly posits 'subject' as positing, and thereby making explicit what is merely implicit in Parmenides . The question of making thought as object can only be for a positing and production of the subject, is what marks the determination of Being as representation or reflection, or as production of subjectivity .In this way, Hegel remained oblivious of the historical transformation of the thought of Being as *Aletheia* in Greek philosophy to the determination of Being as *subiectum* in modern philosophy. It is in this oblivion of the transformation of the meaning of Being from *Aletheia* to *subiectum* that the entire Hegelian philosophy is built upon. Parmenides did not have any idea what is *subiectum,* which is an idea to be found only in modern philosophy. But Hegel understood what Parmenides meant by Being in terms of a modern concept of *subiectum.* Parmenides' thought of Being as *Aletheia* remains, thereby, unthought in Hegel's philosophy of identity. Being originally thought

as *Ousia* came to be determined in the representational manner as production of subjectivity in Hegelian ontology.

2. 'Reason': The word for Heraclitus is *Reason*, which means, as Heidegger says, "the gathering which lets everything that is as a whole lie before and appear as beings." But taking another direction concerning the meaning of the word, Hegel understood the meaning of this word as 'Reason' "in the sense of absolute subjectivity, the logic itself is speculative dialectic, through whose movement what is immediately universal and abstract, being, is reflected as what is objective in opposition to the subject, and this reflection is determined as mediation in the sense of becoming. In becoming, what is opposed comes concrete and in this way comes to unity. To apprehend this unity is the essence of that speculation which unfolds itself as dialectic" (Ibid: 329-30). Determined dialectically, once more the meaning of Being as what lies as presence before and appearing as beings came to be understood as speculative unity of opposites: 'Reason' as the truth of Being as becoming.

3. 'Concept': is the word for Plato, which Hegel considers as "the intrinsically determinate universal" (quoted by Heidegger Ibid: 330). *Idea* as 'intrinsic determinate universal' signifies what exists in-itself, beyond the sensible existence; in-itself implying cognizing itself. The Ideas are what to be "brought forth within the spirit through cognition" (Ibid) since they are not immediately present to consciousness. Commenting on this speculative determination of Idea, Heidegger says, "This bringing- forth, producing, is conceiving as the activity of absolute knowing, i.e., "science" (Ibid).

4. 'Actuality': is the word of Aristotle which Hegel translates as *actualitas*, more determinately *entelecheia,* meaning that "which is in itself end and realization of the end", as "pure efficacy from out of itself". "Only energy, form, is activity that which effects, self-relating negativity" (Ibid).

Quoting these lines from Hegel, Heidegger again brings out the speculative determination of Being as absolute subjectivity, and shows how in Hegel's speculative determination of Being, the original meaning of Being is forgotten:

> Here actuality is also thought on the basis of speculative dialectic as the pure activity of the absolute subject. When the thesis is negated by the antithesis, and the latter, for its part, is negated by the synthesis, there holds sway in such negating that which Hegel calls "the self-relating negativity". It is nothing negative. The negation of negation is rather that position in which spirit posits itself as the absolute through its activity. Hegel sees in the actuality of Aristotle the first stage of the absolute self-movement [266] of spirit, i.e., of actuality in and for itself (Ibid: 331).

We have seen that in these four words for the four Greek philosophers respectively, Hegel presents the first stage of the history of philosophy, namely the stage of thesis when Being is not yet determined in its absolute self-consciousness, and yet the thought of this absolute subjectivity is already implicit in its posited-ness and productivity: - this speculative-dialectic determination of the history of philosophy constitutes the thought of Being, in the very meaning of 'speculation': the production of posited subjectivity in its absolute concept. In this way, the enigmatic resonance of the very truth of Being in its original meaning as *unconcealing* came to be determined in terms of *certainty*, and while, this *certainty* is thought in terms of representational thought of identity. In *The End of Philosophy*, Heidegger's *destruction of ontology* (in terms of history of beings, and no longer in terms of hermeneutic-transcendental-phenomenological horizon as it was thought in *Being and Time)* discloses this unfolding-transformation of metaphysics as history of beings. Here Heidegger shows the transformation of the thought of Being in its unthought origin as *Aletheia* to the speculative determination of it as production of subjectivity; and he shows the transformation of original meaning of the thought of the principle of identity of Being and thought as it is conceived by Parmenides into speculative meaning as truth in terms of subject-object correlation (thus, Hegel does not radically transform Kantian philosophy). Being as *Aletheia* as it is originally thought, is now determined as 'production' of subjectivity in Hegel; truth as 'disclosing' in its original meaning has now become the knowledge of self-reflection in Hegel. The identity of Being and Thought in Parmenides has now become the identity of subject and object through synthesis. In this transformation of thought, Being and truth in their metaphysical determinations, thus Heidegger argues, the original meaning of Being is forgotten which is already presupposed by metaphysics; the *ontological difference*, thus, remains unthought in the history of metaphysics. Hegel's determination of subjectivity is forgetful of the fact that for the Greeks, there was no thought of the Subject; the problematic of the Subject came historically only when truth as *Aletheia* is transformed into *certainty*. Only when truth came to be determined as certainty, the question of the objectivity of the object has come to be. Thus, 'Subject', 'object' and 'certainty' are intrinsically related in the philosophy of reflection, and they are determined as such only when the problem of consciousness (hence, representation) is posed for modern philosophy (Heidegger 1975b: 61). Only for a philosophy of reflection that can only think what is identical and cannot think the very ontological difference as difference:

> Reflection is bending-back, and as such it is the explicitly accomplished presentation of what is present; explicitly, that is, in such a way that what is present is presented to the representer. The bending-back, putting-back, that is, the representation of what is represented which presents *itself* in advance *to itself*, in which what is represented is represented as this and that, and is. The "what" itself in its sameness and posited-ness, constancy.
>
> For this reason reflection strives for the identical, and for this reason reflection is a fundamental characteristic of concept formation (Ibid: 60).

It is this striving for the identical—the light of the speculative—that strives to bring back into its fold only what is identical. Hegelian philosophy is a philosophy of light, and as such, it is a philosophy of the same: it can't think difference *as* difference. The meaning of the word of Heraclitus, *Reason*, in its original meaning as *presencing* of what lies before, has come to be determined as dialectical becoming. In this way every determination is posed speculatively, and the original meaning of Being itself (in all these appearing through these four words) are forgotten. The problem of 'Subject', 'object' and 'certainty' came much later in the history of beings, and, therefore, we cannot understand metaphysics in its essential origin in such terms as *subiectum*. *Destruction of ontology* or overcoming of metaphysics is this un-building (*de-struere*) of metaphysics in terms of history of beings, tracing to its forgotten essential origin. Hegel's philosophy belongs, in this way, to metaphysics because it only thinks what is identical in its utmost possibility, and. for that reason, is incapable of thinking difference as such. Despite Hegel's endeavour to think philosophy in its totality, Hegel could not release the thought of Being as *Aletheia* because his thought, shaped by history of beings as metaphysics, couldn't not determine Being as production of subjectivity and couldn't not think identity as identical. The thought of Being is inescapably 'subjectivized'. Heidegger asks: "Must the human being—which is what is being thought here—necessarily be determined as subject? Does "for human beings" already unconditionally mean: posited by human beings? (Heidegger 1998: 334)

Heidegger's meditation on Hegel's speculative interpretation of Greek philosophy shows that the thought of Being with which philosophy begins as the thought of identity "unfolds essentially as presence only as far as *Aletheia* already holds sway, and yet *Aletheia* itself remains unthought with respect to its essential provenance" (Ibid: 335). We, however, wonder, whether Heidegger's mediation on *Aletheia* itself not governed by certain thought of identity inasmuch as it is question concerning the meaning of Being?

But let me retrace our discussion of Heidegger reading Hegel. Heidegger argues that philosophy begins with the thought of Being as the thought of identity, and yet the principle of identity remains unthought in its essential origin: in the *thought-thought* of metaphysics, the thought unfolding of Being in its historicity gets determined as subjectivity. Heidegger's overcoming of metaphysics requires not only to think as 'the recollection in metaphysics' but also to think ahead of metaphysics at the end of metaphysics. Such recollection in metaphysics is thought in *The End of Philosophy* in its essential origin. The thought of identity is re-examined in *The Principle of Identity* in its essential beginning of philosophy, while ontological difference is thought as the thought ahead of philosophy itself as *step back* from the onto-theo-logical constitution of metaphysics. In the following part we will examine the two lectures published together in *Identity and Difference* to show how Heidegger thinks the thought of identity in its essential origin and the thought of difference as the thought ahead of metaphysics (that is, *step back* from metaphysics). That the unthought thought of ontological difference stems from the essence of identity can be thought only when we take a *step back* from onto-theo-logical metaphysics which determines Being as *ground* of beings, and which determines Being as identity of the self-same subjectivity. Here Heidegger argues that the onto-theo-logical determination of identity as self-sameness of productivity arises when the thought of identity is thought as 'belonging *together*' of Being and thought rather than '*belonging* together' of Being and thought. Thinking historically, though Hegel saw in Parmenides' thought of identity as the genesis of philosophy and its ground, he did not really think metaphysics in its essential origin as the *belonging* together of Being and thought. In this way, the ontological difference that is implied is never brought out but remains unthought in the history of beings.

What does Parmenides mean when he says: "Being and thought are the same"—a thought in which Hegel saw the beginning of history of philosophy, the very beginning that is the beginning of philosophy itself? Hegel interprets this saying as: "This unity [of the subjective and objective], however, only receives its perfect form in speculative Reason; for *only* what is thought by *this* is true in regard both to its form and its content—a *perfect* unity of thought and Being" (Hegel 1971: 129). And in the following lines the unity of this being and thought is determined in terms of identity and difference:

> On the one hand we must, of course, distinguish *being* which is absolutely immediate, indeterminate, undifferentiated, from *thought* which is self-differentiating and—by the reduction of difference to a moment—self mediating, that is from the 'I'; yet, on the other hand, being is identical with thought, since the latter returns from every mediation to immediacy, from all its self-differentiation to serene unity with itself. The 'I' is, therefore, being or has being as a moment within it. When I set this being as another over against me and at the same time as identical with me, I am knowing (*Wissen*) and have the absolute certainty of my being (Ibid: 154).

The following points are to be noticed here:

1. Identity (of Being and thought) is determined (speculatively) as *unity* (of subjective and objective). Identity is, determined speculatively and dialectically, *unity*.

2. That the difference which thought introduces to Being is only *self-difference*, a reduction of difference in-itself to a moment of Being, and hence thought always returns to Being and is identical with Being.
3. Identical *with* Being means it is a *mediating unity*: they belong *together* (unity). In this togetherness (unity of manifold representations) the sameness of Being and thought is to be thought speculatively.
4. What unifies is the ground that grounds, accounts for the ground, and hence grounds itself: the mediating identity of thought and Being is the mediating unity of what ground is, and what is to be grounded. Determined speculatively, identity of Being and thought is the matter of giving ground, for that sake of ground. Since for Hegel, the matter of thinking is thinking itself—of what he calls 'Idea'—this unity as ground is absolute ground on Idea or Idea as absolute ground.
5. That identity, in this way, belongs to Being and characterizes Being.

Does Parmenides mean the same by the thought of identity in this way—as self-mediating, self-returning dialectical unity of Being and thought that grounds, in the name of Idea, of what is to be grounded? Heidegger does not think so. It is for the following reasons:

1. Unity came to be determined as such only at a particular historical moment in the history of beings, namely, when with the determination of truth as *Aletheia* becomes certitude of self-consciousness, and when the objectivity of the object becomes a matter of unity for an epistemological subject in the philosophy of representation. In other words, only when the question of subject and object becomes an epistemological problem for a philosophy of representation, then the question of *unity* comes into being in the history of beings. But this problem came much later in the history of beings and one cannot ascribe this same problem to Parmenides who neither had any idea of subject or object or representation of the manifold.

2. Therefore unity as giving ground does not occur at all to Parmenides', because the problem of ground occurs only when truth as *Aletheia becomes* certitude that secures self-certain knowledge and guarantees the security of the system. In the thought of unity as ground, the truth of Being as *Aletheia* is forgotten. Identity is neither giving ground for Parmenides nor is it unity of manifold representations that accompanies all representations in the Kantian manner.

Then where is the thought of Parmenides to be found if not in Hegelian thought of identity as mediating-grounding unity of subject-object? Heidegger expresses Parmenides' thought in the following way:

1. Since identity cannot be thought as merely identical (it will be a tautological), philosophy understands this problem as connection or *belonging together*—both in metaphysics (as in Hegel) and in Parmenides. Hegel understood this problem of identity as 'belonging together' in the manner of belonging *together* because history of beings already determines his thought to demand a ground in terms of unity. Metaphysics prior to him already determines his thought to understand this identity as unity because metaphysics could think 'with' (Being is same *with* thought; there is no point of saying A=A because one does not need to have two terms to assert what is identical) only as unity. This has led Hegel to determine identity as characteristics of Being.
2. Metaphysics can't think identity other than as unity. What is unthought in this history of thought is not some transcendental origin but what is concealed in metaphysics itself. Thus Heidegger interprets Parmenides' thought: "For the same perceiving (thinking) as well as being" as "Thinking and Being belong together in the Same and by virtue of this Same" (Heidegger 1969: 27). It means that:
3. *Being together with thinking belongs to Identity*. Understood this way, Parmenides' thought is meant to say that Being (with identity) belongs identity and that Being is the characteristic of identity; while for Hegel, identity (as unity that grounds) belongs to Being. Thus, difference between Parmenides' and

> Hegel's thought is infinitesimal and yet, too far away. The unthought of metaphysics is too near to what is thought in metaphysics and yet, for that reason too far from it. When identity as *belonging* together is emphasized, we get the thought of Parmenides, and when this identity is thought with an emphasis on belonging *together*, we have the Hegelian identity as unity of the manifold. While in the former sense of *belonging* together Being is the characteristic of identity, in belonging *together*, identity characterizes Being in the sense of Being grounding beings. Metaphysics is characterized by this ground giving where Being grounds beings. In this sense, Hegelian identity belongs to metaphysics, or, constitutes itself as such, and in this constitution it forgets what it presupposes itself: the *belonging* together of Being and thought. Unlike the belonging *together* of Hegelian philosophy where belonging is determined by *connexio*, Parmenides thought of *belonging* together means thought and Being belong to each other, held towards each other and in this holding towards each other in the Same.

Heidegger asks us to understand this identity of *belonging* together in the relation of man and Being: man and Being belong to each other. Understood this way, the thought of *belonging* together is the thought of Being as characteristic of identity: this belonging together is the thought of *appropriation*. Metaphysics, on the other hand, thinks identity as characteristic of Being in the sense of belonging *together*. Modern technology, in the sense of calculative representative thinking, is thoroughly metaphysical; technological man challenges Being which presupposes that identity is the characteristics of Being. The step out of metaphysics is a leap that has to think metaphysics to its essential origin. At this point, identity would no longer be thought as characteristic of Being but as this thought of *spring* itself:

> The law appears at first in the form of a fundamental principle which presupposes identity as a characteristic of Being, that is, of the ground of beings. This principle in the sense of a statement has in the meantime become a principle bearing the characteristics of a spring that depart from Being as the ground of beings, and thus springs into the abyss.... Principle of identity, means now: a spring

> demanded by the essence of identity because it needs that spring if the belonging together of man and Being is to attain the essential light of the appropriation (Ibid: 39).

Heidegger asks us to think identity as *leap* out of metaphysical determination of identity as unity (Hegel in particular here): identity is to be understood in an originary manner as *spring* that departs from Being (Being as the ground of beings). Reading Hegel's *The Science of Logic*, Heidegger argues that every time metaphysics constitutes itself as onto-theo-logy (in Hegel, the onto-theo-logical constitution of metaphysics is Logic), it aspires to constitutes Being as the ground of beings: it presupposes the ontological difference of Being and beings which it cannot think, which remains unthought in the history of beings. *Therefore, difference as difference, the ontological difference of Being and beings cannot be thought within metaphysics but only as step back*: "the origin of the difference can no longer be thought of within the scope of metaphysics" (Ibid: 71). To think difference as such would then be overcoming of metaphysics itself because only by tracing the trace of forgetting, what is unthought is to be thought in non-representational manner. In this sense, Heidegger's tracing difference as unthought is not to be thought as to retrieve origin in its pristine purity in an idealist manner; it is rather to think what is unthought of onto-theo-logical constitution of metaphysics. In the following part I examine how Heidegger investigates the onto-theo-logical constitution of metaphysics in terms of Being giving ground to beings which presupposes the ontological difference of Being and beings that remains unthought in metaphysics. By presenting the case thus, through Heidegger, we propose to think *difference as difference*, difference other than the essential constitution of metaphysics of Being giving ground to beings; and at the same time we would pose, before ourselves, whether there remains far more profound unthought thought of difference other than ontological difference of Being and beings. Heidegger asks:

1. What is the matter of thinking for Hegel, and what is it for us?
2. What is the criterion for conversation with the history of thinking for Hegel and what is it for us?

3. What is the character of this conversation for Hegel, and what is it for us? (Ibid: 46).

Heidegger answers these questions:

1. While for Hegel the matter of thinking is Being thought in the sense of absolute concept; for Him, Being is to be thought in its difference from Beings: in other words, *difference as difference.*
2. While for Hegel, "the criteria for conversation with the history of thinking" is to think that history as dialectical unfolding though various stages of progression which will culminate in absolute thinking, incorporating all that has been unfolded in the self-externalization of idea; for Heidegger, it is to think all that has been thought only to think what remains unthought in that history and not that will lead to accumulative absolute thinking.
3. While for Hegel, the character of the conversation with the history of philosophy "has the character of *Aufhebung*" that allows to think Being as ground of beings through mediating concept; for Heidegger, it is to *step back* from metaphysics.

In our discussion of the principle of identity, we have seen that Hegel—not in the way that Parmenides thought this principle—determined this principle of identity being characteristic of Being inasmuch as Being is already determined as ground; while "thinking—since it belongs together with Being—gathers itself toward Being as its ground, in the manner of giving ground and accounting for the ground. Being manifests itself as thought. This means: the Being of beings reveals itself as the ground that gives itself ground and accounts for itself" (Ibid: 57). In this way, ground is conceived in Hegel as Being that gathers beings into itself, Being that grounds beings. In our discussion of Hegel's relationship to Heraclitus, we have seen that the word for this gathering is *logos*. In this sense, speculative "Logic" constitutes itself in such a manner that Being grounds beings, gathers beings into itself into its unity, and thus, forming a totality of beings as system.

Now metaphysics thinks beings in its totality. Hegelian speculative ontology is metaphysics in the sense that it thinks beings in its totality;

this totality is for Hegel the system of absolute thinking. In Hegel's thinking of the system, metaphysics reaches its utmost possibility of thinking beings as a whole. This metaphysics constitutes itself as onto-logy when Being as the ground of beings is seen as *universal ground*; and it is theo-logy in the sense that Being as the ground of beings is seen as highest *causa sui* when the ground is determined as the first cause. Metaphysics, thus, constitutes itself as onto-theo-logy that conceives Being as the ground of beings, ground as *unity* of beings and the act of gathering itself.

How in this matter of thinking, that is Being itself as *unity*, difference as difference remains unthought? Heidegger asks us to think the ontological difference of Being and beings in the unthought difference between the meaning of *Being* in the sense of Being of *beings* and the meaning of *beings* in the sense of beings of *Being*. While in the former case, the meaning of Being is to be seen as *genetivus objectivus*; the latter is to be thought as *genetivus subjectivus*. To think *difference as difference* is to think difference as the difference of *genetivus objectivus* and *genetivus subjectivus*.

Heidegger invites us to think the ontological difference of Being and beings transitively: Being as in transition to beings, not in the sense that Being leaves its place to beings but rather in the manner of arriving to beings. This *arrival* to beings is to be thought as keeping itself concealed in its unconcealment. *Overwhelming* is the unconcealment of Being as *presencing* itself and yet, arrival in beings is concealing itself. In other words, Being appear only *this* being or *that*, so that Being conceals itself in its very unconcealment; difference of *overwhelming* and *arrival* as the difference of Being and beings is, what Heidegger calls, *perdurance*:

> Being in the sense of unconcealing overwhelming, and beings as such in the sense of arrival that keeps itself concealed, are present, and thus differentiated, by virtue of the Same, the differentiation. That differentiation alone grants and hold apart the "between", in whom the overwhelming and the arrival are held toward one another, are borne away from and toward each other. The difference of Being and beings, as the differentiation of overwhelming and arrival is the perdurance (Austrag) of the two in *unconcealing keeping in concealment*.

> Within this perdurance there prevails a clearing of what veils and closes itself off –and this prevalence bestows the being apart, and the being toward each other, of overwhelming and arrival (Ibid: 65).

By the word 'Same' Heidegger meant other than identical. Thus in *Identity and Difference*, Heidegger says: "...the same is not the merely identical. In the merely identical, the difference disappears. In the same the difference appears, and appears all the more pressingly, the more resolutely thinking is concerned with the same matter in the same way" (Ibid: 45). Difference of Being and beings is the difference of perdurance: the 'between' of *overwhelming* and *arrival.* Metaphysics presupposes this difference of *perdurance* when Being is determined as the ground of beings, yet, this difference remained unthought in the history of beings (also see Heidegger 1978: 383-84). *Perdurance* is the openness where Being appears in such a way that Being is conceived as the ground of beings:

> The perdurance of that which grounds and that which is grounded, as such, not only holds the two apart, it holds them facing each other. What is held apart is held in the tension of perdurance in such a way that not only does Being ground beings as their ground, but beings in their turn ground, cause Being in their way. Beings can do so only insofar as they "are" the fullness of Being: they are what *is* most of all (Heidegger 1969: 69).

To what extent Heidegger can himself determine that this opening beyond the closure of metaphysics cannot but be a contaminated opening that brings into itself always unaccountable remnant of the very trace of metaphysics itself (that it tries to overcome)? In what sense can the Heidegger's sayings of Nietzsche as the last metaphysician and thereby excluding himself from the closure of metaphysics be justified if the opening from the closure of metaphysics is but a contaminated opening? If that is so, we should be able to reconstitute how Heidegger's thinking is constituted in proximity and yet in distance from the history of philosophy as such, and at the same time, with the same gesture, to point out the necessity that is working in Heidegger's thought of unthought. Thus in the following section, I present the following propositions:

1. That from Aristotle to Heidegger through Hegel, philosophy has always thought of difference (whether Hegelian speculative difference or Heidegger's ontological difference) on the basis of a certain determination of presence (*presence* as in Hegel, *presencing* as in Heidegger). 'Difference', 'non-Being', 'time' is thought on the basis of self-sufficiency of Being as presence: the meaning of Being as presence, or, presence of Being to itself as *meaning*. 'Being', 'meaning' and 'presence': all these determinations are inseparable and they constitute Western metaphysics as the *metaphysics of presence.* At stake here is to determine to what extent in Heidegger's careful dissociating of his ontological difference (as *presencing*, *Aletheia* as disclosure, as unthought for *Being for whom the meaning of Being is at stake*) from Hegelian onto-theo-logical difference (as that which is to be thought on the basis of serving to the self-presence of the 'ground', difference whose meaning or truth is the self-presence of unity as synthesis), the very logic constitutive of onto-theo-logy is reduplicated in such a way that Heidegger's overcoming of metaphysics still belongs, in a necessary way, to the very metaphysics from which he is trying to overcome. Is not Western metaphysics always asks the meaning of Being on the basis of presence which implies certain self-sufficiency of Being? Or, asks the meaning of meaning on the basis of self-presence of Being to the extent that Being is already determined as presence as a question concerning the meaning of Being? Is it not that difference has always been conceived in this light of Being?: this self-sufficiency of Being would be such (for Hegel, this self-sufficiency of Being would be absolute spirit, identity of what is to be grounded and what is ground; and for Heidegger it is the identity of the Being that questions the meaning of Being) that anything that is other or difference, can only be understood only on the basis of this self-sufficiency of Being.
2. May be, then, there is a far more profound unthought—as Jacques Derrida (1982) suggests—than Heideggerian unthought of ontological difference: the unheard unthought that is no longer to be understood on the basis of meaning or Being, or, on presence; it is that which exceeds Being or meaning

or presence, and unsettles, in its ever differentiation, every question concerning the meaning of Being? Therefore, at stake is not only the problematic of difference and time but also a question concerning the problematic of signification. Difference has always been thought in Western philosophy on the basis of unity of the manifold (as in Kant), and time has been thought as presence, which is the synchronic modality of time (is not it that Being, in order *to be* Being, has to be other than *diachronic* which difference introduces into the heart of Being?). Hence unthought—other than unthought of ontological or speculative difference, unthought exceeding thought, unthought as the limit thought—would be the very excess of thought: diachronic transcendence that exceeds meaning *to be*.

3. Unthought otherwise than Being, then, can no longer be understood as either ground (as in Hegel) or as the meaning of Being; time would then be an infinite departure towards the infinitely Other, and not an eternal arrival to Being that recoils into itself in its absolute recuperation of all difference as negativity (Hegel's circle of eternal appropriation) nor will it be self-sufficiency of Being in its 'hermeneutics of facticity' (Heidegger's Being for whom the meaning of Being is at stake): difference that is other than itself, exceeding itself from the circularity of total appropriation, difference that does not shine against its opposites to mediate and determine itself in the immanent self-presence of intelligible light, difference in relation to the other as other, the *infinitely* other than its own other .The question of ethics would be posed here as a relation (without relation—either as dialectic relation or as ontological relation) to the Other that occurs only as interruption of time: the unnameable interval that would never be accounted by any hermeneutic of speculative reading, the remnant of delay that forever opens forever unreadable caesura of the totality of absolute knowledge.

Difference, time and other

Time and difference in Hegelian philosophy

There is an essential relationship between difference and time which philosophy determines in a manner that attempts to ground philosophy itself on a solid foundation. I would try to show how this decisive gesture constitutes both Hegelian and Heideggerian philosophy, not by showing merely the points of contact between both philosophers. I attempt to show that Heidegger's attempt in overcoming Hegelian metaphysics itself introduces this decisive gesture in a necessary way inasmuch as Heidegger asks us to *step back* from Hegelian metaphysics as a question concerning *meaning* of Being. Insofar as it is manner of asking the meaning of Being, difference and time is already let be thought in the light of immanence and its self-enclosure. It is already light of the same. Transcendence is already reduced to the intelligibility of Being—whether it is speculative light or more originary light of *presencing*—for the *meaning* has always been determined in the history of philosophy as the meaning of Being, as the light of Being which presents itself to itself to grasp itself. Does not Hegel too ask the meaning (or, truth) of time? Is it not that this meaning of time is already presence—that is, the *synchrony* of Being with itself, a certain identity of Being with itself, the proximity of the reflective light, light that bends to re-appropriate itself and to represent itself? We wonder whether in Heidegger also, there governs the possible proximity of Being with its own nothingness in the possible-impossibility of Being-towards-death as anticipation? Is not this anticipation, with time as horizon of Being, is already governed by the synchronic modality of time? As soon one thinks death as *mine*, (in my death only I die: this is what Heidegger says in *Being and Time*) time is already presence, already synchronic, already serving the self-sufficiency of Being even in his own impossibility. As soon as one thinks Being continuous even in the non-Being of time, (as Hegel thinks), one already determines time as synchronic, as presence that infinitely re-appropriates its non-Being (its difference, its other).

In our examination of the Hegelian notion of 'speculation', we have shown how the light of self-consciousness always serves the identity of what it reflects. Here I attempt to show how in Hegel's philosophy, time is also thought in the light that throws itself back into itself, the bending back of the mirror-reflection that always recuperates its own reflection. It is time thought as synchrony, as the eternal return of the *self-presence* of the same. Everything in this absolute system is determined in such a manner that it serves the possible recuperation in its immanent self-presence of identity by reflecting back into itself what is different, its own difference.

Here we will ask how Hegel thought the essential relationship of time and difference in such a way that a certain primacy of identity is affirmed in the name of presence, presence that presents itself in the eternal return of the identical. We will show that the very understanding of his philosophy as 'speculative' determines this essential relationship of time and difference. By 'speculative philosophy' as philosophy of immanence Hegel means as philosophy of negativity. How this is to be thought understood?

Hegel begins with identity pure and immediate, identity that of Being and Thought in which identity presents itself as substance or as indeterminate givenness. But this identity, thought in its truth, immediately passes into difference (because it has not yet actualized itself as identity; it has to be actualized, that means, it has to determine itself as mediated. This determination is already negation), is negated by itself and sunders itself. Thus, the truth of identity is its other, this very negativity that sunders itself, and this passage itself of passing. In other words, identity negates itself so as to be its other, difference, which is its own externalization (see Hegel 1970: 34-36). Since this is nothing but the very passage of becoming other, is the very *time* of the passage. In this very process of *othering*, of self-differentiating, of self-negating, time already there as *self-differentiating* or *self-externalizing* of the Subject. Time is the negativity that *differentiates;* but this difference too, since it cannot maintain itself as such (because it cannot present itself. Only mediated identity can present itself. One can see that presence is already inseparable from the concept of identity), is again negated. With this negation of negation, time of difference or difference of time cancelling itself, identity returns to itself as presence, presents itself as presence, reinstalling thereby the identity of Being and thought once again. This process, the very movement of time presents itself as circle where the result is in the beginning but it is also the cancellation of the circle, to the extent that it is cancellation of the very constitutive process of time. Unity as ground is ground only because it is this becoming of negativity, the process which becomes, and yet it is the ground as the very cancellation of this process, of the circle of becoming. The truth of the absolute Subject is the actualization of its identity—actualization being this process of a-sundering, time that is Being thrown out of itself, and yet pointing towards beyond this passage by again annulling itself. *Difference is this passage of time*, time that appears as difference; or, rather, this difference itself that would be sublated into identity. Time, in this way, is the appearing of the Spirit, is Spirit's self-externalization, is Being out of itself that needs to be negated. Spirit in its subsistence and persistence, negates itself, throws out of itself from itself as time –time is this a-sundering and "utter dismemberment" of Spirit, this passage of difference itself. But this time would be negated again as difference and would be sublated as presence. Sublation is (which is unity of identity and difference) is the sublation of difference as time or time as difference. This sublation is the *self-presence* of eternal self-sameness of Being. This sublation, thus, through annulling time, restores the self-sameness of Being:

> This 'I'='I' is the movement which reflects itself into itself; for since this identity, being absolute negativity, is absolute difference, the self-identity of the 'I' stands over against this pure difference which, as pure and at the same time objective to the self-knowing self, has to be expressed as Time. So that, just as previously essence was declared to be the unity of Thought and Extension, it would now have to be grasped as the unity of Thought and Time (Hegel 1998: 489).

The Spirit appears in time, as the movement of self-differentiation only as long as the Spirit has not grasped the Notion. Therefore the Absolute Spirit, as the absolute grasping of the pure Notion, is this grasp itself and nothing but this grasp: it comes to itself by abolishing the very movement which makes itself possible:

> Time is the Notion itself that is *there* and which presents itself to consciousness as empty intuition; for this reason, Spirit necessarily appears in Time, and it appears in Time just so long as it has not *grasped* its pure Notion, i.e. has not annulled Time. It is the *outer*, intuited

> pure Self which is *not grasped* by the Self, the merely intuited Notion; when this latter grasps itself it sets aside its Time-form, comprehends this intuiting, and is a comprehended and comprehending intuiting. Time, therefore, appears as the destiny and necessity of Spirit that is not yet complete within itself (Ibid: 487).

Thus in speculative philosophy, difference as time, or time of difference is thought only *in sight of* its *sublation*. Difference of time—or, time of difference—is not thought as such and cannot be thought as such in speculative philosophy precisely because being 'speculative', it cannot think time as anything but in terms of presence. The question of time—time that is difference appearing as phenomenological consciousness—would always be asked and determined only in terms of presence as identity or identity as self-presence. The Absolute Spirit as abolition of time is the absolute self-presence of self-same Being; it is the truth of time, the meaning of time itself: in other words, the truth or meaning of time is negation of time itself, negation of difference; it sublates sensible non-Being of every particular 'now' (that means presence is sublation of time, meaning as sublation, or signification is the sublation of sensible, etc.). Therefore, whenever the question of time is posed, it is always posed as question concerning the *meaning* of time; whenever time is thought, it is always thought in terms of *presence* (because presence is meaning itself); whenever this question of time in relation to difference is posed, it is always thought in terms of unity as presence. Unity as presence is recuperation or gathering of all the negativity of Spirit; it is the acts of Spirit's penetration and digestion of all that appears as time. The Absolute Spirit, as absolute unity, is this gathering of the entire wealth of time into its self-presence; it is the appropriation of every difference and other of the spirit. But how time, time that Spirit appears in its self-difference, is thought in terms of presence? In response to this question, we propose the following thesis:

As mentioned above about the essential relationship of the problematic of meaning and presence, that philosophy thinks time only as presence because philosophy that aspires to think time, cannot not ask the meaning of time. Metaphysics of presence is, therefore, always metaphysics of signification; it is Being that presents itself as signification: this logic operates in any philosophy that understands time and difference as a question concerning the meaning of time. In this way, time and difference (time and difference as Being thrown outside of itself, Being to whom time and difference yet does not belong, Being that has not yet recuperated its non-being, its negativity and therefore, is not the grasp of Absolute Notion) would be a question of Being, question for Being. Non-being would be thought in terms of Being; time as non-being would be thought in terms of presence; and in both ways, difference would be a property of the Being that differs; and difference that, thus, belongs to identity. Ontology—whether Speculative ontology or Fundamental ontology (other than classical ontology, Heidegger's project on *Kant and the Problem of Metaphysics*) is nothing but this: Being thinking it's other at the limit of its being, thinking non-being in its being. To think time in presence by representing time, to think time as presence—presence that ties Being to its thought: such is ontology as question of Being. The possibility of thinking non-being, nothingness and death, possibility of thinking the abyss of difference (where being is outside of itself) and thinking the "Now of the Night": on this possibility, ontology rests its foundation and its truth. Therefore thinking time and difference at once poses impossibility for philosophy to think, a limit of thinking and its poverty, and precisely, because of it, to be able to think the unthinkable also constitutes its richness and its absolute truth. Thus, the problem of time has always seemed to bring irresolvable aporia to any philosophy that thinks time in terms of its meaning. Who, more than Hegel, apart from Aristotle, is aware of the aporia that time brings to philosophy: that time, the instant that appears as soon as vanishes, and this appearing and vanishing itself, does not have its truth as being, *is not*? But it is this being itself, so Hegel says, (that does not have its truth of being, whose being is not to have being and that is its being) that must be thought:

> The Now is pointed to, *this* Now; 'Now'; it has already ceased to be in the act of pointing to it. The Now that *is*, is another Now than the one pointed to, and we see that the Now is just this: to be no more just when it is. The Now, as it is pointed out to us, is Now that *has been*, and this is its truth; it has not the truth of *being*. Yet this much is true, that it has been. But what essentially *has* been

> [*gewesen ist*] is, in fact, not an essence that is [*kein Wesen*]; *it is not*, and it was with *being* that we are concerned (Ibid: 63).

Time is thought that *is not*: with the *sense* of *non-being*, time is already thought, already secretly determined in terms of being. Because it is a question of *truth* of time, the truth of time *is*: time *is not* truth, time *is not* signification. Therefore, truth of time is not time; it is other than time, yet not timeless as absolute other as well which can be outside time. The meaning of time, the truth of time, is: time *is not;* it is sublation of time as *presence* that has the character of negativity in general. To understand this problem, let us follow that Hegel himself invites us to think:

Suppose the 'now' of the *sensible* time, the 'now' of the instant that appears only to vanish at the very moment of uttering 'Now', is Night. If one asks what is 'Now'? Hegel invites us answer: "Now is Night". But the moment one writes down this truth, one already finds out that it is no longer 'Night'. Yet, this 'Now' of 'Night' has not become a Day either but is preserved its truth in that 'it is Night' (without remaining Night of the sensible)in the face of the Day. The truth of Night (Night is the *sensible* 'now') is preserved in *sense*, and yet, the Night itself no longer remains *sensible* 'now': this preserving and permanent 'Now' that is other than either Day and Night, yet it *is* through the fact that Day and Night *is not*. As such, this 'Now' ('Now' as that has become sense and other than itself, yet through the sensible 'now' of Night which is preserved in this negation)is indifferent to either Day and Night, is permanent 'Now' as, what Hegel elsewhere calls, *presence*. I quote Hegel:

> The Now that is Night is preserved, i.e. it is treated as what it professes to be, as something that is; but it proves itself to be, on the contrary, something that is not. The Now does indeed preserve itself, but as something that is not Night; equally, it preserves itself in the face of the Day that it now is, as something that also is not Day, in other words, as a negative in general. This self-preserving Now is, therefore, not immediate but mediated; for it is determined as a permanent and self–preserving Now through the fact that something else, viz. Day and Night, is not. As so determined, it is still just as simply Now as before, and in this simplicity is indifferent to what happens in

> it; just as little as Night and Day are its being, just as much as also is it Day and Night; it is not in the least affected by this its other-being. A simple thing of this kind which is through negation, which is neither This nor That, a not-This, and is with equal indifference This as well as That—such a thing we call a universal (Ibid: 60).

This process—preservation while negating—is, as we know, the work of 'sublation' (*Aufhebung*). The sense of 'Now' is sublation of the sensible 'now'. In 'Now' as sense, which sensible 'now' passes into, is negated, and yet is preserved as 'Now': this 'Now' is an infinite 'Now' of presence, which has non-being (Day and Night) as its being. Presence *is* through the fact that Day and Night *is not*; it's being is to have non-being in it's being: such is the nature of it's being. Sense *is* inasmuch as sensible *is not*; sense is sublation of sensible that sublates the now of Night. Sense *presents* itself as sense or rather presence *presents* to itself as sense, as universal language that says not what is meant but the universal as truth:

> It is as a universal too that we *utter* what the sensuous [content] is. What we say is: 'This'; or, the *universal* This; or, 'it is', i.e. *Being in general.* Of course, we do not *envisage* the universal This or Being in general, but we *utter* the universal; in other words, we do not strictly say what in this sense certainty we *mean* to say. But language, as we see, is the more truthful; in it, we ourselves directly refute what we *mean* to say, an since the universal is the true [content] of sense-certainty and language expresses the this true [content] alone, it is just not possible for us to ever to say, or express in words, a sensuous being that we *mean* (Ibid).

Thus sense is not what we mean of sensuous being; it is the mediated negation of the sensuous being as universal. The continuity of the present 'Now' that persists and continuous in the appearing and vanishing of every sensuous 'now', is the sense of time, its truth as universal. Sense, as the utterance of the universal, is *Being in general.* Sense of the presence as continuous 'Now' persisting in before 'now' and after 'now' and through them remaining self-same and yet, indifferent to both, has this characteristics of *Being in general.* Finally, representing time as presence, time would be thought as sense, which has the characteristics of Being. Time can only be thought as presence in Hegelian philosophy; non-being allows itself to be thought only in terms of Being: speculative signification, which has characterizes of Being in general, is thus (because it is appropriation of sensible now), the arrest of time itself: it assimilates every non-being and reduces every asymmetrical difference into thinkable presence of self-identical Being. Sense as infinite negativity is negation of negation that forever makes return of the identical possible. The possibility of presence (as sense which is sublation as it is) is the possibility of the self-preservation of the self-same 'Now'; it is the possibility of the eternal return of the self-same 'Now' to its eternal self-repose. This *re-turn* always presents itself as circle that comes to reach the very beginning at the end, where beginning meets its end, and thus closes itself. Being maintains its self-sameness despite the caesura of time, which introduces only to the extent that the end infinitely regenerate in the beginning and the beginning meets the end: the mythical figure of this return is the cunning Ulysses—self-preservative, narcissist, always longing for home. This movement of the circle accomplishing itself is a gathering of many 'nows' into its unity all taken together; as such, 'Now' as presence is a synthetic unity of various 'nows'; presence is the eternal return of the self-same subject:

> The return of the line is the circle; it is the Now, Before and After which have closed together in a unity in which these dimensions are indifferent, so that Before is equally After, and vice versa. It is in circular motion that the necessary paralysis of these dimensions is first posited in space. Circular motion is spatial or subsistent unity of the dimensions of time. The point proceeds towards a place which is its future, and leaves one which is the past; but what it has left behind is at the same time what it has still to reach: it has been already at the place which it is reaching. Its goal is the point which is its past; and this is the truth of the time, that the goal is not the future but the past. The motion which relates itself to the centre is itself the *plane,* motion as the synthetic whole in which exist its moments, the extinction of the motion in the centre, the motion itself and its relation to its extinction, namely the radii of the circle. But this plane itself moves and becomes the other of itself, a complete space; or the reversion-into-itself, the immobile centre, becomes a universal point in which the whole is peacefully absorbed. In other words, it

> is motion in its essence, motion which has sublated the distinction of Now, Before and After, its dimensions or its Notion. In the circle, these are in a unity; the circle is the restored Notion of duration, Motion extinguishes within itself (Hegel 1970: 43-44).

The 'now' of the sensible negates itself (because the moment it occurs itself, it becomes other and passes into non-being) and this negation, because it is nothing but *has been* and *is not*, is again negated. With this negation of negation, 'Now' returns into the first 'Now', but as mediated. With this return, the Now that is maintained here as presence, maintains this presence as being through the negation of its own nothingness. As such, this 'Now' is the unity of the 'nows' of the very appearing and vanishing before and after. Hegel points out this movement of the eternal return of the same as circle, which negates its own negation to return to itself as being in the following way:

> (1) I point out the 'Now', and it is asserted to be the truth. I point it out, however, as something that *has been*, or as something that has been superseded; I set aside the first truth. (2) I now assert as the second truth that it *has been*, that it is superseded. (3)But what has been, *is not*; I set aside the second truth, its *having been*, its super session, and thereby negate the negation of the 'Now', and thus return to the first assertion, that the '*Now' is*. The 'Now', and pointing out the 'Now', are thus so constituted that neither the one nor the other is something immediate and simple, but a movement which contains various moments. A *This* is posited; but it is rather an *other* that is posited, or the This is superseded; and this *otherness,* or the setting aside of the first, is itself *in turn set aside*, and so has returned into the first. However, this first, thus reflected into itself, is not exactly the same as it was to begin with, viz, something *immediate*; on the contrary, on the contrary, it is *something that is reflected into itself,* or a *simple* entity which, in its otherness, remains what it is: a Now which is an absolute plurality of Nows... The pointing-out of the Now is itself the movement which expresses what Now is in truth, viz, a result, or a plurality of Nows all taken together; and pointing-out is the experience of learning that Now is a universal (Hegel 1998: 63-64).

Thus the movement of the circle is the unity of heterogeneous moments of many instants: the circle is the geometric-temporal figure of reappropriation of its very other: it maintains its self-sameness throughout this process of Being passing into nothingness and nothingness passing into Being. With this thought of presence (as unity of various 'nows' and 'Now' as abiding in passing), the unthinkable heterogeneity of temporal instants would be determined in sight of the 'Now'. With this *semiology* of presence, the condition of possibility of experiencing non-being of time for a phenomenological consciousness would be achieved, and all the aporias that non-being of time brings, would be resolved and sublated: such is the desire of Hegelian *speculative semiological-phenomenology of presence.*

In *The Philosophy of Nature*, which forms the second part of the *Encyclopaedia*, Hegel presents the aporias that time brings on two accounts:

1. That every instant of sensuous 'now' *is* only to the extent it is already always *is not* and is *not* of *yet to be*: each instant is *simultaneously* its other and therefore is *non-simultaneous*, non-co-existing with itself; and at the same time, it is also non-co-existing of other nows that precedes this 'now' and follows this 'now'. Time is: not the fixity and arresting of points that distributed in co-existing space but rather the perpetual restlessness of the negative that negates the given fixity of space. Therefore, time appears as the truth of the space, space that negates itself and sublates itself; in negation, which is already becoming of this negation, space is already time. Time is the impossibility of the fixity of the space; or, rather, as restless truth of the negative of space, time cannot be thought as arresting identity of each instant as 'now'. Rather time is difference that has stepped out of identity as perpetual appearing and vanishing. For speculative knowledge to be possible, Spirit self-externalizes itself by introducing this difference and interruption as time, between time of writing (by pointing out of 'Now', the sense of 'Now' as presence) and time of every particular 'now' (of the Night). By releasing difference (which is the negation of the indifference of the given)—time as the interval between subject of experience

and object of experience—is the condition of possibility of speculative knowledge (Here Hegel is the heir of Kant but here, unlike Kant, the condition of possibility of knowledge is not transcendental but this very time itself as experience and not a pure form of intuition). But this very condition of possibility of speculative knowledge, that is, time itself—precisely because it is releasing of the restless difference of the negative—can only *be* as non-being, can only be in relation to what is non-being of being. At each instance 'now' is only to the extent that there are 'nows' in relation to which this 'now' which is already 'not now', in relation to which this 'now' (of the Night) cannot co-existent. Speculative knowledge—thought on the metaphysical model of identity of Being with itself and *co-existence* of itself with itself—precisely because it needs difference for knowledge to be possible, brings to itself its impossibility by opening itself to time of difference, time that brings various instants (there is no Now, there are 'nows') that exclude each other, and are *non-co-existing*. This is first aporia of time: its non-co-existence is required for speculative knowledge, and yet, this in turn halts speculative knowledge by introducing unaccountable non-co-existences of many 'nows'. Time seems to have become at once the condition of possibility and impossibility of knowledge. The semiology of time as uttering the universal, must leave behind something what does not have the characteristics of Being in general: as a result, something always is left behind unuttered, and for this reason, sense of 'Now' can never co-exist with its own process of becoming sense. The rift remains open like a tear, a wound un-remedied. This remedy of this aporia demands that there should be—for speculative experience of time to be possible—co-existence of what do not co-exist with 'now': that is, there must be simultaneity of what are non-simultaneous nows.

2. Because time is the restlessness of the negative and releasing of difference by negation of indifference of space, time is very *becoming* of the Notion's self-externality: of being passing into nothing and nothing passing into being. In order for speculative knowledge of this 'being passing into nothing and nothing into

> being' to be possible, the Notion should be able to grasp this very *becoming*; it must abide, persist, and subsist in this perpetual very non-abiding, non-persisting and non-subsisting becoming. This is now the second aporia: speculative knowledge of time to be possible (which is Notion in its *eternal* self-presence of Being), it must be able to persist and subsist in its self-presence; and yet, it cannot be absolute knowledge either if in its knowledge the restlessness of the becoming gets erased in the process: in other words, absolute knowledge must be both persisting and continuous, and yet, at the same time, be irreducibly restless and radically discontinuous. Sense *Now* is sense only on the condition that sensible *now* negates itself and becomes sense *Now,* but this very negation itself cannot be sublated, so that what the Notion seeks to grasp, *this* and *now*, slips away in its grasp. The separation of Notion (as the eternal grasp) from ungraspable becoming, —this very gap between the sensible *now* and sense *Now*—is required for speculative knowledge; and yet, ambiguously, speculative knowledge also requires the closing up of this caesura and must return, like a circle, to its eternal self-sameness. This rift, this gap can only be closed on the *necessary condition* that that *sensible* now and *sense* Now co-exist together in peaceful identity without any remnant: it is on this condition, speculative spirit would reach absolute knowledge. Therefore, the remedy of this aporia requires that time should be conceived as at once continuous and discontinuous, abiding and perishing; or, rather, there should be something that continuously persisting in the perpetual destruction of each moment by another moment, something abiding in the very process of disappearing.

Both the aporias, mentioned here, are, in fact the same. Speculative knowledge to be possible—by addressing these two aporias—time must be conceived as (1) co-existing, contraction, simultaneity of many nows in sense Now, and (2) There must be the *Now* that should be continuous and persisting in every passing nows. *That means the knowledge of the time-consciousness itself demands time to be conceived on the synchronic modality,* Time identical to itself, and therefore, by a necessary gesture, point towards thinking time on the basis of certain metaphysics of identity. Hegel conceives this synchronic modality of time—*Now* as contraction of many nows and continuously abiding nows—as *Presence*. Time, would be thought in Hegelian philosophy as presence. Presence: the sense of time, the being of time, and the universal being of every particular sensuous non-being. How, then presence is determined as contracting various nows in their becoming and as the abiding in every passing nows?

It is not that Being is imposed on non-Being but that time as non-being, the self-external differences themselves must negate themselves, must pass over, and must sublate themselves: this sublation has the truth of time itself which is presence. In his early essay, "Ousia and Gramme" in *Margins of Philosophy*, Jacques Derrida examines how the determination of time as presence constitutes the fundamental structure of Western metaphysics, and shows how both in Hegelian and in Heidegger's critique of Hegelian philosophy, this privilege of presence constitutes their thoughts. Thus Derrida writes about the privilege of Presence as Now which is continuous in every sensuous passing nows in the following way: "The impossibility, when barely formulated, contradicts itself, is experienced as the possibility of the impossible. This impossibility implies in its essence, in order to be what it is, that the other now, with which a now cannot co-exist, is also in a certain way the same, is also a now as such, and that it co-exists with that which cannot co-exist with it. The impossibility of co-existence can be posited as such only on the basis of a certain co-existence, of a certain simultaneity of the non simultaneous in which the alterity and identity of the now are manifested together in a differentiated element of a certain same" (Derrida 1982: 55). Here Derrida shows how in Hegelian thinking of time in terms of Presence determines difference in the name of a certain Now as *Same* to the extent that this Presence as ontological possibility of impossibility already determines presence as Being (or, Being as presence!) to the extent that Being always already is determined as possibility. In Hegelian philosophy, Time—which seems to be unthinkable and whose aporias Aristotle brings out in his *Physics*—seems to be resolved by itself. Like Aristotle, as Derrida shows in this essay, Hegel in his dialectical way, affirms the very unthinkable contradictions inherent in the concept of time (that time *is* to the extent that it is not, and it *is not* to the extent that it *is*), and thereby escapes from the very contradictions themselves. Such is this ruse of Reason in Hegelian philosophy.

The heterogeneity of various nows of the many dimensions are heterogeneous only to the extent that these various nows are also, to certain extent, nothing but the *same* Now (Derrida 1982): Now that continues in (a) the now that has become non-being of the past now, (b)in the non-being that is anticipated being of the future and (c)as the negative unity of ever vanishing and appearing now of the present (it is negative unity because it is its own negation of 'already non-being' and yet to be negated of anticipatory being and in this sense, both the non-being of the being and being of the non-being would be thought on the basis of *is* of the present). The non-simultaneousness and non-co-existence of the various nows are only to the extent that Now is *present* in the now of past and now of the future. This singular present as Now is—as *differences* resolving of themselves through negation of the negation—is at once the continuous Now: that is, *presence* which is present in and with the ever non-continuous nows:

> The dimensions of time, *present, future*, and *past*, are the becoming of externality as such, and the resolution of it into the differences of being as passing over into nothing, and of nothing as passing over into being. The immediate vanishing of these differences into *singularity* is the present as *Now* which, as singularity, is *exclusive* of the other moments, and yet at the same time completely *continuous* in them, and is only this vanishing of its being into nothing and of nothing into its Being (Hegel 1970: 37).

The singular presence of Now as the continuity persisting in non-continuity—this simultaneity in non-simultaneous, the eternal presence in various appearing and vanishing of various nows, the identity of the self-sameness in differences—is not time itself, but yet, not outside time altogether. Determined as such, this truth of time is eternity, eternity that presents itself as *presence*.

> The present *is*, only because the Past is not; conversely, the being of the Now is determined as not–being, and the non-being of its being is the Future; the Present is the negative unity. The non-being of the being which is replaced by the Now, is the Past; the being of the non-being which is contained in the Present, is the Future. In the positive meaning of time, it can be said that only the Present *is*, that Before and After are not. But the concrete Present is the

> result of the Past and is pregnant with the Future. The true Present, therefore, is eternity (Ibid: 39).

In this determination of time as presence, in this thought of time in the name of presence, both the conditions of the possibility of experience of time (both in fact amounts to the same, as we have seen)—the possibility of thinking time as continuous and the possibility of thinking presence as simultaneous—is seen to be fulfilled. Henceforth, everything in Hegelian philosophy—Notion, Spirit, Idea, Truth, Sense, Subject, Absolute—would be thought on this metaphysical determination of time as *presence*: the *Aufhebung* of time as eternity, on the synchronic modality of time that gives itself as its own identity as *re*captured, *re*cuperated negativity in the *re*turn of self-sameness of I=I: return that *re*-turns to the same by forming the circle, as far as the beginning infinitely regenerate its result in the end. Therefore, the metaphysics of time as metaphysics of presence, always conceives itself as the metaphysics of the circular path of *becoming* to *be*, this *is* of *presence, this* I=I of Notion where difference (the *diremption* of Notion) is sublated. In Hegelian philosophy, difference props up, bringing the vertiginous abyss into the self-sameness of Reason and time brings its inevitable delay in this *re* of the return of the same *only in sight of its own impossibility, only as far as difference is not captured yet, only as far as time is not recuperated yet.* Therefore, Notion (this eternity of presence as the recapture of time and difference) is the power over time. The Notion, the singular presence, is eternal because it is the recapture of time:

> The real is certainly distinct from time, but is also essentially identical with it. What is real is limited, and the Other to this negation is *outside* it; therefore the determinateness in it is self-external and is consequently the contradiction of its being; the abstraction of this externality and unrest of its contradiction is time itself. The finite is perishable and *temporal* because, Unlike Notion, it is not in its own self total negativity; true, this negativity, is immanent in it as its universal essence, but the finite is not adequate to this essence: it is *one sided*, and consequently it is related to negativity as to the power that dominates it. The Notion, however, in its freely self-existent identity as I=I, is in and for itself absolute negativity and freedom.

> Time, therefore, has no power over the Notion, nor is the Notion in time or temporal; on the contrary, *it* is the power over time, which is this negativity only *qua* externality. Only the natural, therefore, is subject to time in so far as it is finite; the true, on the other hand, the Idea, Spirit, is *eternal* (Ibid: 35).

Philosophy, understood speculatively, is this eternal comprehension of time where temporality is comprehended as eternity's *immanent* self-diremption: the Absolute posits itself to itself *its own* other, the Absolute identity it posits *its own* difference, the Absolute Present it posits its other as time; and since this 'time', 'other', or 'difference' cannot maintain itself its identity, it must negate itself and sublate itself into the self-sameness of presence. In this way, Hegel's speculative philosophy hopes to reconcile philosophy's unreconciled dualism between eternity and time, between infinite and finite, between identity and difference, between Being and other. Philosophy constitutes itself in this reconciliation as this reconciliation, constitutes its *arche* and its *telos*, its ground as self-presence. The whole self-engendering movement of becoming Absolute, and thereby releasing of time and difference, presents itself as this circular mode of appropriating and recuperating its own negativity. If philosophy is the eternal comprehension of time, then the Absolute Present would not be conceived as outside time (if so, then eternity would not be eternal either), but it cannot be temporal either (if so, eternity would not be eternal again);but rather time must be conceived as *immanent* self-othering of eternity itself. Philosophy before Hegel could not reconcile time and eternity, Being and other, Identity and difference (so Hegel believes) because they are seen to be transcendental to each other (here Kant's transcendental philosophy is the main target of Hegel's critique) but also because (both are in fact the same) they are seen to be self-subsistence entities or substances; instead Hegel conceived time as *immanent to eternity* and difference as contaminating negativity (that being must pass over into nothingness and nothingness must pass over into being) which sublate themselves:

> ...Eternity is not before or after time, not before the creation of the world, nor when it perishes; rather is eternity the absolute present, the Now, without before and after. The world is created, is now being created, and has eternally been created; this presents itself in

> the form of the preservation of the world. Creating is the activity of the absolute Idea; the Idea of Nature, like the Idea as such, is eternal. (b)In the question whether the world or Nature, in its finitude has a beginning in time or not, one thinks of the world or Nature as such, i.e. as the universal; and the true universal is the Idea, which we have already said is eternal. The finite, however, is temporal, it has a before and after; and when the finite is our object we are in time. It has a beginning but not an absolute one; its time begins with it, and time belongs only to the sphere of finitude. Philosophy is timeless comprehension, of time too and of all things generally in their eternal mode. Having rid oneself of the conception of the absolute beginning of time, one assumes the opposite conception of an infinite time; but infinite time, when it is still conceived as time, not as sublated time, is also to be distinguished from eternity. It is not this time but another time, and again another time, and so on (Ibid: 15-16).

Time is no longer the immobile form of *pure intuition* that is transcendental to experience; it is rather this very movement of becoming. Kant, by determining time (which is pure intuition) as *transcendental* form of inner sense (form without form, what Kant calls pure form) and transcendental to *possible* experience as such, could not (precisely because of his determining the condition of possibility as *transcendental* which is supposed to make knowledge of experience possible) reconcile the gap between the experience and time (in which experience is supposed to have been given), a reconciliation that is demanded (to close the gap between the condition of possibility of knowledge and the experience whose condition time is)if synthetic a priori judgment were to be possible. Now Hegel claims to have been able to reconcile (this is the object of philosophy, as Hegel says) the gap between the condition of the possibility of knowledge and experience itself whose knowledge we seek by conceiving Notion (which is absolute knowledge) as the eternal comprehension of time in which time *immanent* to the Notion itself. For Hegel, time itself is, then, this very becoming, and not pure transcendental form in which experience is given (Ibid: 35). As Notion that is eternity, time is *immanent* to it; and as Notion, time itself is this eternal: unlike Kant, the condition of possibility of knowledge (if we are still allowed to use this phrase) is not only *a priori* but also *a posteriori*, not only *synthetic* but also *analytic*. In other words, Notion (as both *a priori* and *a posteriori*, both analytic and synthetic) is Absolute. By thinking time as immanent to Notion (and thereby reconciling the gap between time and eternity, between infinite and finite, between subject and object so and so forth.), Hegel thereby excludes any diachronic relation of time to a transcendental other (Ibid). One can see in the following cryptic additional note in *Philosophy of Nature*, the whole Speculative philosophy is at stake, namely, how the whole conceptual schema operative in speculative ontology is built around the modality of thinking time as Presence, as eternity of *Aufhebung*.

> But in its Notion, time itself is eternal; for time as such —not any particular time, nor now—is its Notion, and this, like every Notion generally, is eternal, and therefore also absolute presence. Eternity will not come to be, nor was it, but it *is*.... The universal as law, also has a process within it, and lives only as a process; but it is not a *part* of the process, is not in process, but contains its two sides, and is itself processless. On its phenomenal side, law enters into the time- process, in that the moments of the Notion have a show of self-subsistence; but in their Notion, the excluded differences are reconciled and co-exist in peace again. The Idea, Spirit, transcends time because it is in itself the Notion of time; it is eternal, in and for itself, and it is not dragged into the time- process because it does not lose itself in one side of the process (Ibid: 36).

The Notion is eternal; it is the absolute reconciliation of being and thought: with this metaphysical determination of Being as *presence*, speculative philosophy is supposed to have reached its closure. From Aristotle 'Unmoved mover' via Kantian 'Pure Sense' of transcendentalism till Hegel's determination of Notion as the extinction of the very circle of time, time (which is non-being, being out of itself, difference as Notion's othering) would be thought in terms of Being.

Is it not that for Heidegger too there is the proximity of the being (that questions the meaning of Being) and the meaning of Being (that is questioned) has an essential relationship of identity, as implied in his notion of what he calls 'hermeneutic of facticity'? Is this not the whole stake of the question that is raised, in *Being and*

Time, about the meaning of Being? Is it not that Heidegger too repeats the very gesture of the time as circle that constitutes onto-theo-logical constitution of metaphysics, not of course in the name of eternity, but as the constitution of the thought of the very finitude of Dasein's 'being towards-death'? Is not that the unthought of metaphysics, the ontological *difference as difference*—which cannot be thought within the closure of metaphysics—is nothing but *presence* to the extent that presence is already determined as Being? If so, then Heidegger's delimitation of metaphysics—the history of beings that has runs its course from Plato to Nietzsche, while exempting Parmenides on the one end and himself on the other end—becomes a highly problematic issue that we have to address.

Time and difference in Heidegger's thought:

Let us establish our point of contact with Heidegger once again. In *Being and Time*, Heidegger conceives one of his two fold tasks of working out the question of Being as "an original explication of time as the horizon of the understanding of Being, in terms of temporality as the Being of Dasein which understands Being" (Heidegger 1978: 61). Dasein (time is the horizon to understand this Dasein who understands itself) is the Being for whom the *meaning of Being* is at issue, as the *being there*, the fact *it is the-there-of Being*. This self-understanding and *self-sufficiency* of Dasein for whom the meaning of Being is at issue, is called '*the hermeneutic of facticity*' (Heidegger 1999). The question of time is asked as the horizon for the understanding of the Being as a question concerning the *meaning* of Being understood in its self-sufficiency. The meaning of Being for the Being that asks this question of its Being has this '*facticity*' as its proper self-sufficiency: Dasein is the Being (who questions its meaning) who, in the fact of being there, is *self-sufficient* in its being there. Being is the self-sufficient being there whose proper being is that it understands its Being: it means, the *meaning* of Being is proper to Being! Time as the horizon for the understanding of Being, thus, is understood in the name of *self-sufficiency* of Being, in the name of Being who is *identical* with the meaning of Being that it asks. Being is self-sufficient and identical in so far as it is a question of the meaning of Being which it poses for itself, and in the same way, as we have seen in our discussion of

Hegel, the question of meaning is posed insofar as it is the question of Being. Each time the question of time as the horizon within which this meaning of Being is to be asked is posed, is posed in as much as it is a question of *meaning* and of *Being*, inasmuch as it is for the understanding of the *self-sufficiency* of Being which is *identical* with its understanding. Time here is already understood in relation to meaning, and in relation to certain self-sufficiency and identity of Being with itself. Time is relation to meaning: with this determination of time, as we have seen in Hegel's case, time is presence. In *Early Greek Thinking*, Heidegger thinks time in relation to truth as becoming unconcealment:

> What is to come also become present, namely as outside the expanse of unconcealment. What presents itself as non-present is what is absent. As such it remains essentially related to what is presently present, in as much as it either comes forward into the expanse of unconcealment or withdraws from it. Even what is absent is something present, for *as* absent from the expanse, it presents itself in unconcealment. What is past and what is to come are also *eontia*. Consequently eon means becoming present in unconcealment (Heidegger 1975c: 34-35).

Would it radically depart from the onto-theo-logical determination of time as *presence* where the non-being of time would be determined (with the various dimensions of time of that 'has been' and as a now 'coming forward') on the basis of being? Heidegger does not think time negatively as *Aufhebung* but time is still thought in relation to the meaning of time: *Aletheia* as *presencing*. Heidegger's overcoming of metaphysics (that asks the question of time in relation to the truth of time and as a question concerning the meaning of Being) inhabits, to a certain extent, and repeats the very structure of on-theo-logical determination of time and Being as presence (Derrida 1982: 51-52). Thus we see in Hegel's onto-theo-logical determination of time, presence is immediately linked a question of the *sense* of time, that has the characteristics of 'Being in general'; the same thing happens in Heidegger's delimitation of metaphysics in his very claim to think Being and Time otherwise than negativity.

In his later writings, however, time no longer appears as the horizon of the question of the meaning of Being, but the meaning of Being is never abandoned. Time does not disappear, however, but it becomes a question time and Being in relation to the epochal transformations of Being. Time is thought in relation to *Appropriation* that temporalizes, whereas the *Appropriation* is understood as the framework "in which man and Being are delivered over to each other, that is, we must enter into what we call *the event of appropriation*...The event of appropriation is that realm, vibrating within itself, through which man and Being reach each other in their nature, achieve their active nature by losing those qualities with which metaphysics endowed them" (Heidegger 1969: 36-37). What happens then to *difference as difference*, ontological difference? In the thought of *Appropriation* as *belonging* together of man and Being, ontological difference already appears as *perdurance*. How can the ontological difference be thought as *perdurance*?

It has brought us to our reading of *Identity and Difference* where the ontological difference is thought as unthought in metaphysics as history of beings. Thought rigorously, the ontological difference between Being and beings, the very unthought of metaphysics, is the difference of a 'between' (this is already implied in the thought of *belonging* together, thought in relation to Appropriation) "in which the overwhelming and the arrival are held toward one another, are borne away from and toward each other. The difference of Being and beings, as differentiation of overwhelming and arrival, is perdurance (Austrag) of the two in *unconcealing keeping in concealment*. Within this perdurance there prevails a clearing of what veils and closes itself off—and this its prevalence bestows the being apart, and the being toward each other, of overwhelming and arrival" (Ibid: 65).

Unconcealing keeping in concealment: truth as *Aletheia*, *presencing*. Ontological difference between Being and beings as perdurance is *unconcealing keeping in concealment*: with this thought, ontological difference is already thought in terms of the truth as presence or presence as truth. Truth as unconcealing keeping in concealment, *Aletheia* as presence: presence is seen here as movement of differentiation, which is what Heidegger calls as '*step back*' from metaphysics. This *step back* consists of Being thought in terms of the difference. But Being is thought in terms of difference only as much as difference is already thought as presence, as *unconcealing keeping in concealment*; still it is question of the truth of Being and nothing but this. Whether time is thought as the horizon for the question of Being or not in his later thinking, the thought of presence still holds sway in the thought of ontological difference. As one cannot separate the truth of Being from the being that asks this truth, determination of ontological difference in terms of presence and of truth, therefore, is already linked to Being. To the extent that difference still is thought in relation to the an opening (that opens for the sake of presencing), and to the extent that difference still is thought in relation to truth as presence, ontological unthought of metaphysics would still be inhabited within the closure of metaphysics that it seeks to overcome. In that way, the relation between the onto-theo-logical determination of difference (here Speculative difference of Hegelian philosophy) and overcoming of this difference as ontological difference, becomes much more problematic than what Heidegger himself may have been able to think. Therefore, the exceeding of metaphysics would not be point to another presence or another truth, but in relation to entirely other texts. As Jacques Derrida remarks,

> Therefore the sign of excess must be absolutely excessive as concerns all possible presence-absence, all possible production or disappearance of beings in general, and yet, *in some manner* it must still signify, in a manner unthinkable by metaphysics as such. In order to exceed metaphysics it is necessary that a trace be inscribed within the text of metaphysics, a trace that continues to signal not in the direction of another presence or another form of presence, but in the direction of an entirely other text. Such a trace cannot be thought more metaphysico (Derrida 1982: 65).

Trace: difference otherwise than Being and otherwise than presence–absence, otherwise than light and its negativity, otherwise than time thought as negativity, otherwise than ontological difference, otherwise than thought in the name of Being of self-sufficiency and identity with its questioning (see Derrida 1982: 38). It is thus a response to an entirely Other, Other as Other, infinitely Other, beyond any totality (whether the speculative totality or the totality formed as identity of the Being with its meaning). Time would, then, no longer be thought as negativity of the self-externalization of the Idea that would be annihilated when Notion grasps its very effectuation, and thereby completing its process of consciousness's I=I; temporality will then rather be thought as an infinite *departure* towards an Other which no discourse of ontology can master. Trace of the face of the Other in (non) relation to whom time can no longer be seen as synchronic to my time, but a time that is radically *diachronic*, asymmetrical to any immanence of Being. Diachronic time is not ontological time of eternal circular self-appropriation but an irreducible difference, more ancient than any light of Being and its self-presence, deferring any possibility of closure, exceeding any name of presence or truth, sense or negativity, Being or its meaning. Difference: interruption in the circle of the same, an inevitable delay that never synchronize itself with itself, never is present to itself, time that never returns into the same. Such an unthought of difference would be other than either Hegelian speculative difference or ontological difference, difference older than Being and negativity:

> Perhaps difference is older than Being itself. There may be difference still more unthought than the difference between Being and beings... Beyond Being and beings, this difference, ceaselessly differing from and deferring (itself) would trace (itself) (by itself)—this differance would be the first or last trace if one still could speak, here, of origin and end (Ibid: 67).

In the next chapter, we will consider the unthought of difference and time other than speculative and ontological difference, in relation to an entirely Other. Such a thought of time should be able point towards the problematic of ethical question at the limit of philosophy, the 'question' that has remained unthought in the history of being.

Interrupting/Disrupting Speculative Time

The problem

Ontology, that has always determined time on the basis of Being, is the very possibility of the philosophy: it determined Being as synchrony of the self-same! In this way, the Other as Other has remained unthought in the history of Being, an unthought more profound than the unthought of ontological difference, the unthought that cannot be reduced to the *meaning* concerning Being. Synchrony here is determined either as the ground that constitutes onto-theo-logy, or is thought to be he phenomenological horizon for the question of the meaning of Being (as in early Heidegger. Later, however, Heidegger renounces this project of fundamental ontology in relation to the phenomenological horizon of time in which the question of Being would be asked): in either mode, synchrony is always the oblivion of the call of the Other, a call that comes from an immemorial past that has never been retained in the present, a call from future that can never be understood in the light of the present (in the light of Being present, in other words, the call that comes from the future that can never be anticipated in the name of presence). *Retention* and *protention, anticipation* and *(re) presentation* of 'what has been' and what is yet to pass and would pass, are modes of synchronization. This is what we have seen in the case of Hegel where this synchrony of various dimensions of time is understood as problematic of *simultaneity* and *continuity* in which Being presents itself even in non-being. *Simultaneity* and *continuity* are the modes of contraction of heterogeneity of various dimensions of time, which makes possible for unity of the manifold representations (this is the task of any philosophy of representation: how to unify manifold representations into the self-sameness of Being. Thus philosophy of representation is always the philosophy of the same, despite Hegelian pretensions to be a philosophy of difference). Inasmuch as one aspires to represent the manifold, difference and heterogeneity on the modality of time as synchrony, it only serves to reinstate the sovereignty of the same. This synchrony of 'the manifold (in Hegel, it is heterogeneity reduced to *immanent* contradiction, and while in Kant, the heterogeneity is that of *transcendental manifold*) is, thus, the condition of the possibility of knowledge, the very condition of possibility of the identity of Being and thought that makes absolute possible. If the task of philosophy—as Hegel conceives and which he finds the beginning of philosophy in Parmenides' doctrine of the identity of Being and thought, and of which his philosophy is only the final result of actualization—is the actualization of the identity of Being and thought, then the whole labour of philosophy would be thought on this synchronic modality of time that would synchronize itself, that would bring other to its self-same by representing the manifold, and in this way, recuperating the heterogeneity of the other into its unity. Thought is possible for ontology only as synchrony; it is true even in Heidegger's fundamental ontology where for Being-towards-death—the finitude of Dasein—is still the possibility of impossibility. Because for Dasein, finitude is the anticipative (which is one of the modes of synchronic time) mode of time, Heidegger's great meditation on the finitude is already always a synchronic modality. Therefore it is not surprising that for Heidegger, death is always Being's *own* death, of what Heidegger says as the innermost 'the possibility of impossibility'. Ontology, the effacement of transcendence that makes death itself a possible thought, remains only a thought of death. The death of the Other remains unthought and the unthinkable scandal in philosophy. To think time on the basis of death is to think death and time as possibility, even though it is a 'possibility of impossibility'. Therefore Heidegger's thought is incapable of thinking the death of the Other inasmuch his question is always that of asking the *meaning* of time. What remains unthought thereby is the thought of time in relation to Other which is neither the speculative negation of Being that would be recaptured (as in

Hegel), nor the anticipation of Being-towards-death which Dasein's *own* (as in Heidegger; in my death only I die. It constitutes at once *my* possibility and impossibility in that, in my death I am not there). Therefore, any ethical thought of responsibility towards the Other—the Other that cannot be reduced to the thought of negation, or, to that of inauthentic death—proceeds by putting into question the very synchronic modality of time that privileges *presence* on the basis of which thought of Being has been thought as possible and intelligible. Responsibility towards the Other is neither *retention* and *protention* of the past nor is the anticipation of the future. Both retention and protention of past and anticipation of the future is time thought on the basis of presence. To think time as responsibility towards the Other should be able to think time in radically other manner than either the Hegelian negativity, or, other than phenomenological time as form or meaning. Only when this synchronic time is put into question—this privilege given to presence—only then what is unthought in the history of ontology is thought, and only then, exceeding the thought of totality of the self-same Being, ethical responsibility as infinity towards the Other may be affirmed.

In this chapter we would argue that the ethical thought of the Other is possible when freedom itself is put into question by justice. Justice, then, would have to be thought as irreducible to the synchronic thought of presence or to the work of negativity (the latter constitutes history wherein the Same effectuates its ontological freedom). To put into question the violence of negativity, which history assumes and which is called freedom, it is necessary to think that the Other exceeds this negativity itself. In the next section, we would examine how the very notion of *phenomena* in Hegel's phenomenology is an ontological notion par-excellence, which is seen by Hegel as effectuation of ontological freedom, that needs to questioned and to be opened up to the other irreducible to phenomena of the same.

Phenomenon and temporality

What is the condition of possibility of appearance of Being?: this question that a phenomenology asks is the ontological question par–excellence, if appearing of Being constitutes the very *esse* of ontology inasmuch as one substitutes the formal structure of thought by introducing *movement* into thought itself. In response to Kant's transcendental philosophy—that left unreconciled *noumena* and *phenomena*, synthetic and analytic, *a priori* and *a posteriori* and all the distinctions which Kant introduced and could not reconcile—Hegel introduces content into the formalism of Kant as the very process of becoming itself. Henceforth, truth that would be thought as absolute or absolute as truth (Hegel 1998: 47), would be the truth which would present to itself as absolute in the very process of its becoming. Henceforth, the response to the question what is the source of reason, Being and truth would no longer be that of 'pure form' of the intelligible that does not appear to sensible intuition but the very process of becoming intelligible in the appearing of the sensible; in other words, the Absolute must be intelligible as well as sensible, synthetic as well as analytic, *a priori* as well as *a posteriori*. Henceforth, the intelligible will no longer be determined as transcendental to the sensible—as form to content; the *esse* of being will no longer be thought as transcendental but immanent to the constitutive *becoming* of being absolute. Henceforth, the phenomenological question of *appearing* is an ontological problematic par-excellence inasmuch as appearance of Being is immanent to the very constitutive becoming of Being. As such phenomenology is also ontology (yet not entirely identical. Hegel still makes distinction between *appearance* and *essence*, which, however, are going to be reconciled in absolute knowledge at the end of History): here time is understood as the mak*ing* possible of the absolute, time that however is going to be annulled (the annulment being the *telos* of this becoming); in other words, *telos* of this becoming absolute is the annulment of this very process of becoming (the process that makes possible the *telos*). Time—or, finitude—is the mak*ing* possible of Reason, truth, Being, Absolute (whatever name Hegel assigns to it), but the absolute possibility of Reason or truth or Being makes impossible this very time itself:

> The experience of itself which consciousness goes through can, in accordance with its Notion, comprehends nothing less than the entire system of consciousness, or the entire realm of the truth of Spirit... in pressing forward to its true existence, consciousness will arrive at a point at which it gets rid of its semblance of being burdened with

> something alien, with what is only for it, and some sort of 'other', at a point where appearance becomes identical with essence, so that its exposition will coincide at just this point with the authentic Science of Spirit. And finally, when consciousness itself grasps its own essence, it will signify the nature of absolute knowledge itself." (Ibid: 56-57)

Henceforth the problematic of time, time as the mak*ing* possible of Reason, intelligible, Being or Absolute (as the very constitutive process of becoming), would be a problematic of utmost importance for any ontology that constitutes itself as the philosophy of immanence and takes into account the phenomenological appearing of the Absolute Being to account *how* Reason is what it is, *how* Being is what it is, or, *how* truth is what it is (for it does not accept Reason or Absolute Being as given from a transcendental, unaccountable, mysterious source of which Reason itself cannot look back and discover its secret). The critique that Hegel makes against Kant is that Reason is not Reason if Reason does not know its own secret of being what it is, that is, as Reason; and when it knows itself as such, it is already Absolute and then, there is no point of going on making transcendental distinctions of *noumena* and *phenomena*, *a priori* and *a posteriori*, analytic and synthetic, not because there would not be any more distinctions but because, *these distinctions would no longer be transcendental.* They would rather be immanent contradictions which, however, would be annulled at the end of the process (this is what Hegel calls—these immanent contradictions—as 'dialectical oppositions'). Kant could not reconcile, so Hegel argues, *noumena* and *phenomena*, thing that appears and thing-in-itself because he (Kant) did not know that he solved the problem already, because he did not see that he has seen. Therefore, Kant's transcendental unity of apperception which cannot look back, unlike Descartes' cogito, to see its own reflection (that would have made possible absolute reflection); Kant could not reconcile what his philosophy already made this reconciliation because Kant still thought time as 'pure form 'in a formalist manner (which his own formalism demands), and not as the very process of reconciliation. Therefore Kant could not answer *how* Reason is what it is! To account for the *how* of *how* Reason is what is, is already to renounce the tautological form of knowledge (A=A); it is already to substitute the formal structure of thought of transcendental philosophy with the introduction of movement into thought itself, so that it is no longer a question of the formal reconciliation of two subsistent, fixed, transcendental entities which somehow would be reconciled by unknowable principle, but is precisely the opposite: not being able to remain subsistent and fixed, truth presents itself and sublates this presentation as the *eternal restlessness of negativity* (which is time). Therefore, time has become for speculative philosophy, not the Kantian 'pure form, empty and content-less, but an account of *how* Reason is possible: if it not to be tautological identity, it must be able to account *how* difference comes out of identity and *how* identity maintains itself in difference.

Time: *how* of Reason, mak*ing* possible of Reason. Is it not that time has always been thought in Western ontology from Plato to Kant as the impossibility of the Absolute itself so that the very gap would remain open, like a never curable wound: between faith and Reason, between essence and appearance, infinity and finitude, transcendence and immanence, intelligible and sensible, concept and intuition? Hegel, with all the ruse of dialectical Reason, has turned this very impossibility into a possibility by affirming both—and this manoeuvre is what constitutes the very gesture of dialectical rigor of thought—and yet, making possible their reconciliation as Absolute thought. This he has done not by excluding time from the Absolute and pushing time outside of Absolute, but by introducing time into thought itself, into Being itself, into Absolute or Reason itself. Is ontology anything other than this safeguarding of the intelligibility of Being?: its self-maintenance in the form of its eternal return to its self-same home, a light that will illuminate its own light and its presence to itself, identical to itself even in difference, closest to itself even in distance, and precisely because of this distance? Does ontology know anything other than this immanence where transcendence of the Other—irreducible to Being—is either forgotten, or is seen in the service of the sovereign Being (which releases time from its source only to realize its possibilities of Being, draws back into its fold time that it unfolds, gathering into itself its sundering moments)? Ontology knows only this immanent time of synchrony that makes possible of Reason. It is true that Hegel opens up the possibility of thinking the diachrony of time (by substituting the formal structure of thought by introducing movement into thought itself so that time no longer remains 'pure form ' of thought but the very coming-to-be and passing-away of becoming Absolute), but this releasing of time from the grasp of given synchronic 'form' did not radically interrupt the venerable tradition of ontological intelligibility of Being: this is because this releasing of time is determined only in sight of *Aufhebung* of time itself, as the cancellation of this very releasing, returning thereby to its synchronic self-sameness. In other words, by introducing movement into thought though Hegel opens up the possibility of thinking diachrony of difference, this opening up is introduced only to the extent that it would be cancelled, and would reinstall the synchrony of Being in relation to itself in the form circular return of the time: time that finishes itself by itself by returning to its origin at its end. Ontology is this synchronic time of finitude that makes possible of Being.

It would be argued here that to think otherwise than the time that makes possible of Being, we need to think diachronic time that cannot be reduced to the synchronic time of return: not the pseudo-diachronic time of the immanence of self-presence but diachrony opening to transcendence, finitude opening to infinity, infinity that interrupts any possibility of return of Being; not the temporality returns to its self-same home but that which never presents itself to Being, temporality that eludes any possibility of recapture and anticipation, and any possibility of gathering into the homogeneity of synchronic self-sameness. Reading Lévinas, we would argue that such a diachronic time of irreducible heterogeneity can only be thought as responsibility to the Other that begins in a past that has never been present, and would end in an infinitely distant future that would not come to 'pass', that cannot be gathered into the simultaneity of synchrony. Not being present, the face of the Other does not appear in the domain of the intelligible, nor in the sensible (which would be sublated into the intelligibility of Being); as such, the face of the Other is neither the phenomenality of Being nor is it phenomenality of the other in the immanence of Being's interiority. It is rather of a relation to an entirely other than negativity, other than the immanence of Being and its phenomenality: a relationship with transcendence per-excellence. Such is the diachrony of infinity which the face of the Other introduces in Being! The question of phenomenality of Being which Hegel presents in his *Phenomenology* is an ontological event par excellence inasmuch as phenomenality is determined as the manifestation of consciousness to itself, that presents itself to itself as identical itself to itself in its self-diremption : such manifestation, then, has an essential relationship with the synchronic modality of time which privileges presence. Manifestation presupposes presence, presence that manifests itself to itself. Therefore, phenomenology as ontology of manifestation—or, as manifestation of consciousness to itself—always privileges presence. Reading Hegel's *Phenomenology of Spirit*, I would like to show that Hegel's phenomenology as the philosophy of consciousness—inasmuch as it constitutes itself on the synchronic modality of time which his characterization of Being as phenomenon—cannot think infinity in relation to transcendence without reducing the Other to the discursive totality of immanence. As such, we point towards the possibility of thinking infinity other than dialectical negativity of Hegelian phenomenology. Reading Lévinas in this connection, we would like to think this infinity as the face of the Other which is not phenomenal in the sense that Hegel determines phenomenality in his *Phenomenology*. But how does Hegel determine the relationship between the phenomenality of phenomena and presence? How does he determine the essential relationship of Being and its manifestation (whose secret is the time itself as synchrony) in such a way that infinity is remained unthought in Hegelian philosophy and wherein the Other is either repressed or is reduced to the thought of Being?

Being is what appears and what manifests itself. This manifestation of Being, which belongs to Being, is that which consists the *esse* of Being *as* being, and is the condition of possibility of its very intelligibility. The intelligibility of Being *qua* its manifestation is not outside of Being, if that outside signifies a transcendental term, but intelligibility or the manifestation of Being is the *self-diremption* of Being which has an essential relationship of *identity* to Being which it manifests. Spirit dirempts itself from itself, sunders itself into moments of appearing in time, in history, but this appearance being only Being's own diremption, are only moments of Being which Being ultimately recuperates, and thereby again returning to its self-same identity: this process of the return of Being to its identity through its diremption is called *actualization*. Phenomenology is "only the appearance of

Spirit"(Hegel 1998: 22), "the immediate existence of Spirit"(Ibid: 21) that traverses the road of "the seriousness, the suffering, the patience, and the labour of the negative" (Ibid: 10); phenomenology is a narrative of the *movement* which Spirit undertakes and which consciousness suffers the experiences of *labour of the negative*, is this process of actualization of Spirit's self-identity with itself. Thus, *phenomenology is only a passage to an ontology*, a movement which Hegel calls "the way of despair" (Ibid: 49), a journey of consciousness which already point towards the Absolute, the self-same identity of Being. Thus thinking phenomenology as passage to ontology, all the moments of this movement of *consciousness*, of the suffering and *experience* which the Spirit undergoes, and which is this of very time of appearing and coming-to-be (Ibid: 15) are determined teleologically by Hegel only *in sight of* securing the Self-sameness of the Spirit. The notion of experience, and along with the consciousness that undergoes these experiences by traversing the whole travails and ordeals of the journey, belong to the ontological order inasmuch as phenomenality must already point towards the self-securing light of the self-present Same.

> The Science of this pathway is the Science of the *experience* which consciousness goes through; the substance and its movement are viewed as the object of consciousness. Consciousness knows and comprehends only what falls within its experience; for what is contained in this is nothing but spiritual substance, and this, too, as *object* of the self. The Spirit becomes object because it is just this movement of becoming an*other to itself*, i.e. becoming an *object to itself*, and of suspending this otherness. And experience is the name we give to just this movement, in which the immediate, the unexperienced, i.e. the abstract, whether it be of sensuous [but still unsensed] being, or only thought of as simple, becomes alienated from itself and then returns to itself from this alienation, and is only then revealed for the first time in its actuality and truth, just as it then has become a property of consciousness also (Ibid: 21).

Substituting the formal structure of thought by introducing movement into thought did not radically question the domination of the Same inasmuch as the movement is only a return to the sovereign self-sameness of Being. Consciousness is the traversal of the travailing Spirit, losing itself in its negative and death, and yet, "in this utter dismemberment wins its truth": such a consciousness has already been determined as acquiring the power of mastery over the terror of the negative, death and its utter dissolution and yet, has its power of maintaining of its self-sameness of its life even in death. "Death, if that is what we want to call this non-actuality, is of all things the most dreadful, and to hold fast what is dead requires the greatest strength...But the life Spirit is not the life that shrinks from death and keeps itself untouched by devastation, but rather the life that endures it and maintains itself in it. It wins its truth only when, in utter dismemberment, it finds itself…Spirit is this power only by looking the negative in the face, and tarrying with it. This tarrying with the negative is the magical power that that converts it into being"(Ibid: 19). Experience is the name of the movement of traversal, of consciousness positing its own limit and exceeding the limit that it posits. Since to exceed its limit is its own limit, it is equally exceeding itself (Ibid: 51). Such exceeding is exceeding only as far as it is its own limit which can be reduced to its immanent self-sameness; in other words, Hegel could only think the limit which can be subsumed again in its re-turn of the traversal, and hence, it is not a limit at all that Hegel could think. Limit that never can be limited, that one always crosses over (in not being able to cross) and cannot yet come back to its self-reposed immanence, movement that cannot be bent like mirror reflection that would make its own reflection possible, limit irreducible to the reflection of the limited, in other words, limit that is infinite limit or infinity as limit: such a thinking of the limit Hegel cannot think without reducing the radical alterity of the limit. This reduction of the alterity is necessary condition of possibility for Hegelian phenomenology of experience, and yet—and this is the paradox—it halts the very dialectical movement of the Absolute inasmuch as this reduction already leaves behind the sensuousness of the object as something outside it. Because any discourse of totality, such as Hegel's, cannot conceive itself without leaving the heterogeneous sensuousness of the very temporal and singular experience, it can never adequately represent itself without an irreducible remainder. Representation, which is the secret of ontology that sublates the possible experience that comes and goes in every singular sensuous 'now' into the universality of the concept, can take experience into account only by emptying away (this is what Hegel calls negativity) the very singularity of sensuousness which every particular experience brings and takes away. As such, representation cannot present itself as *adequate* to the sensible experience itself without reducing the object of representation, which already, in the very act of representation, would leave behind this very *singularity of sensible.* Hegelian phenomenology cannot account for this sensibility, and its singularity without transforming the object of its own experience:

> *Inasmuch as the new true object issues from it*, this *dialectical* movement which consciousness exercises on itself and which affects both its knowledge and its object, is precisely what is called experience [*Erfahrung*]...Consciousness knows something; this object is the essence or the *in-itself*; but it is also for consciousness the in-itself... the first object, in being known, is altered for consciousness; it ceases to be the in-itself, and becomes something that is the *in-itself* only *for consciousness* (Ibid: 55).

The *in-itself* that consciousness alters is nothing but an act of reduction of the alterity of the in-itself, the singularity of the sensibility that Hegelian phenomenology always leaves behind, which is heterogeneous to the very *adaequatio* of concept to the thing-in-itself, so that—because of this inadequate correspondence between object-in-itself and its representation—the whole system of Hegelian philosophy comes to a halt, and remains wide open towards a heterogeneous unthought of the outside. Hegelian phenomenological account of experience is only a dead experience, emptied of all singularity and sensibility, is not (lived) experience at all. Reduced to the homogeneous dead time of impersonal concept, the Hegelian system is the cold, anonymous totality that says nothing but announces its own impossibility. What is entirely other, the living signification of *saying* itself, the heterogeneous singularity remains outside, unthought and irreducible to the said (see Lévinas 1991: 31-60). Such a saying cannot be thought as ontological or as phenomenological but rather as something that ontological or phenomenological cannot account and must appeal to: the pre-ontological and immemorial time of the Other which irreducibly heterogeneous and outside the system.

But that's not all. We, however, wonder whether Hegelian determination of experience as alteration and reduction of the in-itself to the homogeneous and impersonal totality of the system is not itself violence to the Other, to the singularity of the heterogeneous sensible, a murder (is it not that Hegel himself conceives concept as the murder of the thing, the negativity of the thing, which would assimilated and devoured to nourish the same) of what is outside the system and thus, reducing of the life of the other's *sayings* to the *said* of the system, so that other can be assimilated to the impersonal order of cold tyranny? To think the Other without violence and murder is to work out another thought of experience irreducible to the phenomenal experience (which Hegelian phenomenology presents), another thought of singularity and sensibility irreducible to consciousness and inassimilable to the system, another modality of signification other than the said of the Same; we must rather think of a saying that must put into question the very tyranny of the said in which the Same presents itself. To put into question the violence as experience, or, the violence of experience, is not a question of negativity at all; it is rather to work out another modality of substituting the formal structure of thought with introducing other movement into thought itself (other than Hegelian substitution).

Phenomenology as manifestation of Being is Being's self-diremption, which would be sublated and annulled into the identity of Being to itself in its self-presence. Therefore, phenomenology appears as a stage of dialectical development of speculative ontology in Hegel's *Encyclopaedia*. Being is what manifests—Being manifests itself and is this very phenomenality—in various dimensions of what has passed by, what is already passing in its coming-to-be, and coming-to-be that would soon pass by; in other words, manifestation, in so far as it manifests in/as a given instant, has an essential relationship with the very temporality of time. Philosophy, which is not mere formal unity of thought and Being, must take into account the essential moments of becoming itself—the evanescent appearing and passing away. Hegel says,

> Philosophy, on the other hand, has to do, not with *unessential* determinations but with a determination in so far as it is essential… it is the process which begets and traverses its own moments, and this whole movement constitutes what is positive [in it] and its truth. This truth therefore includes the negative also…the evanescent itself

> must, on the contrary, be regarded as essential, not as something fixed, cut off from the True and left lying who knows where outside it any more than the True is to be regarded as something on the other side, positive and dead (Hegel 1998: 27).

As it's appearing and coming-to-be, Being has already step out of its mere immediate unity and has become temporal. Being manifests itself as time; manifestation is temporal; it is the self-diremption of the auto-engendering Spirit. Phenomenology, then, must seriously address the problematic of time inasmuch as time is not only constitutive possibility of any experience as such for consciousness, but also is the constitutive possibility of knowledge of these experiences, which manifests as temporal, and is this very time itself. In various dimensions in which Being appears as becoming, even in the non-being of past and future whose negative unity is the manifesting Being of the present, what is not manifested would be understood in relation to manifestation as already manifested, and yet to be manifested of past and future. As we can see that manifestation presupposes presence, a privileging of presence, and everything that is non-manifestation would be understood only as *attenuated* variations of present manifestation that would be thought together as synchronic contraction/simultaneity of these various dimensions. Here already the thought of manifestation serves as the prima thesis of ontology: that is, the identity/synchrony of Being to itself, its presence to itself that presents itself by reducing non-manifested into the manifestation of presence. Auto-presentation: that is the secret of ontology in general and of speculative ontology in particular; it is what is determinant of the thought of phenomenology as auto-manifestation. Only what manifests itself to itself present itself to itself, as self-donation is the possibility of sense-bestowal or signification or intelligibility of experiences as such. *Phenomenology privileges synchronic modality of presence*, and is reduction of non-presence, because, presence as the constitutive possibility of manifestation of Being, is possibility of Being as such, if thought of Being is inseparable from its intelligibility and manifestations. Here, however, appears an insurmountable aporia which any phenomenology that constitutes itself as ontology confronts:

Any ontology, whether Hegelian speculative or Heideggerian ontology, that maintains the inseparability of Being and its intelligibility, Being and its manifestation, is nothing but an investigation of the fundamental structure of our experience, its relationship to the knowledge of them in the light of Being that illuminate these experiences that appear as time. Phenomenology as an investigation into the fundamental structure of experiences, is an investigation into the fundamental structure of time itself in its various dimensions of which Being manifests as 'here' and 'then', 'now' and 'then'. But this structure itself of phenomenology must be other than any 'now' and 'then' of every particular temporal determination in which Being manifests in its particular shapes; in other words, this structure of phenomenology itself must be other than temporal and therefore, a rigorous distinction is all the more necessary for a phenomenology—in order not only to conceive the becoming of Being's manifestation but also the pattern of the manifold of manifestations—between eternity and time. Being manifests itself as temporal but the hermeneutic (that is, the understanding or intelligibility) of the structure of these manifestations cannot be temporal, though Being's manifestations must appeal to time for their intelligibility. Being's manifestation in particular temporal determinations, by a necessary gesture, a necessity that I cannot explicate here and which Hegel brought out in his argument against any philosophy of immediate intuitive knowledge of ineffable Being (see Hegel 1998: 42), yields to (sublate themselves, in Hegel's words) something other than itself by negating itself by itself to sublate this negativity into a structure which is not temporal at all. Thus a difference should be inscribed between temporal determinations of manifestation, and the self-repose of Being. The condition of possibility of knowledge of experience that manifests is the difference between the self-repose of Being and it's temporal manifestations.

But this difference itself turns out to be the condition of impossibility of knowledge at the same time if this difference is to remain truly difference: the phenomenal experience remains inappropriable, or, remains outside of the intelligible structure of Being. All manifestation of Being—since manifestation of Being occurs only in this particular 'now' or in that particular 'then'—is essentially partial manifestation inasmuch as manifestation itself, by definition, is finite. But if knowledge of the Being's manifestations in various dimensions implies the gathering of various dimensions of all particular temporal manifestations (because time is not formal time here any longer, but time that is seen in its essential determinations: in its restlessness of *coming-to-be* and *passing-away*. Therefore knowledge of this very know*ing* should be able to account for all the *passing* and *coming to be* moments that constitute this know*ing*. It is for this reason that Hegel asserts that only absolute is truth and truth is Absolute), then the very gap between the Absolute Being's manifestations, between the infinity of truth and finitude of appearing, between the time of the concept and the temporality of sensuous experience, would make impossible the knowledge of the manifestation of Being. '*To be*' is to be Absolute—which means that Being must point towards being Absolute—whose essence is its manifestation. But manifestations of Being—manifesting being only temporal and partial—cannot be Absolute. If to know is to know the whole or absolutely, and if all knowledge has an essential relationship with appearing of what is to be known, then knowledge can only be of what is finite and partial. To *introduce time into thought*—time of unpredictable coming-to-be and unrecuperable passing-away, the time of diachrony—is thus, to renounce the Absolute (even knowledge itself, if knowledge is knowledge as Absolute). To introduce time into thought is to be skeptic, skepticism that is always defeated and always returns anew to ruin any pretensions of Absolute knowledge (see Lévinas 1991).

From Aristotle to Hegel, even in Heidegger and in Husserl, this aporia will haunt the ontology of light that illuminates everything of human existence in the light of Being's intelligibility. Hegel introduces time in thought so as to remedy this aporia, to make possible once again by exposing Reason to the vertiginous movement of time; but this very condition of possibility of Reason, in turn, pushes Reason to its limitless exposure of unreason that would forever make impossible the possibility of an absolute rationality. Any ontology that hopes to substitute the formal structure of thought with a movement proper to thinking, and yet wants to preserve or accomplish the Absolute (which is the gathering of moments into the unity of the self-same), would confront this irreducible aporia: how to account for the Absolute to manifest in the non-Absolute, and yet to conceive their identity? How to account for the infinity to appear in every finite determinations, and yet to conceive their union? How to account for the reconciliation of the whole and the part, and yet, whose difference must be irreducible to each other, and there must be an essential difference so that any account of this difference itself would be possible? Between the Night of the ineffable in which "all cows are black" (Hegel 1998: 9), but which would negate itself to sublate to the eternity of the concept, there already occurs a lapse of time which interrupts any possible *adaequatio* between the time and eternity, the sensible and the intelligible: a lapse of time that the discourse of Being may have always already left behind and outside of itself, an immemorial time that it has always already forgotten, and which cannot be recaptured in the re-collection of re-presentation. In the consciousness of time, the very instance that the act of representation takes to sublate the ineffable into intelligible, there occurs already an *unconscious lapse of time* that remains infinitely heterogeneous to the synchrony of presence. Such an unconsciousness of time, time that surplus of itself, overflows the economy of the Absolute: an *excess of negativity* irreducible to space, the impossible time of in-between of the hyphen, an interval or interrupting of signs and signs, that *always delayed response of the concept to the sensible thing*; it interrupts the continuity of the progress towards the Absolute knowledge. Call it 'Hegelian blind spot', between the ' meaning' and 'saying' of that meaning, there has already passed away the instance that would not return, and which no philosophy of representation can avoid; it is because this gap at once constitutes the condition of the possibility of knowledge, and the condition of impossibility of knowledge. Signification occurs only as time lapse—between the 'now' that comes and passing, and the saying 'now' that wants to preserve what has already passed 'now'—but this lapse of time always already allows the meaning to slip away, and which it cannot preserve. Therefore, it occurs only as *inadequation* of meaning and saying. There has always already occurred difference, which forever makes simultaneously condition of possibility and condition of impossibility of signification. What the saying recaptures is only the emptiness of all 'nows'; ontological signification is only dead time that says nothing. We, however, wonder whether beyond this 'saying' (which says nothing but that 'it says' and its says only itself, which says nothing new), exhausts the possibility of all signification, or whether, exceeding such a closure of ontological signification, there is possible entirely other signification, irreducible to the saying of the same that addresses the wholly Other?

Insurmountable aporia! Ontology has never been able to resolve it—ontology, that is the philosophy of the Same, whose preoccupation is to secure the Same in its own light. Philosophy must know the Other at its limit so as to penetrate into the utmost wealth of the spirit which it invests, so that nothing can be outside of its totality; the Other must be subsumed and taken into its self-same presence so that it can realize the utmost possibility of securing its own light: this ontology whose utmost possibility Hegel realizes by pushing its possibility even to the point of its own impossibility, pushes itself too far, too far into the abyss of the impossibility wherein Reason is threatened by itself to be lost; the Same is threatened by itself to be lost without return, and it thus remains violently open to an infinity that does not return. Such opening (not arriving to a determinable destination) can no longer be determined either as ontological or phenomenological (either as time of return or anticipation, either as time of Being or the time of manifestation); it is rather the time in relation an entirely other, to an irreducible Other. Such Other is not a phenomenon which the Same aspires to dominate by to subsuming/ bringing back to its self-same home by recuperating the *passed-by* and anticipating *coming-to-be* of its finite time; rather, the infinite Other interrogates the violence of the Same, that calls into question ontological freedom of 'to be' in the name of an infinite and inexhaustible justice; the Other calls into question any closure of the ontological discourse of the totality. Ontological discourse of totality would, despite its desire for totality, remain only a *discourse* of totality inasmuch as its aporia always opens itself towards the Other. The ontological discourse of totality never closes into itself because it must always appeal to an exterior, which is its excess: the Absolute must always appeal to the other of the Absolute which is exterior to it, and hence can't never be absolutely Absolute! Therefore, the Absolute of Hegelian ontology can never be absolute enough; the Absolute can never found its own ground and its *telos* in its immanent resource but somewhere else, on some other shore, in another continent. Thus the aporia of any philosophical discourse of totality, by opening any possible closure into itself towards something exterior to itself, must, by a necessary gesture, appeal to the pre-ontological time of the other. Such an excess of totality which de-constitutes itself in the very process of constituting the condition of possibility of the Absolute, thus ruining the very speculative project of ontology, would never be subsumed into the domination of the Same. As such, the time of the Other is not the synchronic time of the Same; it is not the phenomenal time of freedom. Rather time here is diachronic: diachrony as justice!

We should here be able to work out in concrete manner the modality of time in relation to Other. How to think time in relation to justice? How the ethical thought justice (we have to show why it is ethical) is to be distinguished from the ontological thought of freedom (where, in the latter case the Same dominates and presents itself as totalitarian discourse of war and violence)? The task for us to work out, in a concrete manner, how to distinguish the ontological movement of the Same that seeks to assimilate the other (which we shall call 'need') from 'desire', the latter being the movement of transcendence towards an entire Other, irreducible and inassimilable. We should also be able to show how Hegelian ontology presents itself as the philosophy of the need, and how the problematic of need and desire has essential relationships with different modalities of time as synchrony and diachrony, time of freedom and time of justice. 'Freedom', 'synchrony' and 'need': they all constitute the philosophy of consciousness; the Hegelian phenomenology does not call this consciousness of the Same into question, but rather, in its desire for closure, it constitutes itself as discourse of totality. To put into question the violence of the philosophy of the Same is to open time, this infinite time of desire, towards the ethical Other: towards the ethics of peace in which the Other would be thought as Other (not the reduced other of dialectic). What this chapter seeks to do is to open the closure of ontological time towards recognition (this is not to be confused with dialectical recognition which Hegel presents in *Phenomenology*) of the Other as a response to an ethical exigency of our time. We will take up Hegel's *Phenomenology of Spirit* to examine how Hegel's thought on the problematic of freedom and Reason has an essential relationship with the ontological modality of time, which is determined in *Phenomenology* as synchrony. This synchrony, which Hegel determines as history, is thought as realization of freedom inasmuch as freedom is already determined as *auto-constitution and auto-effectuation of Reason*. In the anonymous universal history of Reason in which all individuals would be subsumed and sublated through the negativity of time, the singularity of the Other is violated. To recognize the ethical exigency in the face of the Other is to be able to judge history itself, and to interrogate the violence of the freedom (which history actualizes through the work of the negative). To question the right of freedom is to open up another possibility of thinking time other than as negativity: time must be thought than as the impersonal historical time in which all individuals are dead and subsumed.

Infinity and transcendance

But is it not that Hegel already thought 'infinite' as dialectical synthesis, hence as the unity of infinite and finitude? Is it not that ontology already recognizes the thought of infinity? : whether infinity is thought as that which is beyond the finitude of human Reason as in Descartes', or, as in Hegelian dialectical speculative thought of infinity, which is the idea of synthesis! Is not it that Hegelian thought always already recognizes the thought of the other in the very heart of the same? Is not Hegelian infinity precisely the thought of the other (recognition of the other that cannot be reduced to *this* other or *that* other but the other which is universal)? Is not Hegelian thought of history precisely the thought of the other and Being, in their reciprocal desire for recognition, comes to their mutuality in the name of universal order of Reason in which, all particular individuals renouncing their particulars, *sublate* themselves into universal order? More than anyone else, Hegel seems to be aware of the essential relationship between *time* and *other*.

We have seen that for Hegel the problem is how to reconcile the infinite and finite. The Kantian transcendental philosophy—which reconciles infinity and finite in formal, transcendental terms by positing infinite and finite outside of each other without anything to account how their reconciliation possible—could not resolve this aporia. Therefore, infinity remains for Kant only a matter of faith, or, a hypothetical unity without actualizing or effectuating in real historical, temporal becoming. The result remained one of empty infinity; there are two reasons for it:

1. Infinite thrown outside of finite which it has its limit exterior to it, would not truly be infinite because finite outside of it would limit it, and would make infinite only another 'finite'.
2. Even if Kant conceives infinite, it is only an empty infinite characteristic of all formalistic philosophy, which explains nothing at all, devoid of any content, and which cannot be found anywhere simply because it is outside any historical, temporal becoming of reality altogether. If Kant's problem of infinity is a question of freedom, then it shows that Kant's freedom is not (a) total freedom enough; for total /absolute freedom should be able account not only its eternal concept but its reconciliation with all historical contingencies. Kant's freedom, for that same account (b) is only empty freedom of the concept that does not appear, actualize, effectuate in real historical, temporal becoming of the world. To effectuate the infinite concept of freedom, and also to account for their reconciliation, it will be necessary to account how the idea of freedom comes/manifests/appears/actualize/effectuate in historical, temporal becoming of the world. In other worlds, it should be able to account the concept/infinity/eternity/concept's manifestation—this is what phenomenology as the science of appearing is supposed to do—in/as history, in/as time. This has led Hegel to (c.) an expansion of the concept of Reason/infinity/eternity (because Kant's Reason/infinity is still bounded and therefore, not total, absolute enough), and (d.) to the substitution of the formal structure of thought by introducing movement into thought itself (so as to account for the effectuation of the concept/freedom/infinite in history/time/finite). The way Hegel tries to solve this problem—by substituting the formal structure with movement—is the dialectical movement itself that would also lead to the expansion of Reason.

We have seen that Kant's infinite is not infinite because it does not appear/effectuate in the becoming of the historical world, because it throws finite outside it which limits it, because finite is *transcendental* to the infinite. By introducing (dialectical) movement that should be able to account how the infinite/Absolute/concept/freedom effectuate itself historical becoming, Hegel also makes finite *immanent* to the infinite, and temporality immanent to eternity, and thereby, making Infinity Absolute and total which has its finitude immanent in it: the movement or this process that makes this possible is the process of negativity. This immanent movement of dialectic negativity presents itself thus:

Infinite, to actualize itself as such, must be able to appear itself in time. But if this finitude is not to be absolutely outside infinite (then it would not be total or infinite), it will be necessary to think the finite as *immanent* to infinite (it is necessary to have other pair of infinite as finite. It will be necessary to have another without which it is mere tautology to assert A=A). To have finite as the other of infinite and yet being immanent in infinity: this always already effaces the radical transcendence of the Other (the Other as Other). This effacing—which is the violence of ontology—is a necessary gesture (or, rather condition of the possibility) of immanence. In other words, Hegelian philosophy of immanence must always already presuppose—and must always already appeal to—the transcendence of the Other even if only to violate it. This is what we can call Hegelian 'blind spot'. The Hegelian Absolute that seeks to constitute itself as discourse of totality (or, as the thought of infinity), has to be self-sufficient (only a homogeneous, self-foundational, self-sufficient system can be Absolute and total. Only Same can totalize; the heterogeneous must therefore be effaced to constitute a homogeneous discourse of totality, which is already a violence of the Other); it must always already appeal to something entirely outside the totality, something entirely transcendent heterogeneity (whose effacement and violence is a necessary gesture of instituting the order of the Same). To be the Same is always already to appeal to the other even if only to wage war against 'Him'. The Absolute/totality cannot find its reason of being in itself, whose foundation is *not immanent* in it; thus, it constitutes itself as a discourse of violence, effacing the face of the Other; its foundation is, therefore, only a tyrannical order whose monarch is the anonymous Reason. This is the blind spot Hegelian discourse refused to see: the very moment of instituting the order of freedom, and to reach infinity, is already to efface the Other as Other; the very moment of instituting totality must bring ruin to the totality, because it would always leave something un-totalizable outside.

Infinite makes finite immanent to itself but this finite is only its *own* other (since absolutely other is already a threat to the homogeneity of totality):

> There can be no talk of the going forth of the Absolute out of itself; for only this can appear as a going forth: that the opposition is, yet the opposition cannot pause at its being; rather its essence is the Absolute unrest of sublating itself. Its being would be its terms, but these essentially are only as connected with each other—that is, they are not their own account; they are only as sublated. What they are own account is : not to be on their own account. If the Absolute opposition is separated from unity, then the latter is on its own account just as the former is outside itself, but in this case the opposition itself has only changed its expression (Hegel 1986: 36).

Infinite negates itself (which has the form of sublation) and appear itself as other: this is, for Hegel, the finite. This other is only *immanent* other, is its own internal other (which already left behind in this very moment of negation/reflection/determination, the transcendence other); but when this finitude—since its truth is not in-itself but outside of itself—recognizes its untruth, it negates itself and immediately returns with which it begins, namely, to the infinity itself (Ibid: 35). Infinity is nothing but this process of infinite negation, and through negation (that subsumes its other) returning to the self-sameness: "the annihilating unrest of the infinite is only through the being of what it annihilates; the sublated is absolute just so far as it is sublated: it arises in perishing, for perishing only occurs because there is something that perishes" (Ibid: 38).

This process of negativity, the restlessness through which infinity actualizes itself, has moments of finitude immanent in it; through this immanent negation, infinity brings back its other to its fold. As such, finitude is only self-diremption of infinity; it is the immanent differentiation of the infinite: infinity, then, for Hegel is the name of this totality, the reduction and consummation of difference in its unity (Ibid: 36). The negativity which movement introduces is at once the process of effectuation of Reason in history (the infinite effectuates, appears, presents/realizes itself in finite), but this effectuation also points towards the reconciliation of finite and infinite, history and

Reason, concept and the object. Infinity is no longer the bounded transcendental infinity outside but the Absolute (as in Kant), but unbounded infinity that has finitude within it.

History is the becoming of Spirit; it is the temporal process of self-othering: as negativity which negates this negation (the negation of self-othering), the Spirit becomes absolute at the end of this history. Therefore, the Absolute, while realizing itself by appearing in historical time, must, with the same measure, exceed this very historical time. The end of history sublates all the forms of finitude—of the appearance of the Spirit—and makes Spirit the Absolute. One can see that Hegelian form of infinite is nothing other than the Absolute reinstating its absolute self-sameness through self-diremption: appearing but going beyond that appearance! Infinite is, thus, sublated finitude: Hegel calls it "infinite negativity"; here the self-othering (which is time itself) would be sublated into the self-sameness of Being. Here, infinity is the thought of Same, serving the sovereignty of the Same in which all finitude would be engulfed and enclosed within the totality of history. The Hegelian infinity is Absolute because it encloses anything that is *its* other, reducing the very alterity of the other into the self-sameness, which forms thereby a totality of significations: such is the Hegelian thought of infinity which is *totality* in the name of the same: infinity negating its own negation, and nourishing itself by devouring and assimilating its own other.

We, however, wonder whether the thought of infinity that is totality and which, in the name of Being, presents itself as a discourse of violence, exhausts the meaning of the human, and whether, beyond such a discourse of violence (which makes any particular others only as moments of an impersonal Reason) does there exist the thought of infinity infinitely infinite, of a past that cannot be remembered and of a future infinitely remote and would not come to pass. Such a thought of infinitely cannot be thought as Absolute (or, on the modality of the Same), because the Absolute itself must presuppose infinity that is exterior to itself. The openness to the transcendent Other—which is metaphysics par excellence—is necessary and irreducible: to think this infinity—which is other than Hegelian infinity—is not to think infinity as immanence but as radical transcendence opening to an infinitely other. To think infinity as transcendence is to question the very Hegelian project of system: the question of ethics—if the openness towards the transcendence be called 'ethics'—arises as this questioning itself, as sobering up the slumbering Being. Consciousness would no longer have the meaning, as in Hegel's understanding of phenomenology, of mastering the experience that it undergoes, but consciousness would be sobering oneself towards the right of the Other. If the effectuation of freedom is necessary, it must be understood as only to effectuate the freedom of the Other, to recognize the right of the Other even before myself.

Justice and freedom

In the last section we have examined how in Hegel's notion of infinity, which is the work of negativity that has finitude in its immanence, the heterogeneity of diachrony is already 'constricted'; and we have seen that the incommensurable difference of the already lapsed—the passed time of unrecuperable past—and of un-protention time of future is already pushed up to dialectical contradiction (which reduces difference and re-institutes the immanence of self-presence). This has led Hegel to conceive not only the reduction of the Other to the sovereignty of the Same, but also leads to the legitimization of the violence which negativity asserts itself on the other: it justifies, as necessary evil, the war of negativity which constitutes its homogeneous order of faceless Reason! Therefore, we must introduce another thought of infinity other than the terror of the negative, an infinity where the height of the Other is not reduced to faceless particulars with an anonymous order of universal Reason. To think Other as Other is to put into question this universal mode of traversal of consciousness which, through the work that negativity puts into effect to transform the given and to produce its own self-recognition, gives a name to this process itself as 'history': to think the Other as Other is to judge this violence of history, to interrogate this process of production (the process that transforms the diachrony of the heterogeneous into the immanence of self-presence).

At the beginning of the chapter we discussed how Hegel substituted the formal structure of thought by introducing movement into thought and we also examined how for Hegel, this movement of thought means none other than the negativity of time, the restlessness of the becoming itself which would again be annulled to the repose of the Same, the effectuation of infinity of itself through diremption in finite. Infinity is seen as the liberation, *freedom* from all heterogeneous finite which, being *mere* other, immediately be sublated to infinity of self-sameness. Freedom is thus freedom *from* heterogeneity of all particulars, from all *mere* others (which is nothing but being in its self-diremption) to assert the autonomy of the self-engendering, self-moving, self-foundational Being; to assert this self-foundational Same is to carry out the work of the negative, since only in the form of *work* the given heterogeneity could be/negated transformed into the self-same presence of the concept. It means to say that the concept is already delayed: thus, there already occurs the problem of accounting the inevitable *delay* between the heterogeneous time of sensible, and the homogeneous time of the concept. This *delay* is necessary for the concept itself: labour presupposes time, the time of '*not yet*', but this time, in this pointing towards the 'not yet', must presuppose a past that must have gone by (if there is 'not yet', there is no point why there needs be transformation/negation at all). Work is the difference, gap, caesura, the in-between of always already passed time of the sensible and the never-to- be-passed time of the concept. Again this is the same problem of the accounting the gap or difference of restlessness of the finite and self-repose of the infinite. This gap is the necessary condition of possibility of the concept—this time of work or work of time—but yet, it brings *inadequation* between sensible and concept, and hence, at the same time, the condition of impossibility of Absolute.

Like Aristotle, Hegel affirms both by showing that concept is already there in the sensible; in other words, concept in immanent to the sensible itself: the sensible negates itself, sublates itself, and becomes the concept realized, and the third term that unites them both is *sign*. *Sign* is the synthetic *unity* of sensible and concept, the very work of negativity. Sign is temporality, which means, it is the restless movement of sublating sensible into concept, and yet, sign is also spatial, because it is the arrest of the very restlessness of sensible: it is the sublated self-repose of the concept. In fact, the sign is the unity of both the temporality of the sensible and yet, it must always point beyond itself to the eternal rest of the concept. As unity of the sensible and concept, sign is a condition of possibility of the Absolute, the *adaequatio* of the sensible and the concept. Let us return to the discussion of time and signification in the first chapter.

Death, signification and time

It is the problem of 'now'. 'Now', the word, the concept, is the *sense* of the *sensible* 'now': the sensible 'now' negates itself and sublates itself into the sense of 'now'. In this very process of sublation (negation), time is already the sublating itself: not only what is to be sublated is time, but that this sublating itself is time. Sense, the concept 'Now', is possible only because the sensible 'now' is finite: sensible 'now' dies itself (negates itself), and yet, is preserved in this very nothingness (its own emptiness, its death) in the signification of 'Now'. Sense, or, concept is, thus, the work of negativity, the work of annihilation and violence, the murder or destruction of the sensible; in signification, or, in the concept, the immediate and sensuous particulars die, and are subsumed to the infinity of the universal 'Now'. Thus, the concept or signification which the work of negativity realizes by destroying the natural given, does not refer to anything but only to the nothingness of things: it is the dead time of the concept, the effacing the face of the living, itself empty and a void. Signification is this anonymous order wherein all living face of the Other is erased, negated, and violated to subsume to the empty totality of dead time. If negation is essential for signification and for effectuation of Reason, then signification and History is essentially violence, the effacing of the face.

Now let us take up a word 'Dog'. The word 'Dog' signifies itself only as far as it is not the 'dog' that barks, shits and breeds: the concept 'Dog' negates the finite and sensuous 'dog'. As such, the concept 'Dog' is infinite, always remaining same despite all the appearing and vanishing of the sensuous dogs. The life of the concept 'Dog'—as if a second life after death—is the death of the life 'dog': this second life, the life of the concept, is what Hegel calls the life of Spirit, the life of consciousness that knows 'dog' because by killing and negating the real, living dog, it transforms this immediate sensuous particular being to the universal life of the Spirit; it elevates it to the consciousness that knows dogs (hence also knowing that it knows). All consciousness of things in the world, and hence self-consciousness, is this work of negativity. The following points are to be noted here:

1. Sense 'Dog' signifies itself only inasmuch as it *constricts* the heterogeneity of the sensible 'dog', only as far as it already leaves behind the remnant of something of the very sensible 'dog' which the concept 'Dog' cannot sublate; despite self-sameness of the concept, it leaves something outside of its totality, something heterogeneous. Only as much as heterogeneity of the sensible is *constricted* to the homogeneity of the concept, that the Absolute realizes itself as Spirit. To be Absolute is already to die, to know how to die and yet, to maintain itself in this very negativity, in its own nothingness and in this terror of its death; to signify 'I', to have knowledge of itself, to have self-consciousness is not only that this immediate, natural, sensuous *I* has to die but also in this 'utter dismemberment' (Hegel 1998: 19), in this abyss, to find another life, the life of the Spirit. Not only Hegelian phenomenology but the whole Western tradition of ontology is based on this paradigm of the work of death, on this work of negativity: this terrible power that converts even the most dreadful nothingness to the realization of the Same, that transforms the heterogeneity of the sensible into the most synchronic, homogeneous faceless order of Reason.[1]

Philosophy is this work of death. All possible sense or signification, all possible realization of freedom and Being, thought and consciousness

1. In Jean-Luc Nancy's words: "If Death has fascinated Western thought, it is to the degree that Western thought believed itself capable of constructing upon death its dialectical paradigm of pure presence and absence. *Death* is the absolute signified, the sealing off of sense. It is the *name*, but "to be born" is the verb.

It is certainly neither false nor excessive to say that all production of sense—of a sense making sense *in this sense* –is a deathwork. It is thus with all "ideals", with all "works", and it is also thus, remarkably, with all philosophies. Philosophy distinguishes itself by the unique way it profits from death—which is also a way of assuring its own perdurability. Philosophy is ignorant of true mourning. True mourning has nothing to do with the "work of mourning": the "work of mourning", an elaboration concerned with fending off the incorporation of the dead, is very much the work of philosophy; *it is the very work of representation*. In the end, the dead will be represented, thus held at bay.

But mourning is without limit and without representation. It is tears and ashes. It is: to recuperate nothing, to represent nothing. And thus it is also: to be born to this un-represented of the dead, of death" (Nancy 1993: 3-4).

is this work of death. Yet, dying that refuses the meaning of 'work', what has been irredeemably lost, and would not be recuperated by memory of consciousness, that which occurs only as the lapse, and would not be converted into being and thought: mourning for such dying is endless, stretching toward an infinite past, a dying that cannot be represented in any concept or idea, a dying that philosophy cannot mourn. Philosophy is incapable of mourning this death; as such, the mourning that constitutes philosophy itself is nothing but a theatre of death, which Bataille has so much to speak of. Hegelian death is only a spectacle of death, a pseudo mourning agony over its own death and nothingness, its ceaseless preoccupation with its own sense and non-sense. Thinking with Bataille, we can say that to think 'dog' Hegel needs a theatre of the death of dogs; in other words, representation of dog is necessary to have knowledge of the 'dog', but this theatre already loses what it seeks to know. Absolute knowledge is only empty, homogeneous signification that signifies nothing, and whose totality is only the empty time of discourse. Totality as such, can only be 'discourse' that says nothing about the 'dog' itself without reducing its very sensuousness that makes the dog a dog. It makes itself thought of death, which is only a spectacle of death that has lost its sting and has been rendered powerless: only by rendering death such powerless, philosophy can claim to look death in its face. The other dying, however, remains impossible for philosophy.

How to think of this signification, which is not the work of death and which philosophy, let alone Hegelian philosophy, cannot think? How to think this 'impossible death' that exceeds the work of death, and even the possibility of thinking itself, the mourning which always exceeds the comedy of the speculative spectacle that Hegelian speculative philosophy sets up? To think this impossible death, irreducible to knowledge and consciousness (that never appears to a phenomenological consciousness), is to think another thinking of death, other than as negativity and as work, without 'concept' and without 'Spirit'. Does the face of the Other, where dying appears without work, allow itself to be converted into 'my' concept, and represented in 'my' world? : The face of the Other—the singular sensibility, or sensible singularity—cannot be subsumed into the universal order of anonymous Reason. Here Emmanuel Lévinas' reflection on death and significations in relation to Other is immensely important to us. Not: the death of the Same, the work of negativity that the whole tradition of ontology puts into work to effectuate its freedom! To respond to the face of the Other with its irreducible signification that signifies his death is to put into question the terrible injustice of the Universal order of anonymous Reason.

2. That time is this passage of negation, this restlessness of sublating the sensible, sensuous 'dog' (which barks) to the freedom of the concept: it is freedom to the extent that it elevates the immediate, mere animal sensuous existence to the eternal life of Spirit. If self-consciousness is what distinguishes a man from being mere animal, this self-consciousness would itself be realized, negatively, by negating the mere, immediate, sensuous being to transform himself to the full consciousness of *Logos.* It is through the labour of the concept that the human is transformed from the mere sensuous being into spiritual life If negation is essential to the concept—this *work* of death that transforms the given sensuous to elevate to the higher form of spiritual existence—, this is insofar as only man is capable of death. Only for man death is a 'possibility'; in this possibility not only would humanity be realized in history but the very consciousness of this project of history. Thus, philosophy is this *deathwork* itself: all ideals of sense are based on this work of death. Sense, in this sense, is death-work in which the possibility of being self-consciousness is realized, the *logos* wherein man recognizes himself by negating all immediate, contingent animal existence.

We, however, wonder whether in this sublation of the sensible—wherein sensible disappears to make sense appear—this sense itself carries within itself the traces of the sensible because the very *materiality* of the signifier would be, in this very negation of the sensible, essential for the sense itself. If sense is the work of death, then signification itself is possible only to the extent that it bears the very trace of the sensible. The word 'dog' signifies not only because it is the negation of the real barking dog, but also because it itself is only a word, a materiality, has a sensuous mode of being. Thus the negation of the sensuousness of the 'dog' is not exhausted by the negative-negating sense/concept of 'Dog' but rather negativity exceeds this very negativity of the concept in the materiality of the signifier. If sense is this self-consciousness of man, and it makes possible realization of man's negative-negating freedom from mere sensuous existence, then sense inevitably brings into itself an impossibility of absolute annihilation of the sensible.

Now this is what precisely Hegel argued against any philosophy of intuition: Hegel shows, against F.H. Jacobi, of the impossibility of the ineffable to maintain itself as ineffable (because the ineffable must inevitably pass over into the concept). Philosophy is sense, the work of *logos*, of making sense of oneself and the world by negating-negativity of the; to renounce sense altogether and yet to philosophize—Hegel goes on to argue—is to claim to know one does not know what. But sense, the non-material that is the negation of materiality, can be realized only in the word which itself is material: such is the aporia, the excess which negativity itself brings to itself. Absolute sense in which Spirit has penetrated into all the wealth of the Spirit, and that has exhausted its work of negativity by transforming every sensuousness to the eternal self-sameness of the concept, can only be—if one pushes this logic to its own limit—Absolute non-sense itself . To reach the closure of history wherein reason and human freedom is realized totally, would be to renounce even the sense (if sense always carries traces of the sensible in its very materiality of signification) of being Absolute. Therefore, pushing Hegelian logic to its utmost possibility, we reach the other end of the Hegel which Hegel himself has not been able see: that Absolute, which is 'infinite negativity', exceeds its own sense, and always already going towards non-philosophy: what Absolute knowledge discloses is none other than the impossibility of the Absolute itself—the absence of sense, and absence of the Book! Not being able to say anything (since it is negation of all 'here' and 'now', 'this' and 'that'), it only murmurs its own impossibility of saying, its own death and its incessant othering. Concept, the concept of all concepts, the Absolute idea or even, the Book, the book of all books, is this empty, homogeneous saying of the law that says nothing and that in every endeavour of saying, unsays itself thereby. Absolute is the death of sense, death of meaning, the death of the Book: the Book of all Books where the beginning and end of human history is made eternal, and where freedom is made possible. Such a book is possible only as 'discourse', only in a discourse, despite Hegel's hope that he is recounting effective human freedom in real historical time, *hic et nunc*. History where human freedom realizes itself through the work of negativity (by transforming the given natural world to human world of culture, and making possible thereby his self-consciousness in his own product), this historical world can be accounted only in the sense of the 'Dog', only in a signifier, and nothing but only in a 'discourse'. Absolute is only a discursive product and end of history is only a discursive project, an assemblage of signifiers to constitute the Book of books, Hegel's *Encyclopaedia*. Such a system says everything and yet nothing. It destroys its own possibility while all the time constituting its own possibility. The Book is the name of such a system, totality that inscribes its possibility only by erasing its presence, absents itself in its presenting, in representing itself. Not only that philosophy does not seem to have been able to ground itself on itself, and thereby to derive its signification from its own immanent field of concept but also that, in this very desire for grounding itself on itself, philosophy opens itself up to an entire Other, and incessantly and interminably is exposed to its own impossibility.

Philosophy, thus, is not only its product of its own labour but *undoing* of itself in this very doing, undoing that does not belong absolutely to doing and yet, cannot be posited as transcendent ontological ground. It is dying without work, absent in presence and present in absence that does not have Hegelian third synthetic unity which can bind them together: such absence-presence, such "insane game" of sense cannot be totalized; infinitely erasing, absenting itself from itself, it never returns to the self-sameness of the concept. Such is the face of the Other: the face of the Other is a trace that cannot be recuperated in any immanence of self-presence; it cannot be reduced to the synchrony of the Same: it erases its own presence in the very appearing, differs in the very moment of identification, eludes itself in the moment of grasp of the intellect. Saying would, then, no longer be seen as the self-satisfying time of the concept; it is the very trace of the Other, the enigma of his face that eludes every attempt of negation. It puts into question the violence of the negative in its unconditional commandment: "thou shalt not kill".

3. Thus, all discourse, all writing is addressed to the untotalizable Other. If from Plato to Husserl reminiscence constitutes the condition of possibility of knowledge—reminiscence through which representation takes charge of its work of gathering into unity the manifold, then

it must be said that this reminiscence is founded upon the forgetting of the Other, a prior forgetting which allows the Same to remember itself to be the Same accompanying its representations (as in Kant's transcendental unity of apperception). Forgetting: the unthought of the metaphysics of presence, not the forgetting of Being which metaphysics as the history of Being forgets but a forgetting even prior to this oblivion of Being, forgetting that exposes us to an infinitely distant future of the 'not yet'. Not a forgetting that cannot be realized as nothingness of death, nor a recoverable forgetting at the origin of memory, but an origin that is always already forgotten. Philosophy cannot mourn this death, this incessant forgetting which (de) constitutes memory, this infinite absence from the horizon of time in which the question of Being is posed. Thus philosophical discourse of totality itself can never be totalized: it must always remain open to the Other who does not come in any representable time of synchrony. Always to come, the 'not yet' time of reading, a deferring and differing 'not yet' time of promise: saying has this relation to this time of future, which the negativity itself must always presuppose as its very condition of being.

It is from Emmanuel Lévinas we learn that 'saying' is irreducible to the self-present time of the Same, and is essentially addressed to the Other. To address the Other, offering him the meaning of discourse, is to respond to his death and to his finitude. It is what Lévinas calls, Justice. In the next section we will examine the thinking of negativity as the problematic of freedom, and we will ask whether Hegelian notion of freedom adequately addresses the problematic of justice. We will ask whether, in the name of Reason, Hegel subsumes singularity of the Other to the impersonal order totality. It appears that Hegel preferred the second where freedom is always actualized in the rational order of law, and maintained by law: this freedom is always grounded on the ontological right 'to be'. Freedom is always seen as the *ontological freedom* that can be exhaustively realized in the rational order of law that sublates every particular *sensible* to the *sense* of universal right. We wonder, whether this establishment of rational, homogeneous, universal order of law always leaves behind—like unaccountable remnant which Hegelian Absolute leaves outside of itself—the justice to the Other. For Hegelian metaphysics of history is grounded upon metaphysics of violence: a philosophy of war where human freedom is the result of the life and death fight for recognition; it is the philosophy of sense which through the terror of negativity de-faces every face of the singularity, reducing thereby to the homogeneity of universal sense. Reduced to the faceless particular moments within the anonymous order of cold Reason, Hegel's effectuation of freedom is only an abstraction, an empty assertion of the right 'to be', and freedom for everybody and for nobody. Such is the paradox of Hegelian order of universal Reason: that it renders abstract, as the law itself which it conceives, the humans whose freedom this homogeneous order would seek to effectuate. If the total reconciliation as desired by Hegel is between the law and freedom on the one hand, and the human on the other hand (whose freedom history tries to realize), then the Hegelian human being would be nothing but only as faceless and dead as the law itself. The history of the Hegelian man is the freedom of the dead man; or, rather it is the dead freedom of the dead man—not because man should actually be killed to realize his freedom, but that his death from his immediacy of natural existence is necessary for even to conceive his freedom 'to be'.

We propose here, following Emmanuel Lévinas, that the singularity of the face of the Other cannot be rendered in these terms of history; that we need to open up another time, another thought of justice so that this very gap between the time of freedom and the exceeding time of justice, between the time of history and diachronic time of eschatology, would allow us to think the very unthought of metaphysics: difference which violence of the Same cannot render appropriate to itself, the thought of the Other that would put into question the closure of history. This gap, this difference and this un-appropriable excess, is necessary if thought is to open to the infinite justice to the Other, if thought is put into question the violence of the universal order of Reason.

Death, desire, and labour

Signification is a work of negativity, the eternal restlessness of the negative that sublates (Hegel 1998: 490-91) the immediate and the natural, transforming the given animal existence to the eternal life of the Concept: negativity is itself this passage from the mere particular sensible to the self-repose of the concept(that maintains its self-sameness even in this restlessness) (Ibid: 490). As negativity, sense or signification is the assimilation, re-appropriation, recuperation of all the wealth of the sensible; it is an eternal hunger that assimilates its own heterogeneous other to nourish its lack, eating and devouring what it produces through its work of negativity.

Signification that is manifested in the face of the Other, that responds and addresses to the singularity of the Other, cannot be thought as need and return to the Same but as surplus which, going from the subject, desists any form of absolutisation. The temporality of signification that is opening to the Other is the *diachrony* of the sensible: an inassimilable asymmetry between the addressed and the addressee, without dialectical synthesis that will include the two within an overarching order of totality. This desistance does not have the verbal resonance of movement that is initiated by the need, the fulfilment of which is the *telos* of the movement; it is rather a pre-ontological event of opening : the intelligibility that schematizes/thematises this event of Being must already appeal to the pre-ontological saying which is not at all verbal resonance of a movement of negativity, but the desistance that always already is a lapse of time. In the naming of the intelligible saying, therefore, something is always already lost: this inadequation forever interrupts any possible totalization, and resists any possible representation of it. This excess, which is also its poverty, is necessary for any signification to be possible: for it is not the verbal resonance that is its condition of possibility of itself, but the address to the Other that always exceeds every Said!

Philosophy, then, cannot derive its signification from its aboriginal ground, but from a wholly Other that bestows its sense by giving the movement of the verbality of resonance; to be able to assume this act of signification, it must always already address to the Other: this 'sense–bestowal' is an overflowing gift, a surplus beyond any economy of norms and equivalences of values. Philosophy cannot ground its own signification; this very act of signification, philosophy desists its own grounding, opening thereby to the infinite Other to whom its appeal to justify itself. Unlike Hegel whose philosophy is the work of negativity (the labour that negates the heterogeneous 'nows' of the *sensible* to the homogeneous principle of *sense*, the universal order of anonymous Reason which will have the characteristics of being in *universal*), the address to the Other is the excess of this anonymity of faceless Reason, that exceeding its own totality:

> European thought has always combated, as skeptical, the idea of man as measure of all things, although this idea contributes the idea of atheist separation and one of the foundations of discourse. For it the sentient I could not found Reason; the I was defined by reason. Reason speaking in the first person is not addressed to the other, conducts a monologue. And, conversely, it would attain to veritable personality, would recover the sovereignty characteristic of the autonomous person, only by becoming universal. Separated thinkers become rational only in the measure that their personal and particular acts of thinking figure as moments of this unique and universal discourse...But to make of the thinker a moment of thought is to limit the revealing function of language to its coherence, conveying the coherence of concepts. In this coherence the unique I of the thinker volatilizes. The function of the language would amount to suppressing " the other", who breaks this coherence and is hence essentially irrational. But in its expressive function language precisely maintains the other—to whom it is addressed, whom it call upon or invokes...Language, far from presupposing universality and generality, first makes them possible. Language presupposes interlocutors, a plurality. Their commerce is not a representation of the one by the other, nor a participation in universality, on the common plane of language. Their commerce ... is essentially ethical (Lévinas 1969: 73).

In Hegel's philosophy of signification, signification that fulfils the need of the same by negating the other, would amount to the suppressing of the other. Knowledge as such, for Hegel, is the absolute hunger of the human consciousness; human consciousness attains its full-satisfaction only when Spirit attains its Absolute knowledge, the totality of self-consciousness of the whole process of constituting pattern of becoming Absolute. Knowledge is possible as the Spirit attains the consciousness of the other and thereby consciousness of itself through the work of negativity which constitutes *sense* or signification. One can never attain the full consciousness of the dog if the dog is not yet a *sense* or concept and in this consciousness of the dog, if Spirit itself is not itself conscious of its knowing the dog. Therefore knowledge always point towards, must point towards Absolute knowledge if Absolute knowledge is not only knowledge of the other but Spirit's consciousness of itself knowing its other. Knowledge as signification is this work of negativity, the work of death and the work of violence, the work of transforming the heterogeneity of the other to the self-sameness of the homogeneous self-consciousness, the work of eating and devouring and self-satisfaction of the nourishing Same. Signification or knowledge (philosophical knowledge precisely because only philosophical knowledge can attain Absolute knowledge, can carry out this work of death and negativity) is *work* because only human work is negativity, because only humans know how to die, is capable of death, because only for human, death is a work and possibility.

But signification which is addressed to the Other—address that is inadequate to the addressee where one, addressing to the Other always says more than what is contained in the saying, where address is always the surplus, overflowing of all that can be contained in the labour of the addressee—is overflowing of labour which death introduces us to produce meaning. In the address to the Other, the production overflows the labour: labour cannot re-appropriate it because, in recuperating would amount to produce more surplus. Thus, language, exceeding any labour of production and consumption, rather disrupts the economy of intelligibility of Being. If one calls this surplus of the address (that resists any appropriation to the economy of Being) as 'ethics', this ethics would be the very modality of signification which exceeds the economy of Being. Perhaps this necessity to depart from signification of economy, or economy of signification—based on the intelligibility of Being—would amount to leaving behind the atmosphere of Hegelian theatre of signification (where death is put into work that produce the profit of meaning). To exceed the labour of signification is to give one's home to the Other: Lévinas thinks this *offering* is an *ethical* act, act without action (of negativity):

> Language *effectuates* the entry of things into a new ether in which they receive a name and become concepts. It is a first action over and above labour, an action without action, even though speech involves the effort of labour, even though, as incarnate thought, it inserts us into the world, with the risks and hazards of all action. At each instant it exceeds this labour by the generosity of the offer

> it forthwith makes of this very labour. The analysis of language that tend to present it as one meaningful action among others fail to recognize this *offering* of this *world*, this offering of contents which answers to the face of the Other or which questions him, and first open the perspective of the meaningful (Ibid: 174).

Language is a gift, an offering of possessions and home; it is the gift of the world that is constituted through the labour that negativity put into. Work is the production of the world, the human world: the eternal restlessness of the negative transforms the alien, heterogeneous natural world to the home of the self-sameness. In producing the world—in producing the sense 'Dog' by negating 'dog'—Spirit posits itself in this positing; it comes to itself in this self-engendering movement of self-consciousness. Signification as such is a product of death work in Hegel where self-recognition is possible for the Spirit: to produce sense is to create its home wherein Same secures its own site.

Is not this creation of home, production of its site where the Same produces itself by negating the alien, heterogeneous others already a violence to the Other? For Hegel—and for ontology as such—history is the domain of sense where the sensible is already *usurped* by this negating time of consciousness: this philosophy is metaphysics of eating that maintains itself by transforming all others into its own. Hegel calls this negativity of hunger as desire. But language which is irreducible to hunger that would be satisfied by the profit of meaning; addressing the Other is irreducible to the labour that produces the world: it is rather an infinite! As such, the originary dimension of language is not reducible to sense that has the characteristics of "Being in general"; it does not subsume the heterogeneity of sensible under the maximizing fold of the concept (Ibid: 76). The gift of language is not peace pact arrived through conditioned negotiations after the life and death struggle for recognition. The gift given to the singular Other is rather rupture of this very totality of universal Reason; it cannot be reduced to the moments of within the overarching totality of universal history (Ibid: 182).

The hunger, which initiates the Same to set the movement of labour is what Hegel calls 'desire'. Hunger is negativity, the lack in being, the nothingness of what is 'not yet', for thing which is not 'yet presence'; the gap between this nothingness in Same and nothingness of the 'not yet', 'not yet present' is the delay, the restlessness of time which labour assumes to transform the negativity of the object by negating this negativity itself to fulfil itself. Desire is this *movement* of negativity, the passage of transforming *sensible* to the *sense* (signification is this time, the time that necessary for labour to satisfy desire, which is a lack, a nothingness on the Same). Time is the *negation* of the mere self-repose of fixed, immediate, natural existence (the universal '*Night where all cows are black*'); in this very self-repose of the given existence, desire introduces the restlessness in the Same, propels him to initiate action that transforms the given existence to satisfy its hunger. Work is this negative-negativity of action, the project of transforming the given alien world of the sensible to recognize its own self-consciousness by building its own world—the world of history and not mere nature. The time of desire, which means the time between the nothingness of 'now' and nothingness of 'not yet' (this gap is necessary for desire if desire is nothing but this distance of 'not yet' of concept and nothingness of hunger), is also the time that work assumes: it converts this nothingness of 'not yet' into the fullness of the Same. Distance which desire introduces, the diachrony which the labour of the concept would soon assume, would soon be converted into the synchronic time of presence. As such, 'distance', 'gap', 'diachrony' is introduced into the very heart of the Same only to convert this diachrony into the synchrony of the self-satisfying nourishment! Already diachrony is reduced to the possibility of a synchronic time of the self-satisfying Same. Ontology as the philosophy of hunger and labour, cannot address the problematic of diachrony without reducing it to the synchrony of self-satisfaction. Desire, understood in Hegelian sense, is the negativity, which assimilates the heterogeneous outside to transform into the interiority of the self-same subject; what is the irreducible outside, irreducible to the interiority of the self-same remains to be account by the Hegelian philosophy.

To think this infinite Other, it is necessary think the relation of the same to the Other other than as 'lack' (as negativity that initiates action to assimilate the other for its self-satisfaction): here desire as infinite desire, irreducible to satisfaction and nourishing and irreducible to the desire for self-presence, remains unaccountable in Hegelian philosophy of the same. It could not have been otherwise. The erotic of philosophy has always been only this desire for presence, and for synchrony of being: desire for the proximity of being identical with itself. This is true whether in Hegelian form of dialectical identity, or in Heideggerian manner of hermeneutic identity: ontology is incapable of thinking the irreducible diachrony of difference which infinite distance introduces. Hegelian speculative philosophy only realizes—without putting into question radically its philosophical *eros*—the utmost possibility of philosophical project of attaining the self-presence.

The metaphysics of work has the ontological possibilities which more than any others could Hegel see. After Hegel it is no more a question of mere desiring (passive desiring for an impossible presence which defines the predicament of the 'beautiful soul' or even for Kant, where desire for the impossible constitutes the desired object as merely hypothetical one) but *effectuation of desire,* by putting desire into action, so that desire would introduce into being its utmost possibility of fullness of Being. The moment work is introduced in desire, it already becomes an instrument of self-satisfaction. Desire is necessary but it is only to satisfy desire. With Hegel onto-theo-logy realizes its utmost possibility in seeing the desire itself as 'possibility'—of the fullness of Being. But the irreducible desire that exceeds the very satisfaction of realization would remain unaccountable because Hegel's ontology cannot think desire other than as nothingness that has its *telos* its annulment. We wonder, whether irreducible desire does not exceed any projection of *telos* or *arche*', for desire irreducible to satisfaction of hunger would be infinitely stretching towards indefinite future, towards an infinite postponement of satisfaction (it would no longer be a matter of satisfaction then), and which, therefore, without being able to return to oneself through recuperating the negativity, would only be departure towards this infinite Other: the very sense of diachrony itself! Infinite desire would not then be understood as circular return to the self-presence of oneself; infinite desire is rather the movement of traversal that would not return to the self-presence, but only a *departure* that is incapable of negativity. Incapable of assuming the negative-negating time of labour, such an infinite desire for the other is a *radical passivity* that does not recognize its presence of nothingness in its desire; it cannot assume even the nothingness of desire: such is the passivity of desire; its time is not the restlessness of negativity but passivity of diachrony itself. Not being able to effectuate desire into action, it is incapable for any *arche* or *telos* for itself. Rather it is the tragic play of existence whose consequences it cannot foresee, results that exceed every ontological project of realization. Desire, which is infinite, is therefore tragic. Emmanuel Lévinas brings out this tragic dimension of desire relation to the Other: the tragic exceeds every determinant realization of ontological project of 'to be'. It is a tragic destiny that exceeds every determination of a teleological project (which should ensure the self-maintenance of the Same); instead the tragic hero is delivered to an unforeseen destiny that cannot be anticipated. Here, the destiny exceeds the determinative projection; it is the surplus of the work, which, instead of assuring the self-maintenance of the system, ruins the labourer himself:

> The idea of *fatum* accounted for the reversal every heroism in a role suffers. The hero finds himself playing a role in a drama exceeding his heroic intentions, which, by their very opposition to that drama, hasten the accomplishment of designs foreign to them. The Absurdity of the *fatum* foils the sovereign will. In fact inscription in a foreign will is produced through the mediation of the work, which separates itself from its author, his intentions, and his possessions, and another will lays hold of. The labour which brings being into our possession ipso facto relinquishes it, is in the very sovereignty of its powers unceremoniously delivered over to the other (Ibid: 226-27).

History cannot assume its own destiny: such is its predicament! Not being able to contain what work introduces—the very unpredictable surplus of 'not yet' that would not come to pass by –history cannot close itself into itself once and for all. Exceeding its totality is to free time for a future to come what is not synchronic with itself, what is asymmetrical to both particular determined 'here' and 'now' and continuous 'Now' that presents in all 'nows'. It is to think difference, not subsumable to the generality of concept, and not exchangeable with any particular 'now': such singularity cannot be thought within the metaphysics of history. If such a thought has an eschatological dimension, it cannot be thought as a product of negativity, labour and concept but rather as judgment upon history, not by history itself but something entirely other to itself which history cannot contain. If judgment upon history cannot be produced as historical self-consciousness, if such an eschatological dimension frees time from the time of labour—it is every time the time of pure exceeding, it is to put history to its utmost limit, to push the labour of the concept to its utmost possibility. The universal history is the order of Reason where each particular being makes his own death a work at the service of the Universal. Reason—the very realization of the humanity (that human is not mere sensuous, immediate existing but the negative of it: 'the life of the Spirit is the death of immediate existence', as Hegel says)—has its own inhuman dimension where the worker cannot recognize his own face in his product, and it ends by constituting an impersonal order which, with its progressive rationalizing process, effaces every possible singularity, where the social dimensions of responsibility and existing for the Other is reduced to this rational process of instituted rights. It's not for the Other that these rationalizing institutions carry out its effectuation of freedom through law, but in sight of a total homogeneous order that reduces the Good (goodness in face of the inviolable Other) to the calculative machinery of the state apparatus. Even when this historical totality thinks plurality, it thinks plurality by reducing it to equivalence of the many: the radical difference, which makes each one singular and asymmetrical, is reduced to the calculable particulars. Plurality remains unthought in its radical difference and heterogeneity. The constriction of difference into contradiction which is finally reduced to the homogeneity of the impersonal order, is already a violence that constricts singularity: thus the non-thematizable dimensions of ethical responsibility to the Other become objectifiable and thematizable, which then can be manipulated by the effective hand. Wherever the law has its primacy, and wherever sovereignty over the singularity seeks to effectuate freedom through rational institutions, there occurs reduction of decision to the calculative programme with a pre-determined telos; everything that is difference, heterogeneous to this project, is then violated, negated and repressed. To open up this closure of the law and Reason, it is necessary that another dimension, irreducible to law, must be opened up: not because law, Reason, State and all the rationalizing institutions are unnecessary but that their violence needs to be judged and questioned. That history needs to be judged is not to renounce history; it is rather to affirm the singularity of the Other that would judge history in the name of the infinite justice. Thus, history—for that matter philosophy itself—cannot found its possibilities in its immanence; it must always already appeal to an infinite transcendence—of the face of the Other—irreducible the time of negativity; it is to discover diachrony at the very heart of the historical time. If history is what defines the very 'humanity' of the human, this self-consciousness that through negation produces the sense of our existing as labouring animal, then the judgment upon history would be to put into question this humanity of the human itself, in order to think of the 'humanity of the other man'. If tragic destiny puts into question this very humanity of man, and if such a tragic destiny constitutes the very judgment upon history, then it is only this desire for the infinite Other, unassumable by history, that would put into question any totality of history.

Desire that exceeds the metaphysics of *humanism*: such desire is essentially an infinite desire for the transcendent Other. It is from Lévinas that we would learn how to think desire as infinity and as transcendence (not the Hegelian desire as negativity, which Lévinas calls 'need', but desire as the excess of negativity) (Ibid: 117). In the second section of this chapter we examine how Hegelian philosophy is incapable of addressing this infinite transcendence. Other than Hegelian form of infinity, we need to introduce another infinity: such thought of infinity should be rendered in concrete term here. We would call movement to the Other without return as 'desire': not the desire that assimilates the nothingness of the 'not yet' into the fullness of the Same, but a relation to a 'not yet' that would not be converted into the fullness of the Same. Lévinas, therefore, rigorously distinguishes the transcendent infinity of desire as a movement to the Other—the movement that traverses without return to the same—from the immanent Hegelian form of infinity as desire (Lévinas calls the latter 'need'). It is from Lévinas that we will learn how to think the unthought of Hegelian onto-theo-logical desire for presence. No doubt, it will take the form of an interrogation of the whole Western ontology itself that borrows its light from the Greek Sun. Very early, in Plato, philosophy names itself as *desire*: the name of the movement that exceeds itself to the something beyond itself. But this distance that makes desire itself possible (hence philosophy itself) would be determined only to be traversed and recaptured. The philosophical eros only knows this movement of immanence: distance that would be traversed and annulled, which already implies the virility of assimilation of the Other into the self-sameness. Hegelian narrative is nothing but this movement of traversal that sets its own limit, and thereby, traverses its limit itself. In his *Phenomenology*, Hegel describes this movement in the following way,

> The nature, moments and movement of this knowing have, then, shown themselves to be such that this knowing is a pure *being-for-self* of self-consciousness; it is 'I', that is *this*, and no other 'I', and which is no less immediately a *mediated* or superseded *universal* 'I'. It has a *content*, which it *differentiates* from itself; for it is pure negativity or the dividing of itself, it is *consciousness*. This content is, in its difference, itself the 'I', for it is the movement of superseding itself, or the same pure negativity that the 'I' is . In it, as differentiated, the 'I' is reflected into itself; it is only when the 'I communions with itself in its otherness that the content is *comprehended* [i.e. in terms of the Notion]. Stated more specifically, this content is nothing else than the very movement just spoken of; for the content is Spirit that traverses its own self and does so *for-itself* as Spirit by the fact that it has the 'shape' of the Notion in its objectivity (Hegel 1998: 486).

Here also we see, Hegelian concept of desire has an intrinsic relationship with time. Desire is restlessness of negativity, a mode of traversal that supersedes its limit, which it posits: the movement of positing its excess, and overcoming this excess by assimilating its own other. This movement of traversal, which the Spirit undertakes ('this highway of despair' is the journey which the Spirit undertakes), this movement is reduced only to the particular moments of the whole journey: "the movement of carrying forward the form of its self-knowledge is the labour which it accomplishes as actual history" (Ibid: 488).

As the restlessness of superseding, desire is already time. Here though Hegel destroys the whole ontological project of 'substance' by substituting its formal structure by the movement of becoming, the Subject still retains the domination of the Same. Time is restlessness, negation of Space or the negativity of the substance, but this restlessness of time is only a mode of philosophical eros that sets itself into motion to actualize itself through this very process. What has remained unquestioned in Hegel, then, is this very philosophical eros : From Plato to Hegel this metaphysics of presence never radically questioned philosophy's desire for presence. If Hegel has introduced temporality into being, in not very much unlike Aristotlean manner, temporality is determined only on the basis of presence: the Spirit posits its difference—that is, it phenomenalizes itself –only to appropriate its other. Each stage of this phenomenological movement of Spirit presents a veritable gallery of rich images in which it appears in its manifold form.

Beyond the closure of history

Thus, *desire has an essential relationship to history*; the other aspect of Spirit is Space presenting as the form of Nature. In the *Phenomenology of Spirit*, Hegel says,

> The self-knowing Spirit knows not only itself but also the negative of itself, or its limit: to know one's limit is to know how to sacrifice oneself. This sacrifice is the externalization in which Spirit displays the process of its becoming Spirit in the form of free contingent happening, intuiting its pure Self as Time outside of it, and equally its Being as Space. This last becoming of Spirit, Nature, is its living immediate becoming; nature, the externalized Spirit, is in its existence nothing but this eternal externalization of its continuing existence and the movement, which reinstates the Subject (Hegel 1998: 492).

Time is sacrifice, the self-externalization of Spirit but it is not mere sacrifice but also a *knowledge of sacrifice itself*. For a long time, more prominently from Georges Bataille' analysis of sacrifice and recently from the work of Philippe Lacoue-Labarthe (Lacoue-Labarthe 1998) we have come to know how the theatre of enacting sacrifice constitutes the metaphysics of desire for presence, and how speculative idealism is based on this paradigm of the work of death. If philosophy is to construct upon death its paradigm of knowing, and if knowing is nothing but knowing of death, then this knowledge is possible only (in other words, if philosophy is this knowing itself) from the enactment of certain spectacle of death. The knowledge of death is possible only when one is still alive, but to be alive and still conscious of being alive is already not to know death. To be alive and still to know death: such is the spectacle of sacrifice functions as the dialectical paradigm of Absolute knowledge. As such, time is only a spectacle of sacrifice. Every time death threatens to destroy the very spectator—and suppose it is Hegel himself—there occurs the impossibility of advancing of any further than what it can represent itself to itself. It, thus, already leaves behind another death, which it cannot maintain and which it cannot endure the impossibility of death which is irreducible to any project of knowledge. Not being able to put into work, and not being able derive profit out of it (profit of meaning or signification, for instance), not being able to assume this terror of death (more terrible than the terror of dialectical negativity), the other death refuses the *adaequati*o of representation. At the summit of experience there opens up an excess—a movement of traversal—that never returns to its home. By putting death into work, philosophy comes across another death that it cannot *look into face and still to maintain itself.* The Universal history, whose temporality is that of the impersonal Reason, subsumes all finite appearances, is thus torn from within: the gap between being and nothing here does not know dialectical synthesis; rather, this dying is for us a passivity of mourning, an anguish that like a tears into the system of dialectical unity of knowledge.

Therefore, Plato has this profound wisdom that *mimesis* is dangerous: there is something excessive, but also something impotentiality about mimetic representation; mimesis always produces a surplus that it cannot contain once and for all; the work of negativity produces its own surplus that exceeds the system of signification. Incessant mourning of pure loss, the interminable death agony that cannot be closed in a determinable point of reference: mourning exceeds the consolation of work and resurrection through work. Not being absorbed in historical time, mourning incessantly interrupts every form of historical closure. Lévinas expresses it beautifully,

> ...Interiority is the refusal to be transformed into a pure loss figuring in an alien accounting system. The death agony is precisely in this impossibility of ceasing, in the ambiguity of a time that has run out and of a mysterious time that yet remains; death is consequently not reducible to the end of being...Dying is agony because in dying a

> being does not come to an end while coming to an end; he has no more time, that is, can no longer wend his way anywhere, but thus he goes where one cannot go, suffocates—how much longer… the non-reference to the common time of history means that mortal existence unfolds in a dimension that does not run parallel to the time of history and is not situated with respect to this time as to an absolute…Death—suffocation in this impossibility of the possible—opens a passage toward descent (1969: 56).

Mourning refuses to enter into the economic system of profit and loss. Hegel does not know true mourning, this endless mourning and beginningless mourning without concept and without knowledge (Hegel 1998: 492).

Here is what Hegel calls "Absolute knowing", the end of this restlessness itself, as the end of history. If this enactment of the theatre of sacrifice is the necessary condition of possibility of absolute knowledge (which, consequently, delivers the Absolute knowledge into the vertiginous abyss of eternal repetition), then, history itself would be infinitely postponed, and its temporality, instead gathering into presence, will extend to infinity beyond any totality. The task of thinking after Hegel is to think this impossible closure of history: the diachrony of excess (infinitely delayed and lapsed, infinitely stretched towards a future which cannot be closed)! If desire to be thought rigorously—infinite desire irreducible to the work of negativity, irreducible desire of non-satisfaction and of unrecuperable negativity, as time of departure towards a transcendence without return—then desire is to be thought as this excess itself: surplus of totality and the impossibility of the end of history. Beyond the closures of history, there has to be thought of another time of worklessness, the passivity of endless time, which makes infinite desire possible. Exceeding the meaning of work, desire has to be thought as impossibility of dying—an unsacrificiable dying, whose meaning is given in the Biblical commandment: "thou shalt not kill"! If desire is to be thought in its irreducibility to need, this desire for the Other, then desire should be thought in such a way that it must put into question history. To put into question the end of history is to interrogate the totalizing Reason of universal history that subsumes singularities into the anonymous order of the concept. Desire that is irreducible to the negativity, the unproductive pure desiring which in its very movement exceeds itself its limit, puts into question the tyranny of universal history by responding to the Other that history always leaves behind : it is the face of the Other. Not the desire that recoils into its self-same fold but limitlessly stretches towards an immemorial time of the past and the un-anticipation of the 'yet to come'. Unproductive, this desire does not yield the profit of sense: the abyss of sheer groundlessness of Being, suffering which Lévinas calls 'passivity'. Desire always repeats itself, calling other desires that again repeat ad-infinitum, which cannot look back to recognize its own face: diachrony as transcendence! To desire is, thus, to open oneself to the unthinkable; to desire the other is to lose time, the lapse of time without value and without profit. Desire is this impossibility of memory: if memory is the constituting ground of history, then desire opens history to the immemorial outside of history. History is recollection of dead time, time that has passed by and yet preserved in memory: as such, in Heideggerian terminology, history is metaphysics insofar as history is conceived as gathering into unity (which is the ground, thought onto-theo-logically) of all moments of non-simultaneity. Memory: possibility of all impossibility—that converts even the nothingness of passing 'now' into the recuperating presence by representational act of the same—all philosophical possibilities of meaning and totality is based on the modality of remembrance. Even in Hegel, history is the recollection of the shapes of Spirit: Phenomenology of Spirit is nothing but a remembrance, a recollection of what has become; it is the history of the Spirit (Ibid: 492-93). From Plato to Hegel, the philosophical eros for presence and the primacy of memory has never been radically questioned. In the case of Hegel, the question of desire and memory has become a problematic of the actualization of freedom in the human world of history. Once the desire for presence remained unquestioned, memory remains the ontological modality of thinking time: for memory is the ontological possibility of re-collecting, recuperating, gathering into unity that makes simultaneousness of non-simultaneous thinkable, the synchrony of the Same possible. The primacy of the Same over Other is maintained, and secured once again. Even in Husserl, this is never questioned in any radical manner, despite his careful maintenance of distance from Hegelian phenomenology. To desire the infinite Other is to put into question this primacy of the Same (which maintains its identity with itself through remembrance). To think death on the basis of time is to push the labour of remembrance to its limit, and to deliver remembrance to forgetting. The infinite desire for the transcendence Other cannot be effectuated by the labour of memory but rather marks the limit of time: 'my' desire for the Other exceeds any act of remembrance, having began in an immemorial past, exceeding towards the infinity of diachronic 'yet to be'. Such is the inexhaustible desire that constitutes 'my' responsibility to the Other that brings rupture to the unity of knowledge (which 'I' seeks to maintain through memory).

Again it is from Emmanuel Lévinas we learn how to think death on the basis of time. In his two courses of lectures before his death that are published together as God, Death and Time, Lévinas is engaged in confrontation with three master philosophers of death—Hegel, Husserl and Heidegger—arguing that whether death as the work of negativity in Hegel, time as retention and protention of lived experience in Husserl, and the thought of death as 'possibility of impossibility' in Heidegger, death is always seen as ontological possibility, thinkable and graspable to Reason whereas time as diachronic infinity, irreducible to the work of death, has remained unthought, or rather is thought on the basis of death as possible effectuation of Being (Hegel), as possible effectuation of retaining through memory of the lived experiences (Husserl), or as virile affirmation of Being-towards-death as anticipation of its nothingness (Heidegger). To respond to the call of the Other is to have time, to postpone death, to defer and defer time itself so that time is this very infinity of responsibility that has began before any retention of particular moment of birth, and it exceeds all anticipation of Being-toward-death. In other words, to respond to the other is not to negate nothingness to convert in my Being, but it is Other's death which cannot be negated and sublated into my time: as such, it is death that is to be thought on the basis of time. To subsume this modality of difference—that defers and differs to infinity—to the thought ontological discourse of totality, is to subsume the ethical modality of responsibility to the ontological time of synchrony (Lévinas 2000).

Outside the Book

In the sections above, we have examined Hegel's notions of history, Reason, Desire and Death to show how Hegel's philosophical discourse of totality is grounded on metaphysics of violence (violence that is carried out by individuals in their desire for recognition) and how, in such impersonal order of Reason, the goodness of the other and the singularity of his face is effaced. By showing the limit of this historical closure we recognize the exigency of thinking another modality of time other than dialectical modality of time as synchrony. The following pages argue that the Hegelian concept of freedom, which is inextricably bound up with his concepts of Reason and History, needs justification, not in the name of freedom itself but in the name of what Lévinas calls 'justice'. Insofar as Hegel determines freedom as that which the self-conscious humanity produces in history through his work of the negative, freedom remains bound up with the establishment of rationalizing institutions that effaces singularity of the Other in the name of a homogeneous universality. As such, freedom is always the freedom 'to be': the domination of Same (not the individual Same but the universal Same) whose sovereignty is ensured by the rational institutions of the State. On the other hand, the face of the Other clamours justice that each time exceeds the ontological freedom 'to be'.

Hegel's great meditation on 'freedom' recognizes the insufficiency of (Kantian) thinking of freedom: freedom as mere hypothesis, merely to be hoped for, freedom to be realized in a transcendent beyond of any historical 'here and 'now', something that can only be a horizon of all possibility but cannot itself be actualized in any real, historical world. The task of philosophy, for Hegel, is to account how the actualization of freedom can be made possible in the historical becoming in human consciousness. Freedom, therefore, cannot be understood as mere 'noumena'; it must actualize itself by manifesting in real human world of history. Freedom must be actualized freedom 'here' and 'now'; it cannot be a mere transcendental a priori condition, but absolutely immanent in the order of human consciousness, and in the historical becoming of the world where human consciousness recognizes its own freedom from mere animal being.

Already Immanuel Kant determined freedom as 'autonomy': freedom is freedom from 'heteronomy'. However, Kant could not account how it is to be actualized in historical world where the human exists and for whom freedom must be. If freedom is not to be mere formal freedom (as in Kant) where oppositions are laid side by side without reconciling them, it is necessary for Hegel to substitute the formal dialectic of Kant with the very negative action of Aufhebung, by which Hegel shows the actualization of freedom as immanent in the very progress of universal world-history. Through the negative work which desire sets into motion, Spirit frees itself from mere animal condition to the life of the Spirit. This negative labour is the transformation of given heteronymous condition present in the sensible Being into the life found in Universality of Reason. As the life of the 'Dog' (the concept/discourse/sense) is the death of the 'dog(sensible), so freed from the mere contingency of animal existence (which is prey to natural decomposition and death), Spirit is the life of sense, the life of actualized freedom: life as autonomy! Here discourse/sense/concept is determined as mastery of mere animal nature, the alien other of nature that threatens the humanity of man to reduce him to the dog's life. Already in this concept of autonomy, in this desire for subsisting in one's being and signification, in this persistence for identity and signification, discourse of freedom smells war and violence; in the name of freedom, the Same takes up the right to usurp the Other.

Thus, history (which is the process of human becoming self-consciousness through labour and thus to be free) establishes certain organization of rationalized institutions to actualize the freedom 'to be': freedom to be one's own, to possess oneself, to ground oneself on autochthony! Freed from the mere animal condition of the sensible, freedom is the life of sense, the logos that has emerged from nature, discourse that derives its meaning from itself alone, that seeks to ground itself on its immanent order of pure existing, by reducing whatever is excess to it, its heteronymous other, to its immanent movement of progress. From then on (freedom that seeks to free itself from the violence from animal existence, from the terror of alien nature imposing its will on the human, freedom that emerges from this violence through gradual mastery over nature through reason), such a discourse of self-sufficiency (which derive its meaning from within itself) perpetrate its own violence and terror, waging war anything that it considers 'heteronymous'. From then on this Book, logos itself, the Book of all books, would seek to derive its meaning only from its own saying—the Book that wants to be closed once and for all—hopes constitutes its own genesis and structure. To actualize its sense in the world, 'here' and 'now', and yet to maintain its self-sufficiency—the Book being the absolute of all sense, the Book of law, which in totality has within itself all particular laws—freedom would thereby reduce the singularity of exteriority. But the Book itself—without essence and empty, the dead time of the concept where from all sensible fled, the time of Minerva's flight which is too late—that would seek to mean everything, would not mean anything (because all dogs will be dead), in-itself without in-itself (without sensible in-itself): a pure loss and pure expenditure of meaning! The end of the Book: Book that absents itself from itself!

The Book of law that actualizes freedom (by rational institutions through which law is imposed on the citizens: individuals who can be 'citizens' only by being faceless and lifeless) is only an empty Book. But this emptiness itself (which are only words, like the word 'Now' from where all 'nows have fled), being free from every 'now' and 'here', is the condition of possibility of the law. Such is the paradox of the Book: the Book that says nothing-in-itself is now capable of saying everything (Blanchot 1993: 433), and can be the source of all violence and terror. The Book that should mean everything (because it is the totality of significations) ends up saying nothing (that it becomes only empty in-itself); but it is only the cunning of the Book, the trick played by Hegel—or might be a mere trap for the Hegel's reader who is already read by Hegel. Meaning nothing in-itself, the Book assumes the sovereignty of this nothing and converts this nothingness into the fullness of its satisfaction and pleasure. To read Hegel is to be already read by him: the Book that is capable of saying everything and condition of possibility of assuming the force of law.

To put this Book into question is not to escape from the Book (As Blanchot says something of this sort somewhere that not to read Hegel would amount to reading of Hegel); it is rather enter into the Book, and yet, inserting the time between Hegel's Book and reading of the Book, to produce an infinitesimal diachrony, little distance between Book to itself almost its utmost proximity, to interrupt the time of representation with the inadequacy of 'some other time', postponing and disrupting every 'here' and 'now', to inscribe another time of diachrony and another movement. To displace the Book from itself is to open the Book little to something that exceeds the Book, that overflows the Book; while pushing the logic of the Book to its utmost limit, and yet, there at this very summit of experience only to betray it by refusing to return to 'here' and 'now'. To exceed the Book, it is important to trace the Book once again by repeating its logic ad-infinitum.

It is this trace that remained unthought in the system, the left behind of the system, the remnant of all sense and concept. Such 'trace' is not the trace of the same that would be recuperated in the unifying act of memory but trace of the other (Lévinas 1986: 345-54): time that is already lapsed in its very representing, the interrupting time of interval between sensible and sense, the lapse that is irreducible to either presence and absence, irreducible to either phenomena and essence, time that is sublated and that does not work: "the patience of time"(Lévinas 2000: 7-8). This diachrony that cannot close itself into itself in the very heart of the Book, remains open to the Other: it is the Other who puts into question the violence of history. To respond to the call of the Other is to be attentive to his judgment; to respond to this judgment is to bring oneself each time to this court of justice. Lévinas says:

> But it is very important in my view that justice flow or issue from the pre-eminence of the Other. It is necessary that institutions required by justice be overseen by charity, from which justice itself issues. The justice that is inseparable from the institutions and thus from politics, risks causing us to misrecognize the face of the other man. The pure rationality of justice in Eric Weil, as in Hegel, comes to make us think of human particularity as negligible and as if it were not that of uniqueness but rather that of an anonymous individuality. The determinism of the rational totality runs the risk of the totalitarianism that certainly never abandons the ethical language and has always spoken—and still speaks—of the *good* and the *better*...it seems to me that rational justice is compromised when the relation with the other is visibly profaned. And there, between purely rational justice

> and injustice, there is an appeal to the "wisdom" of the I whose possibilities perhaps comprise no principle formulable a priori (Lévinas 2001: 223).

To open the Book to the *time of patience*, to the diachronic time of the Other that exceeds the synchrony of totality, and to judge the violence of freedom and history, it is necessary that the inappropriable gap, the difference and diachrony of infinity, this interruption of interval and this lapse of time in-between be inscribed between the Same and Other, between freedom and justice, between the closure of history and what exceeds it, between the closure of the Book and what overflows it. This temporal gap that would not be sublated by any work of negativity can only be understood as trace. Trace: that is neither absence nor presence; neither the light of the universal sense nor the universal night of the pure sensuousness where "all cows are black," but the trace that still retains the sensible for, negativity can never be a total negation. To judge history and its work, it is necessary to show that all the negative work of history is only "constrictive" negation, and thereby to show that there is something that exceeds the Book.

How the judgment upon the Book is to be thought? The judgment upon the Book—the judgment of justice—is neither the judgment of the speculative proposition where the subject passes into the predicate and in this negativity, rediscovers, re-conquests its truth of nothingness; nor is it the formal judgment of transcendental logic wherein the copula is the synthetic unity of subject and the predicate. It is rather the infinite judgment, without synthetic third term, so that the totality of the judgment is forever suspended (never being able to constitute itself as a proposition). Every time the Book puts itself into work, the judgment of justice exceeds the Book, so that a disjunction or discordance interrupts the tranquillity of the Book. Every time law is instituted through rational institutions to ensure the freedom of the worker, it already produces asymmetry, not only between the worker and his product, but also between his work and what the work leaves behind (namely, the sensible itself). In every passing 'instant' of 'now'—this passing and vanishing that defines time, as Hegel himself says so—there already occurs the fissure of thought, a time 'out of joint', the moment one seeks recapitulate the passing 'instant' through the work of memory, the moment one seeks to convert through representation this lapse of time.

Who was more aware of this lapse of time that occurs at the very moment of recapture than Hegel himself? Is not the whole of *Phenomenology* dealing with this—that 'now', at the very moment of saying 'now', has already become 'non-now'? But that is not all. Hegel discovers at the very heart of this heterogeneity, an arbitrary and yet necessary synthetic conjunction, a simultaneity of non-simultaneous of the third term that would unite discordance of 'being' and 'non-being'. That it is possible only within the Book, only by constricting difference and ignoring the interval of lost time between 'being' and 'non-being', only this constriction allowing to create an ontological field of immanence. But the disjunction between the judgment of justice and the Book itself, between the already lapsed time of diachrony and the effectuated time of synchrony, does not know the synthetic copula of speculative proposition. This discordance is rather the excess of the Book, the Other that exceeds the Book, the trace of transcendence that no phenomenology knows how to recover. As such, justice is infinity that cannot be represented any 'here' and 'now' but somewhere else, in some other time, more ancient than any past and more distant than any anticipatable future. If freedom is necessary, and if it is necessary to put into work the rational institutions, it is not because freedom derives its signification from itself alone and be self-sufficient, but rather because there is another time of justice that requires freedom to be effectuated through juridical, political, economic institutions:

> The irrational in freedom is not due to its limit, but to the infinity of its arbitrariness. Freedom must justify itself; reduced to itself it is accomplished not in sovereignty but in arbitrariness. Precisely through freedom—and not because of its limitation—being freedom is to express in its plenitude appears as not having its reason in itself. Freedom is not justified by freedom. To account for being or to be in truth is not to comprehend nor to take hold of…, but rather to encounter the Other without allergy, that is, justice (Lévinas 1969: 303).

It is not that the actualization of freedom through the rational institutions is not necessary and that we must discard any form of action that would transform the existing historical institutions. it is rather to say that freedom is possible—freedom understood as rational effectuation of philosophical-political decisions through institutions—only when decision, singular each time, exceeds the very ontological determinability, exceeds the grounding on any a priori, calculative synthetic unity of apperception, or on any absolute, auto-effectuating, auto-engendering Subject. Every time there occurs the singularity of judgment, it is history itself that is judged so that the singularity of the judgment must be an opening to an opening, to the promise of the 'not yet', to an exterior, irreducible incalculability, to an undecidability which itself does not have its ontological grounding. If the law and its rationality always assume the form of the Book—the system, totality, absolute—it must always already appeal to the future time of the Other. If freedom is not to be separated from its actualization in the historical self-consciousness of the Spirit, it must appeal to a judgment that does not know any phenomenological experience of it. This judgment is incalculable, exterior to the Book and irreducible to experience; otherwise decision itself would be inseparable from a certain ontological notion of *necessity* to which philosophy has always subsumed the thought of justice; otherwise politics, as the realm of the decisions and their effectuation, would be nothing but calculative program of *a prior* determined teleological necessity. This openness is not openness of an ontological concealment—Heidegger's *lichtung* (Heidegger 1978), an opening of a field wherein darkness and light play their enigmatic unconcealment-concealing so that Being, in its own light of intelligibility, illumines itself—but an opening towards an opening, towards the infinite Other. It is opening even to the Book to take place, to constitute its necessity and signification; an opening whose abysmal unthought at once gives and takes away what is 'human' (understood as 'rational animal'), Reason, thought or even the understanding the meaning of Being. Justice, if it is the name we give to this opening, is this opening that gives the Book its name—Hegel's *Encyclopaedia*—and yet, with this same gesture, tears apart the Book, exposes the Book to the vertiginous abyss of its fictional foundation.

In this chapter, we attempted to examine the thought of diachronic time of justice—which is the time of the Other, irreducible to the synchronic time of the Same—at the limit of freedom, at the limit of philosophy itself, if philosophy amounts to this labour of effectuating freedom in historical time which constitutes the human world. But justice, irreducible to the work of concept, cannot be effectuated in 'here' and 'now'; justice thereby exceeds history itself and puts its violence into question, the violence which negativity assumes, and which freedom perpetrates. It is to open up to another modality of thinking time that constitutes the thought of justice, our ethical relation to an infinite Other which can only be thought as diachrony par-excellence.

The Experience of the Limit–I

> I walk among men as among the fragments of the future—that future which I envisage. And this is all my creating and striving, that I create and carry together into one what is fragment and riddle and dreadful accident. And could I bear to be a man if man were not also a creator and guesser of riddles and redeemer of accidents? *To redeem those_who_lived in the past* and to turn every '*it was*' into '*thus I willed it*'—that alone should I call redemption?
>
> —Friedrich Nietzsche (1995: 139)

> You are not any more different from me than your right leg is from your left, but what joins us is THE SLEEP OF REASON—WHICH PRODUCES MONSTERS.
>
> —Georges Bataille (1992a: 113)

Introduction

The following remarks are taken as points of departure:

1. At stake here is the problematic of 'excess' at the limit of Speculative representation. If death has always served in Western thought as the source of all meanings, signification and accomplishment, not merely of philosophical possibility or possibility of philosophy, but the very possibility of human 'thought' which constitutes the 'humanity' of the 'human'; if by putting death into the work of sublating, human realizes its self-consciousness, and philosophy re-conquers its sovereign mastery over its own death (and thereby effectuates human freedom from mere animal condition), death is also,paradoxically, the limit of

this work : there is, exceeding the work of death, the other dying which does not work—the worklessness of dying, without knowledge and without concept. In the following pages I examine whether exceeding the *work* of death (which through labour produces and effectuates human freedom and constitutes human history), there is another dying that is irreducible to work, irreducible to representation: infinite mourning of which exceeds every recuperated closure of representation. If philosophy is incapable of this infinite mourning which it cannot put into work, which exceeds any closure of the representation of death (only by representing death, in other words, by rendering death powerless that philosophy is capable of thinking death), if philosophy assumes death only by putting a spectacle of death (its feigned 'comedy' of which Bataille ceaselessly reminds us), and thereby, putting death at a distance and death '*held at a bay*', then the excessive negativity of the other dying and its infinite mourning (this impossible, unworking, unproductive death) can be seen to limit philosophy itself.

In what way is representation of death determined as realization of the possibility of philosophy? What is the relationship that death has with its representation? As we see that it is a question of *mimesis*, one of the most classical problems in philosophy, and here it is a question of *mimesis* in relation to death in speculative philosophy. In what manner is death represented in speculative philosophy, if death is what is most terrible of all which "requires greatest of all strength"? Why it is that the representation of death is a necessity for speculative philosophy, if death is also one that threatens to destroy the very possibility of thought (and limits the philosophical discourse itself)? Why and how representation death is a necessity, and thus, is the condition of possibility of absolute knowledge? If, on the other hand, there is 'other' dying which cannot be represented, is irreducible to the recuperable 'negativity' and irreducible to the speculative-phenomenological *experience* of death, then what relation this 'other' dying harbours with the problematic of representation? We then wonder whether representation itself (*mimesis*, which is generally seen as unproblematic dialectical paradigm of re-producing and effectuating the ontological-epistemological subject) would not have something abyssal that limits the very philosophical discourse itself. Rather than seeing the problem of im/possibility of philosophical discourse and its limit in some transcendental source purely outside philosophy, it is a manner of asking: how and in what manner, representation (which is the condition of the possibility of philosophy), is also with the same gesture, the condition of impossibility of philosophy? If representation is what is supposed to be constitutive of the phenomenological-speculative subject, *mimesis* also seems to de-constitute this very subject of philosophy (which is the onto-theo-logical ground of all thought and meaning). After all it is the problematic of the philosophy of the Subject: the speculative philosophy is the utmost possibility of metaphysics as onto-theo-logy. In a more general manner, the question of the 'possibility' of philosophy is also a question of the possibility of the philosophical subject.

2. How can death be represented—and thus seen as 'possibility' of knowledge (death that seems to be the 'impossible', most dreadful and that seems to limit all that is 'human')—if not in tragedy which is the spectacle of mourning and death, and where is also played out the drama of the limit of human Reason? It is not difficult to see how tragedy and its aesthetic experience figure here. If philosophy realizes itself as a possibility only by being able to put death into work, and if this knowledge of death (is philosophy anything other than knowledge of death, its own nothingness and its own impossibility?) requires a spectacle of death (in other words, the representation of death), it is not difficult to see why tragedy, which is supposed to be the representation of death, serves as the dialectical paradigm of speculative thought: tragedy, with all its classical notions of *catharsis* of tragic contradictions and *anagora*, presents itself as the paradigm of speculative resolution, which is the very project of speculative idealism! Tragedy not only seems to give the tragic knowledge of death, but also, in this very representation, is the resolution of the tragic contradictions of human existence: of the infinite and finite, necessity and freedom, Reason and fate. Tragedy is, thus, determined as the dialectical paradigm of representing the possibility of philosophical foundation, if the philosophical task is nothing but—as Hegel conceives of it—the unification and resolution of the sundered contradictions of infinite and finite, Reason and fate, necessity and freedom. Who more than Hegel was aware of the necessity of representation of death, and hence the necessity of tragedy, for the knowledge of death (hence,

for the possibility of philosophy itself) to be 'possible' (for death is most unknown of all)? Who more than Hegel was aware that tragedy realizes this necessity, not by only allowing the knowledge of death to be possible, but also allowing the knower, the subject (the philosopher Hegel himself) to maintain his life in this experience of death so that his death is still meaningful for him. From Aristotle to Hegel, despite Hegelian critique of Aristotelian tragic-mimesis, tragedy remains the paradigm of the very possibility of thought, source of all meaning and sense. The philosopher is the *tragic figure*, the *tragic subject* par-excellence (and for this reason, a comic figure—who is always sure of his resurrection through his suffering).

At heart here is the question of mimesis, and the possibility of the tragic *subject* as the subject of philosophy. Tragedy, as it is conceived from Aristotle to Hegel, is the possibility of thought, and is constitutive of the *subject* of knowledge (here it is the philosopher, the knower of death. One can say that it is the possibility of 'Hegel' himself, not the Hegel the individual thinker, the immediate, sensuous, existing Hegel, but the *sublated* 'Hegel' who knows death and is not terrified of it). Is not the philosopher the tragic subject, the tragic hero par-excellence who passing through "the highway of despair", traverses the travails of death and mourning, and arrives at last to its self-consciousness, its home and destiny of self-recognition. This self-recognition always emerges in the form of tragic knowledge, bringing resolution of tragic conflicts between necessity and fate, non-being and being. It is not for nothing that Oedipus is recognized as the tragic hero par-excellence whose fatal self-consciousness brings his own destruction. It is this tragic subject understood as self-consciousness (the heroic subject of knowledge with his *desire* for *recognition* and his accomplishment of self-consciousness), it is this possibility of the subject that Hegel looks for in tragedy. With Hegel tragedy becomes speculative-ontological representation of the experience of finitude. The subject here is the constitutive possibility of metaphysics as onto-theo-logy (the subject who through the bloody fight for recognition engenders the whole historical unfolding of human possibility). Tragedy here is no longer functioning as mere literary genre, but becomes the question of the possibility of metaphysics as onto-theo-logy (the possibility of philosophy and the possibility of human subject as subject of freedom, the historical subject of tragic consciousness who through the labour of death—which tragedy within the enclosure of theatrical space represents—arrives at his self-consciousness).

Is it not Hegelian ontology anything other than tireless grounding of installation of the subject? The speculative subject needs the knowledge of death, and since the knowledge of death requires its representation, it must find in tragedy this possibility of tragic-knowledge. Tragedy is that space wherein death is put into work by making death itself a phenomenological experience; a space wherein death is present (while still being absent; it is still a mere spectacle and nothing more) in all its terror: death thus becomes something lived experience. Through ritual of re-presentations through the tragic spectacle—because repetition neutralizes the dreadful experience of suffering and death—death is transformed and converted to the phenomenological consciousness of being, into the *Aufhebung* of non-being and its nothingness. In this way, non-being is converted into the profit of tragic knowledge, into the meaning of recognition, and unification of subject-object: this is the very task of speculative ontology as Hegel conceived. *Catharsis* is the Hegelian concept par-excellence: it is the synthetic labour of the concept, the *Aufhebung* of contradiction, and production of self-consciousness. One can see how Hegelian logic can exploit philosophically the classical concept of tragedy, despite his significant departure from Aristotelian concept of tragedy. Even Hölderlin, not to talk about Schelling and Schlegels, too thought that there could be aesthetic unification—not the theoretical one—of the subject and the object, finite and infinite, necessity and fate. The whole metaphysics of *work* and *logos* are ascribed to tragedy: tragedy as the space where death is put into work. If *work* and *knowledge* are the two conditions of onto-theo-logical determinations of metaphysics, then tragedy (as representation of death) serves the purpose of speculative thought: that is, the installation of the sovereign subject and securing of the possibility of absolute knowledge. With this, the closure of representation achieved, the subject has re-conquered its death, the absolute knowledge is secured, and all limits are sublated into the supreme heroic-tragic form of human consciousness. Such is the Hegelian ruse of Reason! Tragedy merely serves for him as the detour to this self-consciousness: a feigned death which will anyway be re-conquered; only pseudo-mourning which has turned out to be a mere comic show which, being sure of its profit and gain, has merely played the game of loss and risk by enacting this tragic play of death and suffering. It is this paradox, the comedy of the Hegelian tragic drama that Georges Bataille's analysis brings to articulation. What happens when tragedy is seen to be a mere comic show, when tragedy can no longer be contained into itself but overflows itself, when it exceeds its own limit, and thereby, no longer being capable of turning this impossible of the excess into the possibility of Being? How to think the tragic which exceeds the closure of representation and thereby limits the philosophical discourse itself: the excess of mourning which cannot be recuperated in the self-presence of the absolute subject?

3. At stake here is the limit of philosophy itself—this sovereign discourse of Reason which aspires to form a totality of significations in the name of knowing even death through tragic representations. If mimesis serves as the condition of possibility of absolute knowledge for speculative philosophy, it is also the condition of impossibility of absolute knowledge. What interests us is to understand how mimesis, in the very manner of rendering death representable, and thus constituting the possibility of Reason (which knowledge of death brings), at the same time, in this very constituting, produces its own excess which cannot be recuperated into the fully-satisfied self-consciousness. It is rather this *excess* that would forever make absolute self-consciousness unsatisfied, for the excess would forever be irrecuparable. Instead of a fully constituted absolute self-consciousness, it is rather the infinite movement of deferring-differing of excess which *mimesis* produces (is not mimesis is its own excess?), which is the very condition of the impossibility of the philosophical subject. This de-constitution of the subject in the very constitution of it, this irremediable-irrecuparable loss of the subject in the vertiginous abyss is the most abyssal of all thought. At very heart of thought—the tragic thought that makes thought itself possible, hence is the source of all meaning, sense and subject itself—of tragedy which serves as dialectical paradigm of the constitution of the subject, there is another tragic thought irreducible to the former one. An infinite mourning, ceaseless mourning which is excess of all thought, which is excess of itself; mourning that instead of allowing itself to be re-presented to a phenomenological

consciousness, rather displaces the very phenomenological subject of the experience. Instead of constitution of the *subject* as labouring and knowing subject, it rather brings rupture to it, empties itself out, hollows itself out, tearing it asunder by introducing an eternal abyss into thought in a sweeping vertiginous experience of anguish. It is this madness: mimesis is then madness, the loss of the subject in the face of anguish; terror of nothingness which philosophy, including Hegel's cannot look in its face. This is this tragic thought—not the Hegelian thought of tragedy—that Nietzsche's madness introduces us in his most abyssal thought of eternal return. In the next chapter, reading Nietzsche's writing which opens up this abyssal thought, we examine how his thought of eternal return is the tragic thought that puts into question philosophy itself and limits the very possibility of the philosophy of the subject. Irreducible even to the unthought that which Heidegger speaks of in relation to Nietzsche, the tragic thought of the eternal return cannot even be thought as the question of Being. Following Blanchot, we would call it 'limit-experience' (Blanchot 1993: , 85-284): experience of perils and of travails that does not belong to any phenomenological consciousness. The latter—speculative consciousness—is only a pseudo-tragic experience, which is already sure of the survival and resurrection. Nietzsche's thought of eternal return is the profound experience of the tragic thought whose ethical significance for the post-metaphysical world is yet to be brought out. In the next chapter we will discuss the significance of the philosophical form of madness such as Nietzsche's, which his most abyssal thought of eternal return introduces in philosophy. What is the relationship of madness and *mimesis* and in what sense it is a matter of the limit of the philosophical discourse? In what sense Nietzsche's tragic thought (in other words, it is to understand why Nietzsche calls himself 'the tragic philosopher') is different from the classical Aristotelian-Hegelian speculative notion of the tragedy? In what sense Nietzsche's tragic thought of eternal return and his limit-experience of madness puts into question philosophical discourse itself, philosophy that takes tragedy as dialectical paradigm of thought and Being? To sum up, what interests us is to recognize the importance of another thought of tragic in Nietzsche's thought other than that assumed by Hegelian speculative-phenomenological thought of the tragedy. It is think mimesis in another direction other than as the source of meaning and the subject; it is to think tragic as excess of the Hegelian closure of the speculative representation.

Mourning and philosophy

When Hegel was still young, from the age of twenty- five to thirty, he complained of his fear of going mad and severe depression, some sort of 'hypochondria' that threatened to drown his whole existence. By the time of his writing Phenomenology which was supposed to be the introduction to the system that he has had in his mind, he seems to have already come to terms with his 'hypochondria'; in other words, he surmounted his 'abyss'. Phenomenology seems to have marked a new period of reconciliation, the end of his romantic period of youthful days, even though the language in Phenomenology is still haunted by the lingering intoxications of 'Bacchanalian revel' (1998: 27); but something has changed, even though Phenomenology still abounds evocative images of night and terror. What has happened between the age of twenty-five and thirty that threatened to ruin his whole existence? What ultimately led to the reconciliation with this 'abyss'?

Was it only to do with 'personal' matters of an individual which can only be of interest for the biographer who would consider such 'matters' as 'datum' that might have some kind of influence on his thought, as if an accident that has befallen him, like any other accidents of life! Was it only such a 'matter' that the biographer would trace, like a historian re-constitute the past events, to either his lineage, or to his mental 'make up'! Such an investigation, useful in its own way, however, does not interest us here. What interests us is this: why it is that philosophers often complain of an unbearable anguish that threatens to destroy his very existence? There is David Hume's thinking of himself as an "uncouth monster" and his shipwreck: "Methinks I am like a man, who having struck many shoals and having narrowly escaped ship-wreck in passing a small frith, has yet the temerity to put out to sea in the same leaky weather–beaten vessel, and even carries his ambition so far as to think of compassing the globe under these disadvantageous circumstances." Furthermore, there is Hume's talk of his 'despair' and 'melancholia' which his thoughts have thrown him, as if into an abyss, who fancies himself as " some strange uncouth monster, who not being able to mingle and unite in society, has been expell'd all human commerce, and left utterly abandon'd and disconsolate"(Hume 1978: 264). There is Kant's depression of his later years which we find traces in his later writings. And, how can we forget, there is Nietzsche's abyssal sufferings, which we will have more to say, that led him to the point of madness.

What is at stake here if not the very experience of thought, the perils which thought brings to the thinker, revealing the groundless, bottomless abyss beneath one's feet, the anguish of nothing that thought, in its excess, leads the thinker to the vertiginous movement of sheer 'impossibility' of any possibilities? If to think is to think the limit of thought, is to think at the limit, then thought, pushed to the limit of the possibility, is the impossibility that the thinker cannot assume. If to think is to think the limit of thought, then thinking pushed to the limit, would no longer be a 'possibility' for thinking as such. Hegel seems to have a glimpse of this experience of thought (Hegel knew everything, including his own death. Is it not that it is the finitude of the individual thinker that constitutes the condition of possibility of thought itself? Heidegger too, in his own way, understood this and his Being and Time is a great meditation on this thought of finitude of Being), which he understands as the perilous voyage of ordeals: "the highway of despair" (Hegel 1998: 49), of shipwrecks and above all, that which reveals the terror of death:

> Death, if that is what we want to call this non-actuality, is of all things the most dreadful, and to hold fast what is dead requires the greatest strength...But the life of Spirit is not the life that shrinks from death and keeps itself untouched by devastation, but rather the life that endures it and maintains itself in it. It wins its truth only when, in utter dismemberment, it finds itself. It is this power, not as something positive, which closes its eyes to the negative, as when we say of something that it is nothing or is false, and then, having done with it, turn away and pass onto something else; on the contrary, Spirit is this power only by looking negative in the face and tarrying with it (Ibid: 19).

Hegel calls this perilous voyage, 'experience', a phenomenological concept. In the last chapter we discussed how in Hegel's thought 'experience' conveys a sense of mastery over the ordeals, and even over the negativity that death presents. 'Experience' implies traversing of thought and all the travails that such a movement of traversing brings; it implies traversal of thought to the limit of the possible. Was Hegel not aware of the limit, the very limit of thought? What is absolute knowledge if not this very limit and knowledge of this limit? At the end of *Phenomenology*, there occur these words,

> The self-knowing Spirit knows not only itself but also the negative of itself, or its limit: to know one's limit is to know how to sacrifice oneself. This sacrifice is the externalization in which Spirit displays the process of its becoming Spirit in the form of *free contingent happening*, intuiting its pure Self as Time outside of it, and equally its Being as Space (Ibid: 492).

Hegel was aware of the limit of thought that he calls 'negative': there is his anguish which stretched from his twenty-fifth to the thirtieth year; it is having to 'sacrifice' oneself, having to die so that another life takes on meaning, life beyond death, signification beyond sensible. Here we are at the point, which should be of our concern in this chapter: that philosophy has an essential relationship with the thought of death. Not that philosophy thinks death as it thinks of lot many other things; it is rather that philosophy is the thought of the tragic-comic experience of death. If death is what limits thoughts, ruins human truth and world, if death is what is the limit (that's why it is the most dreadful) of all that constitutes the ideals of sense and meaning, then philosophy, the terrible discourse which aspires even to think the limit of thought, must be able to think even the most dreadful of all; in other words, it must be able to think death, its abyss and nothingness. To think death is to be able to think the limit of thinking, thought's other. Ultimately philosophy will, in its ability of think the limit of thought, conquer death. Death with its negativity will be held at bay. Philosophy is, after all, the knowledge of death: with this assertion, the possibility of philosophy is realized. Hegel's philosophy is after all the philosophy of death, philosophy that has always taken death as the dialectical paradigm for constitutive possibility of all sense and meaning. If nothingness of death, decay and decomposition is the most powerless, it is also, when put into work in service of meaning or sense, assumes the most terrible power that founds human truth, history and his world. Who more than Hegel exploited philosophically this negativity in service of meaning and sense, which found Reason and human truth? But is not that way death itself, the sovereign death insubordinate to any service of meaning or human truth, slips away and becomes death that is servile, in service of meaning and sense that found human truth, death that has been rendered powerless and domesticated? This is towards this question that the entirety of Bataille's thinking turns and towards which we would like to point. Very sketchily we would like to make the following remarks,

(a) If philosophy is the knowledge of death, the knowing of one's limit, in other words knowing of how to sacrifice oneself (Ibid), and if in this sacrifice the very possibility of philosophy is at stake (and consequently the possibility of all human truth, discourse and meaning), then one must acknowledge that sacrifice, that means the representation of death, is the condition of possibility of philosophy itself and consequently, the condition of possibility of human truth, meaning and sense. From researches, such as Rene Girard's (1977) work, we come to understand that it is violence and various sacrificial rituals that have found, at various moments of history, human community. What interests us is the philosophical problematic of violence, that whether the very possibility of philosophical truth, meaning and sense is not founded on the representation of violence, of sacrifice, of death and its anguish. This will bring us to the problem that we proposed to discuss in the introduction, namely, the problem of tragedy and mimesis. If tragedy serves as the privileged dialectical (re)presentation of speculative idealism, it is because Hegel recognizes tragedy as the space wherein sacrifice is enacted, wherein violence is unleashed in its representation, and yet through representation, is at the same time violence is put into work, domesticated and thus made servile with an end in view of meaning. Hegel thus recognizes that violence of death or what he calls, 'the terror of negativity' is necessary for production of human meaning and human truth, that it is the nothingness that is, paradoxically, the constitutive condition of possibility of all human meaning and truth.

(b) But Hegel did not push this most abyssal thought too far to arrive at the truth that the condition of possibility of knowledge, meaning and human truth itself is a bottomless abyss; that the groundless nothing and its unbearable anguish threatens the whole existence of the philosopher himself. Hegel had a glimpse of this profound anguish in his youth—which he calls 'hypochondria'—but it seems he couldn't push it to the limit (could he do otherwise? It is not a psychological necessity that is the issue here but a profound philosophical exigency which Hegel responded); instead he sought to construct the monumental system *Encyclopaedia* wherein, with a desire akin to a desire for immortality (can one forget Hegel's fascination with Egyptian pyramids which more than once he evokes in his writing and which plays a very significant part in Hegel's system), he wanted to give supreme form to his anguish by representing this nothingness itself, this abyssal groundlessness itself *as if it has ground, as if it can be grounded.* In this way Hegel sought to escape from the most abyssal thought of death, compromised his anguish and constituted, in Bataille's words, a *servile* discourse upon death. What terrified the young Hegel (his fear of going mad) is this death which Hegel could not look *in the face,* with which he later reconciled only by turning away the gaze, by enacting a spectacle of death which end up would neutralizing death through its ritual performance (death made bearable, non-objectionable!). Thus, tragedy serves here—as in Aristotle—the supreme form of self-preservative principle that responds to demands which are contradictory, and yet both are to be affirmed, namely: to expose oneself to the violence of death (without which there is no meaning or sense, no human truth or community. Hegel, even before Nietzsche, recognized that the foundational gesture of all human 'truth', meaning or 'community' is the abyssal violence which death brings. Therefore, it is all the more necessary to examine, in a rigorous manner, Nietzschean interpretation of 'truth' and 'community' and Hegelian view of 'truth' and 'community') and yet, not to allow oneself to be ruined by this very abyss so that 'truth' itself is 'possible' and can be grounded, in ontological manner, on itself. Too direct a contact with the abyssal violence, with the groundless impossibility (which one cannot maintain and yet at the same time to be maintained at all costs) would ruin the very possibility of human truth. To respond to the 'ambivalence' of violence—here the word 'ambivalence' is important here by which I mean 'double bind' (that one must avoid at all cost and yet and cannot avoid avoiding)—an indirect mechanism is necessary so that both the contradictory demands can be responded at the same gesture. Is not it the very ruse of dialectical Reason? However, extending Girard's research to the philosophical problematic here I would argue that it is in tragedy as enactment of sacrifice (wherein Hegel found this indirect mechanism necessary to respond to the contradictory demand of violence), that death and violence is rendered powerless and bearable. If this analysis is plausible, then it is difficult not to say that tragedy is onto-theo-logical thorough and thorough. Hegel's speculative philosophy is an onto-theo-logical tragedy, animated by the philosophical exigency of a foundational gesture to be able to conceive sovereignty of the self-grounding Subject. The abyssal experience of thought, which is the very condition of possibility of human truth, is soon compromised, or even set aside for the sake of servile necessity of knowledge. Hegel, having had this glimpse of this abyssal foundation (which is no foundation at all) of thought, and yet, afraid of looking this death in the face, had to recourse to tragedy to save his 'soul'. The entirety of Hegelian philosophy, his *Encyclopaedia,* is constituted by this demand of self-preservative gesture (Adorno calls it 'bourgeois' in his *Dialectic of Enlightenment*) of cathartic *anagora*; his absolute knowledge is this knowledge that emerges only at the price of evading. Could Hegel avoid this avoidance, Hegel who did not want to avoid anything and even avoiding itself? More than anywhere else, it is at this point Hegel seems to have failed here. Something, in this very moment of grasping which is most dreadful and difficult to grasp, escaped Hegel's grasp—something ineluctable, that seems to render powerless the absolute thought of the absolute thinker! Philosophy that subsumes death for the profit of foundation, is incapable to think death in its 'sovereignty' (this is Bataille's term), and is incapable of true mourning. The abyssal character of thought and its anguish would soon be 'employed' (again this is Bataille's word) so that anguish can be made productive to maintain the homogeneous order of meaning, and the servile discourse of profit. Could it have been otherwise?

(c) This raises another disconcerting question: what about Nietzsche's interpretation of tragedy? Anyone who has seriously read his

The Birth of Tragedy cannot fail to notice that Nietzsche's interpretation of tragedy is directed against the metaphysics of tragedy in general that comes down from such classic exponent like Aristotle. We must not fail to notice that it is against Hegelian onto-theo-logical tragedy that Nietzsche re-interprets the tragic age of the Greeks. But the question immediately arises: if tragedy has always been metaphysically defined in general and by Hegel in particular speculatively, how tragedy can still be a 'critique' of the very metaphysics, and all the more so since Nietzsche himself, till the end of his life (thus in *Ecce Homo*, for example) calls himself a 'tragic philosopher'? As one can see, the whole Nietzsche's philosophy is at stake here in relation to metaphysics. Things seem all the more enigmatic when we find Nietzsche himself, after many years of *The Birth of Tragedy*, while looking back this tiny book, remarks that it "smells offensively Hegelian". This may only mean that Nietzsche was aware of the Hegelian spectre haunting in his philosophy; and this shows the almost impossible task to distance oneself from the overarching presence of the Hegelian system (Nietzsche 1979: 78-79). Nietzsche's book on tragedy is directed against Hegelian metaphysics. We have seen Hegel takes tragedy as the dialectical paradigm of all ideals so as to ground metaphysically the philosophical discourse of totality. If tragedy is used to put metaphysics into question by Nietzsche, then we must investigate the radicality of Nietzschean deconstruction: is Nietzschean deconstruction of metaphysics another metaphysics in turn (Heidegger says, the "reversal of Platonism")? It begs the further question: if Nietzsche could recognize the haunting presence of metaphysics in his book on tragedy, why then he still keeps calling himself as 'tragic philosopher' till the end of his career (and at the same time ceaselessly putting metaphysics in question in all his subsequent books)? One can quickly, hastily answer that Nietzsche had an entirely radical, new interpretation of tragedy in his later works which falls 'outside' of metaphysics (it is to say that there is part of Nietzsche's work that does not belong to metaphysics and hence, to rescue Nietzsche from Heidegger's delimitation of metaphysics) altogether, and while his earlier works till *The Birth of Tragedy* (which includes his philological works) is 'inside' metaphysics, and therefore Nietzsche himself was right to concede his Hegelianism of his early philosophy. Whatever the plausibility of such an interpretation, it seems to be too naïve and simplistic for the simple reason that it is very difficult, without reducing Nietzsche's philosophy to absurdity, to point towards the 'precise' point of disjunction and transformation of his thought from a metaphysical thinker to a destroyer of metaphysics. It is not to say that there is an identifiable homogeneous body of Nietzsche's thought, and that there is a single body of Nietzschean doctrine; nor it is a matter of rescuing from the tyranny of Heidegger's interpretation of Nietzsche. It is the question of taking into account the singular 'strategy' of Nietzsche's displacement of metaphysics. This demands—which Philippe Lacoue-Labarthe alls 'detour' (1993: 14-36)– taking up a movement of traversal, a movement of entering into the very circle of which is to be displaced, to produce an infinitesimal difference, to push the centre a little, *almost* to the point of nothing, imperceptibly and unrecognized. It is necessary for Nietzsche to "offensively smell Hegelian": one hardly feels the difference (is not difference far more profound and nuanced than contradiction? Here it is a matter of difference and not contradiction) one could hardly see the distance from the very atmosphere that is to be put into question: one *smells* Hegelian, but one smells *offensively*! As far as answering to the question of how Nietzsche's thought takes this strategic detour of thought—which puts metaphysics itself in question—I will only point this problematic to another direction": namely, the problematic of displacement in relation to the very problem of mimesis or representation of tragedy. It is the problematic of 'experience'—of anguish (which Hegel seemed to have suffered in his early life) of death—of certain 'limit experience' of abyssal character. I would understand such experience as 'tragic' that has something to do with the problematic of 'displacement' of philosophy.

(d) This should be able to bring us to the very heart of Hegel's glimpse into the limit-experience, into which his profound depression threw him, and from which he sought liberation through the 'labour of thought' for the sake of the profit of salvation. In what sense can we understand 'the limit-experience' as a question concerning displacement of philosophy if it has not to do with the very *subject* of philosophy itself? In a certain way, Hegel's 'hypochondria' represents a profound experience of groundlessness, its abyssal sufferings threatening to paralysis his very existence. No longer being able to assume a transcendental source (which will have its ontological ground or foundation as given and from which traditional philosophy drew all ideals of meaning), Hegel was cast shipwrecked into bottomless nothingness from which he had to gather the thought of the possibility of human freedom. With Hegel, in a certain sense, God is already dead! With the effacement of any notion of transcendental 'origin' (whether Kantian *a priori* unity of apperception, or traditional conception of substance) which hitherto has served the ontological ground for human existence, mankind suddenly seems to have been left in bottomless nothing where all hope of salvation is lost. Is it not this is what Nietzsche calls 'destiny' (of mankind) which suffers in him to the point of pushing him to madness? It is this same exposure to the most unbearable void (which the absence of God leaves us with), and it is the same dangerous contact with the brilliant sun of Greece (contact which can appear only in the form of nostalgia, hence not a contact at all) that has led Hölderlin to unreason, an unreason from which emerged some of his most lucid poems. As such, Hegel's profound depression is not mere another depression that one suffers; it rather indicates the limit-experience of 'destiny' which threatens to annihilate the very possibility of thought and the subject of thought (not the individual thinking 'I' of sensuous, immediate self but the philosophical subject, which, in its becoming of the philosophical subject, must already annihilate and destroy the sensuous, immediate condition of the 'human' to constitute itself as the subject of philosophy). With Hegel, without any transcendental ontological ground, the task of philosophy has been transformed into a task to speak as if no language has given to him, to speak as if no one has spoken before. Therefore, at the very beginning of his *Logic*, Being is to be seen inseparable, in fact understood as same as Nothingness. Here we feel as if we are exposed to the most abyssal thought: "Being is Nothing" (Hegel 1975a: 128-136). If the speech of philosophy finds its language only in this very speaking itself, preceded by nothing that would ontologically support it, and if the philosophical subject who utters '*Being*' is nothing but this very speaking of 'Being' itself, then the foundational gesture of philosophy itself seems as if founded on a nothingness (which, at the same time, threatens to engulf the very possibility of philosophy itself). Hegel's abyssal thought of nothingness—his most terrible knowledge that knowledge is founded upon a void and that Being is Nothing—is, at the heart of the matter, a question concerning the ineluctable 'impossibility' of the very philosophical subject. Prior to the act of assuming the movement of speaking (and yet only in the very act of assuming) the speaking subject has already disappeared, already lost in the limitless Night from which no consciousness survives the perils of its displacement. But this is another Hegel—not the Hegel of system—but the unheard Hegel who is absent from the very origin, who appears in his absent only by effacing his face, and yet who, like the Night that illumines with its excessive darkness, brings a tear to his 'system', a wound that would slowly ruin or unwork the entire possibility of his philosophy, hurling, throwing and returning itself again to the nothingness from which it emerged, to that Night where none presents himself even to say, 'Being is Nothing', wherein the very ability to say 'I' is lost from the very beginning in the unnameable anonymity of infinite murmur. Why Hegel—Hegel of the system—tirelessly, with his infinite patience and rigor of thought (the patience and suffering of the philosopher), sought to run away from his anguish, and thereby constructing his monumental system so as to find the last vestige of salvation for his shipwrecked soul? At the utmost possibility of the thought of 'possibility' which determines the whole Western tradition, Hegel suddenly seems to have exposed the entire tradition to the terrible Night from which 'ground' derives its meaning of Being (or Being derives its ground); it is as if there opened a violent opening where the rift of the origin (which is absent from itself and which appears only to conceal) has appeared, but, immediately, it is closed once again, the profit of meaning desired and the servile discourse of work is given all the more firm ground.

The death of God

What I would like to point out here, which is already too obvious, that from Descartes onwards—from which modern philosophy begins, the point in the history of philosophy which Hegel identifies as the beginning of the dialectical process of synthesis, the very task of philosophy that has its *catharsis* and accomplishment in Hegelian speculative dialectic philosophy—the subject of philosophy, or the philosophical subject becomes the condition of the possibility of philosophy itself, philosophy that has assumed as the task of thinking the problematic of *reflection/representation* and the synthesis of the representations and thus, the problematic concerning the origin and source of significations and human truth. Thus, the problematic of representation is inextricably linked with the possibility of the *subject*, which collects, gathers and synthesizes and thus grounds manifold representations. Thus, following Descartes, it is in Kant we have seen how the *transcendental unity of apperception*, which accompanies all representations, is seen as *synthetic* unity, as the very condition of possibility of knowledge. One can say that question of representation is already posed in Plato. This is true but it was not a problem of *subject* at all. As Heidegger points out in his *The End of Philosophy*, the Greeks did not have any idea of *subject* at all .It is rather when, with the question of *consciousness* being posed in Descartes, the problem of subject comes into being which has further, for Heidegger, accentuated the oblivion of Being. All this is nothing new and about which nothing would be discussed here. I can only remark while passing to other points, that from Descartes onwards—philosophy that has now rested its possibility, its ground and its foundation on *consciousness*, philosophical reflection that has drawn inward and has been transformed into the constitutive *interiority* of consciousness or subject—philosophy derives its condition of possibility from the very possibility of *subject*. With Hegel—he describes his philosophy as 'philosophy of absolute reflection'—philosophy of reflection/representation has reached its utmost possibility in the realization of absolute subject reaching absolute knowledge. Absolute *reflection/representation*=Absolute *subject:* this is, to put in the most simple way, Hegel's task of philosophy and its accomplishment inasmuch as Absolute subject is already determined, in the wake of post-Cartesian thought, as Absolute Consciousness.

What I would like to draw attention towards, from the remarks I made above, is simply this: with Hegel, the task of possibility of philosophical representation has reached its absolute in the very possibility of thinking subject as absolute. It is no longer a question here of us being anti-mimetic/ anti-representationalist to read Hegel against himself; in other words, it is not a question of coming out of the closure of representation, placing us outside of the site of the metaphysics of representation while delimiting representation, as if from a distance and having our pleasure of finally getting rid of the grasp of representation altogether. It is rather—and this is what is at stake here, a 'strategy' far more complex and dangerous—a matter of rendering 'representation 'turning back against itself so that representation or mimesis, instead of being able to reach its closure once and for all, the closure of satisfaction or the profit of meaning, remains open to what is outside, what exceeds its closure and what it cannot name, the irrecuparable unnameable. Thus, it is not a question of an anti-mimesis but pushing representation to the limit, to that summit where representation brings its own dissolution, its utter impossibility and its perils, it is to push representation to the utmost possibility of labour wherein, having reached absolute, also sinks into the Night, the excess of light that blinds vision of the absolute, de-constitutes in this very constitution of representation the subject that represents. Such a movement of the de-constitution of the subject, its perils and utter dismemberment, its utter impossibility and sundering from which it never recovers once and for all, we will call 'experience'. Not the 'experience' in Hegelian sense, the perils and dismemberment that has the form of Aufhebung in the concept or sense, which masters its own death and dissolution but experience which is traversing to the limit where absolute sinks into oblivion, not being able to sustain memory, that has lost time and which the work of negativity unworks its own possibility and thereby ruining its projects that define human history. If history is what constitutes the humanity of man, his realm of work and labour of concepts which in producing objects, also produces human self-consciousness—then limit-experience, in the sense we understand above, puts into question the very humanity of man,(this is why David Hume understands himself as 'uncouth monster', the inhumanity of the philosopher) the very self-consciousness that separates humanity from the animal, and its puts into question, finally, history itself. This is to say—which Bataille took so much pain to bring to our notice—limit-experience is problem of end of history, when history has accomplished its labour and desire and when work has given over to 'play' of negative thought. Limit-experience, bereft of any ontological ground or foundation, is an anguish that is also freeing from history, from the servile labour of the concept, from the discourse of slave and its desire for recognition. Nietzsche's madness and his thought of the eternal return can only be understood in this manner—not as psycho-pathological case study—as limit-experience, the impossible anguish at the dissolution of the subject, the thought of the absence of God. Excessive experience or experience of the excess, excess of the thought that thinks and which, not being able to maintain its excess, pushes thought to its limit wherein its brings its utter dissolution and opens thought, reaching its utmost freedom and brilliant lucidity, to the abyss, its bottomless and groundless nothing. What is important for us to notice is that thought, thought that exceeds itself and that ruins the very subject of thinking, is essentially (what kind of essence is this?) fissured, always already a dehiscence, a rift and a tear that never can be closed, an opening to the outside or a caesura between being and nothing which is always transgressed and yet, can never be maintained. Not being able to be lifted in the form of *Aufhebung*, the caesura of the being and nothing remains like an open wound, the void left by the death of God and would not be replaced by a new one. Nietzsche's madness and his, what he calls his 'most abyssal thought' of eternal return is this profound experience of the death of God, experience of the open wound and the incessant anguish and mourning for this death. Hegelian philosophy has never been capable of this experience of death and this anguish, this infinite mourning because reducing this anguish to the work of death, the labour of negativity, Hegel could experience this death only within what comes as possibility of 'consciousness', within the possibility of the 'subject' or as possibility of 'history' for the sake of maintaining 'truth', meaning, profit and production of concept. Hegelian anguish of death and his mourning is an economizing death, an *economimesis* (Derrida 1981: 71-111) of death, which does not push the work of death to the risk of absolute loss, to the dissolution of all meaning and the very subject of meaning. Far from exposing to the utter risk which death brings to the subject of thinking, Hegelian subject enacts only a theatre of thought for the sake knowledge (here we distinguish knowledge and thinking) to be possible and so that being only a spectator, subject of knowledge retains its 'possibility' from which is derived all meaning and truth. Here thought comes as sacrifice—a spectacle of death, or thought as death, which gives knowledge. But is not it thereby, it brings the dissolution of the very thing that it is supposed to yield profit of knowledge? This is towards this problematic we would point towards.

This means there is thinking is not reducible to knowledge. Is not is precisely what Kant was aware of and which despite the post-Kantian philosophical desire to close the gap between thought and knowledge, would always remain open to thinking? There is an excess of thinking which does not yield the profit of knowledge and which exceeds absolute knowledge. Can one call it 'non-knowledge', this anguish that drowns the very subject of experience? Whatever one can call it, limit-experience is experience of thought at the summit, irreducible to knowledge, which one can call 'madness', the sheer loss of the subject of thinking, of the calculative-economical profit making labouring animal called human 'subject' and it is what is excess of the dialectical appropriation of negativity. It is this very 'madness' that Hegel was afraid of when he complained in his younger days of his 'fear of going mad'.

Thus limit-experience is experience of thinking itself and its excess that the subject of thinking *cannot* think. Madness or unreason is proper (yet madness renounces all claims of property and propriety) to thought. Limit-experience is not the thought of Being or Subject that is *capable* of death or for whom death is '*possibility*'; it is rather an experience of finitude of Being and impossibility of subject. Pushing to the limit of humanity, thinking is 'becoming other', 'becoming monster' or may be the obscene and monstrous coupling of god and beast which Greek tragedy has so much to say and which Nietzsche gives the name, 'philosopher': " To live alone one must be an animal or a God—says Aristotle. There is yet a third case: one must be both—a *philosopher*" (Nietzsche 1968a: 23).

The Nietzschean tragic philosopher is not 'human'—the historical, labouring and desiring self-consciousness and hence, not a subject of thinking, the negating-negative subject which through labour, transforms the animal, natural given order and humanizes it by giving it a human form as meaning or sense, the terrible animal that does not turn away from the animal world of death but subduing this death, creates its own world of human possibility. The tragic philosopher is not the philosophical subject who enacts his own 'sacrifice' so that life of Spirit is possible, for whom his spiritual existence is the tragic experience that would have the form of *Aufhebung.* The tragic philosopher is rather name of the limit-experience that pushes all humanity to the limit, always on the verge of and becoming an 'uncouth monster' and who announces, not a human subject of consciousness that can think only within the limit of consciousness, but 'Overman', that exceeds the historical, negating-negative subject of thinking. This is what Zarathustra announces, the coming of 'Overman' who exceeds 'man', who brings dissolution to the labouring, economic-mimetic man of calculative Reason, the historical man of self-consciousness. But for coming of 'Overman' to be possible, the historical, servile man of labour—Hegelian subject par-excellence, the slave who triumphs through undergoing absolute dread of the master who makes the very core of his being shiver, the cowardly, servile slave who cannot risk death and therefore, cannot reach sovereignty of limit-experience—has to die, he has to bring his own dissolution. " Not 'mankind' but *overman* is the goal" (1968b: 519). The subject in question here is the historical figure of anthropomorphic possibility, which, with the wake of Kant, already Descartes behind him, has become the figure of philosophical subject. The Hegelian philosophical subject—despite his desire to make his 'absolute' more than mere anthropological figure—is anthropomorphic figure that engenders its own *arche* and *telos*, in other words, constitutes its own narrative subject of becoming which narrates to the extent that it is about itself which it narrates. What Nietzsche's Zarathustra announces—his madness is only an extreme experience of an excessive thought—is the finitude of this figure of anthropomorphic historical subject. Overman is one who overcomes himself—not to preserve his 'humanity' through servile desire for profit, knowledge and meaning—but one who is 'tragic' in the sense that he brings his own dissolution, exceeds his 'humanity' because he is the extreme possibility who transfigures existence itself to the limitless surpassing of himself, without goal and without meaning. The figure of Overman is the supreme form-giving *transmutation* of existence, who across the abyss which death of God leaves us with, he takes a leap over 'humanity', going beyond the historical, labouring human society and who knows, without anyone being his equal, the icy solitude of the mountaintop from which he looks beneath the servile world of profit and pleasure; the figure of Overman who transfigures existence knows ''how to transfigure himself "(Ibid: 434) and who has also gone beneath all the abyssal depth of a bottomless sea, knows its sufferings and affirms this very suffering without the need to justify life with this sufferings.

The specular/spectacular death

The limit-experience is the experience of the finitude of Being. If philosophy is the thinking of the limit, as Hegel says so, then philosophy is also an experience of this limit: this is what Hegel's *Phenomenology* all about, that philosophy is an experience of the limit, the 'utter dismemberment' (Hegel's phrase) where consciousness is torn asunder and yet, finding its truth in this dismemberment. The philosopher subject, the speculative-phenomenologist is the figure who has survived its 'utter dismemberment', redeemed from it and thus has been able to narrate the story of its Ullyssian dismemberment and his redemption through his own narration: *Phenomenology* is this story of his adventure, suffering of the philosophical subject, his tearing away of Being and the story of his redemption. A few points are to be noted here:

1. The originary gesture of philosophy and the constitution of its genesis and ground is a gesture of violence and of death; that the foundation and source of all ideals of significations, meanings and knowledge, in other words, the very possibility of human truth is that itself groundless abyss.

2. Yet, this violence and abyss never itself appears as such and therefore must be presented in a spectacle—here comes the 'representation' or '*mimesis*'—in other words, in a *simulacrum* of *presence*. It means that the foundation of philosophical knowledge of death is only fictional or figurative and death never appears as such in its originary violence; it means that philosophical knowledge is representational knowledge or essentially *mimetic* (mimesis, which itself does not possess any 'essence'). Representation of death as the condition of the possibility of philosophical knowledge and source of all meaning and truth is also the condition of the impossibility of philosophical knowledge since representation, presenting only the

simulacrum of presence, displaces the very experience that is supposed to be preserved and given meaning or form. What Hegel recognizes is that—here one is reminded of his critique of Jacoby—is there is no or there cannot be any such thing called *immediate* philosophical knowledge; that all philosophical knowledge is mediated, determined or negated. Representation or reflection is mediation and determination and hence, the very condition of possibility of self-conscious knowledge of the object and subject that knows itself by knowing the object. Here Hegel cannot be refuted—neither we are concerned with refuting him—the ineluctable mediative character of representation and its work of determination. What we are concerned here is the closure of representation that Hegelian specular-speculative onto-theo-logy presents us, that Hegel could not push this very logic of representation too far, the logic of representation which is not only mediative but simulacrum, a figural showing that in this very showing dissimulates what is to be shown, a fictional appearing that disappears at the very moment of appearing, the appearing of the subject that de-constitutes itself and already on the verge of throwing itself into an abyss . Hegel did not know or even better to say, he refused to push his knowledge too far to the limit (he must have known, how he could not have known?) and still knowing that the knowledge that he possesses, wise man that he is, is only fictional or figural, is only *simulacrum*, a theatre of feigned knowledge, a mere ruse of unreason, a *mimetic trap* (Lacoue-Labarthe 1998). What it means to say that Hegel could not avoid mimesis and thus fallen into a mimetic trap, the unworking abyss that would slowly ruin his system, always leaving his system open to the limit which cannot be appropriated. May be Hegel knew this and hence his despair but he could not avoid avoiding his 'hypochondria', his despair and anguish. What he refused to push to the limit—could he do otherwise—and thereby constructing his 'work', is the thought of the limit itself, the excessive, abyssal, mimetic simulacra; in other words, Hegel's philosophy, which Hegel understands as 'philosophy of Absolute Reflection' or as philosophy of Absolute Representation, is incapable of thinking representation to its limit, is incapable of thinking *mimesis* to its limit. Like a Greek tragic hero, who is blinded and led astray because of his excessive knowledge and not because of his ignorance, Hegel is delivered over to a fate unknown to him, to a tragic fate unknown to someone who aspires to use tragic spectacle for the profit of satisfaction and meaning. The tragic fate to which Hegel is delivered over is the fate, which is none other than the product of his excessive knowledge, and the surplus of this knowledge. *Mimesis is excessive,* not in relation to anything or anyone in particular nor in relation everything in general that would be subsumed in concept but in relation to itself; *mimesis exceeds itself, unworks itself, dispropriates and displaces itself and always opens itself to this displacement.* Unlike Hegel of the system that sublates all phenomenological experience of finitude into the knowledge of the experience, which has the characteristics of recuperating of negativity, representation pushes this negativity to the limit, which cannot be recuperated. Once more, representation delivers the negativity that works to its unworking—once more, means infinite times—returns the work of death that founds meaning and truth to the bottomless groundlessness, to the foundationless unworking. In this way, the closure of representation is exceeded once more—means infinite times, all the time, incessantly and interminably --the system opens itself up one more time to the bottomless abyss from which it emerges, not in some immediate, primordial manner, the violence that grounds Being, founds meaning, yields profit but through representation, through mediation itself; in other words, it is representation that grounds Being, meaning and truth ungrounds itself, delivers over to an unforeseeable future that exceeds all *telos,* and exceeds the economic character of onto-theo-logical representation. Anguish of infinite loss, incessant mourning of an absolute 'expenditure' (this is Bataille's term): such is the experience of the limit that representation of the subject brings to the subject of representation.

Representation is *excess,* surplus remnant that, unforeseen, unworks the very system to which it is put into work for profit of meaning or knowledge and thereby ruins the negativity constitutive of the 'world' and the production of history. What Bataille means by 'the excess of negativity' (we have to analysis still what Bataille means by this term) is nothing but this: paradoxical immanent excess that exceeds and haunts every immanent ontology and here Hegelian ontology is particular; that the excess is the summit of the *possible* which onto-theo-logical representation of anguish realizes but it is also, for that very reason, the sudden fall from the summit, the overturning of the onto-theo-logical possibility itself. And this is important: representation carries anguish to the limit, to the summit of the possible—not by outside transcendental forces but by the immanent logic of representation itself—and at the very summit, falls into the Night that blinds the speculative subject, not because of the darkness where '*all cows are black*' but of excessive light of the Sun whose dazzling lucidity is not recuperable. What is important for us to emphasize here that there is, perhaps, nothing transcendental outside representation—and therefore (this is Bataille recognizes explicitly) there is no question of limit-experience, which is immediate, non-representational experience and here Bataille, once again, Hegelian to the limit—but that representation itself is limit of itself that, at its utmost possibility, opens itself towards the outside of the closure of representation, overturning all system, all metaphysics based upon the economy of work and meaning. If there is something called 'communication' happens with the other, it is as the experience of the death of the system, experience of the anguish at the finitude Being, the death of the subject that, confronting its ruins, affirms this very ruin as an object of affirmation. Here, as in Nietzsche's experience of eternal return, an experience of the death of God, the anguish of nothingness that cannot be recuperated and that remains, what Bataille calls, 'unemployed', the void in the absence of Being and dissolution of the subject: such a thought is possible when the death of God itself to be affirmed and willed. Here we would only emphasize one point that while for Hegel, despite his glimpse of the ineluctable unworking essence (which is non-essence) of representation as such—and it is not for nothing that Plato banished the poets and above all the tragic poets from republic if it was not for the danger which representation represents for system and for the rational totality of knowledge—made it object of negation, constricting difference to 'contradiction' (we have discussed it in the first chapter while referring to Hegel's Logic) and conceiving the possibility of the philosophical subject as Aufhebung of the sensuous, individual 'I'. Bataille and Nietzsche, on the other hand, made difference an object of affirmation itself (Zarathustra's saying of 'yea yea') and thereby putting at perils and overturning the very possibility of onto-theo-logical metaphysics itself. In that sense, limit-experience is the experience of affirmation itself, affirmation that affirms affirming, the affirmation of the end of philosophy and death of God, affirmation of the most abyssal thought of unworking, ungrounding which puts into question the subject of experience itself and not the experience of what, as in Hegel's, assumes negativity, the servile experience of the labour of the concept, the patience of the slave who assumes works and carries the burden of the world and history. In this profound sense, Nietzsche's experience is tragic-experience, the affirmative experience of even the most abyssal thought of impossibility and the limit of thought itself.

In the next section, we would examine how in Bataille's limit-experience of excess, what he calls somehow paradoxically 'interior experience', the Hegelian onto-theo-logical representation of negativity is pushed to the limit and pushing the Hegelian speculative-representative subject to its own dissolution through the very logic of representation and betraying thereby the very strategy that he fulfils to the limit, the Hegelian strategic thought of labour and history which death assumes. And we will analyze how Bataille undertakes, in a most unforeseen strategy, to take tragedy to the height of its possibility which speculative labour uses as the best means for the profit of the knowledge of death, and at this limit, opens this speculative closure of representation to the excessive experience of death itself, the most terrible experience of violence which no philosophy of representation ever hopes to recuperate again—for it is its own impossibility, its groundlessness to which it is delivered once more time.

Excess of negativity—experience at the limit of speculative representation

Representation is excessive. The whole movement of *Phenomenology* demonstrates that the movement of representation essentially appears as the movement of negativity (or, even better, negativity is *movement* itself). In my previous chapter I attempted the trace the onto-theo-logical aporias that such a strategy of introducing movement into thought brings (which ruins the very project of speculative thought). What is important for us to show here is that movement (which is negative and the movement of representing) is excessive in relation to itself: the incessant working that unworks its own ground, rending asunder the very possibility of thought. Here we find Hegel's profound departure from the atmosphere of Platonic mimesis: while Platonic mimesis is based on the transcendental paradigm of representation in which what is to be represented is transcendental in relation to what represents(and this relation is conceived on the model of 'eternity' which has what is aleatory outside it), Hegel, on the other hand, by introducing movement, seeks to affirm both necessity and contingency in dialectical movement of immanence by conceiving active synthetic principle that negates as well as preserves both the contradictory moments. While movement does not appear in Platonic mimesis, in Hegel it is the very constitutive process of representation. Movement is negative-negating *work* of determination since determination implies positing and representing what 'is not'. Representation is work of negativity: -the work of sundering and gathering back what it loses, the labour of movement which is that of 'being' passing into 'non-being' and converting this non-being' into 'being'. It is the negative work that creates the 'world' as the act of consciousness (Hegel 1998: 294). That's why the philosophical subject is always the figure of the worker. The phenomenological-speculative subject is the onto-theo-logical figure of the worker par-excellence: the virile work of the slave that transforms the given world of nature by mastering and negating what is alien, and sublating it to the self-consciousness of '*human*' world. Hegel's speculative-discursive subject of representation is the '*humanist*' subject which through 'pain' (this "highway of despair"), gathers into itself what is most intimate to itself. 'Recognition'—the sublation of suffering—redeems this suffering of the worker who through work risks his own death. Which is to say that philosophy which constitutes itself as totality of meaning or signification, is the work of slave, servile production for the sake of meaning that needs 'justification' or 'redemption' of the pain and suffering.

Here one sees that Hegel's philosophy of the tragic is not the tragic experience of Greece but the Judeo-Christian experience of 'nihilism' in its historical formation. Nietzsche's critique of Hegel's philosophy of tragic seems intelligible here: onto-theo-logical tragic knowledge that realizes the redemption of life through history is the extreme form of metaphysical nihilism—the saying of 'no' to life that assumes the *negativity* of work, the need for salvation or redemption for the sake of which philosophical knowledge is subordinated, the servile discourse of meaning which slave produces, the one who cannot risk death and cannot overcome himself. 'Life needs to be redeemed and justified through suffering', so says the nihilist philosopher who cannot affirm life, and who seeks salvation of his pain in philosophical knowledge in the form of concept. What Nietzsche's tragic philosophy teaches is not that of justification or salvation of life but that life is to be affirmed. His thought of eternal return is the most tragic affirmation of life that does not aim at the redemptive *telos* of *cathartic* self-recognition through speculative knowledge but that which affirms difference, the abyssal ungrounding of existence:

> The tragic man affirms even the harshest suffering: he is sufficiently strong, rich, and capable of deifying to do so. The Christian denies even the happiest lot on earth: he is sufficiently weak, poor, disinherited to suffer from life in whatever form he meets it. The god on the cross is a curse on life, a signpost to seek redemption from life; Dionysus cut to pieces is a *promise* of life: it will be eternally reborn and return again from destruction (Nietzsche 1968b: 543).

If Hegel arrived at the salvation of the : " seriousness, the suffering, the patience and the labour of the negative", the onto-theo-logical form of tragic knowledge, he arrived it not in the transcendental world above but in history where Reason is realized; salvation becomes historicized and that which can effectuated in 'here' and 'now' through the infinite pain of negativity. One can see here that in speculative philosophy, such as Hegel's, the death of God is not affirmed to the limit, whose possibilities have just been opened up, is once more compromised and closed for the sake of meaning. Hegel's 'hypochondria' takes this speculative tragic form of knowledge that has as its aim the *telos* of tragic reconciliation and self-recognition. *Phenomenology* is the utmost realization of this reconciliation, which, through work, arrives at its final recognition that man, the finite consciousness is this 'becoming' God, the infinite consciousness. Henceforth, an individual lives as if he is nothing but that as if death lives in him, as if he is an empty Nothingness which has its form of salvation in the universal work of Reason for the sake of which the philosopher sacrifices his individual sensuous being, and undergoes his own death. Thus Hegel writes in his beautiful *preface* of his obsession to "tear men away from their preoccupation with the sensuous, from their ordinary, private [einzelne] affairs" (Hegel 1998: 5). Philosophy is sadness, an infinite anguish which he must undergo as if death is no longer possible for him. This emptying out of what is subjective, this loss or disappearance of the ability to say 'I', vanishing of all the certainty of what one calls Being, or truth into the bottomless abyss, this rending asunder of all that appears beautiful human existence, this violence or sacrifice of the what is 'living'—this is the most terrible anguish, the very impossibility of humanity:

> When the pure 'I' beholds itself outside of itself and rent asunder, then every thing that has continuity and universality, everything that is called law, good, and right, is at the same time rent asunder and is destroyed. All identity dissolves away, for the utmost disparity now occupies the scene; what is absolutely essential is now absolutely unessential, being-for-self is now external to itself: the pure 'I' itself is absolutely disrupted (Hegel 1998: 314).

One can cite the whole of *Phenomenology*, which is nothing but a narrative of this "highway of despair". So Hegel knew this most abyssal suffering. But he did not push this 'rending asunder' to the utmost affirmation to push to the point of 'tragic joy', transmuting and transfiguring all that is terrible into its most tragic affirmation. Could he do otherwise? Instead, for Hegel, the vanishing individual 'I' immediately passes onto the universal 'I', into universality of the anonymous concept. Hegel calls this process of negativity *Aufhebung*. The death of the immediate, sensuous subjectivity is not disappeared absolutely but is rather preserved in this negation: there is, thus—so Hegel claims—no absolute loss of the subjectivity, but through the concept the memory of this death is preserved and interiorized. Representation is this work of this 'interiorization' of subjectivity, the work of gathering and collecting the traces of what is 'no more'; it thus constitutes the possibility of conceiving the continuity of Being even in non-Being. The immediate subjectivity of the sensuous 'I' disappears but the 'I' of sense appears, another 'I' takes place, which is that of the concept, the universal subject of philosophy,

> Language, however, contains it in its purity, it alone expresses the 'I', the 'I' itself. The *real* existence of the 'I' is, *qua* real existence, an

> objectivity which has in it the true nature of the 'I'. The 'I' is this particular 'I'—but equally the *universal* 'I'; its manifestation is also at once the externalization and vanishing of *this* particular 'I', and as a result the 'I' remains in its universality. The 'I' that utters itself is *heard* or *perceived;* it is an infection in which it has immediately passed into unity with those for whom it is a real existence, and is a universal self-consciousness. That it is *perceived* or *heard* means that its *real existence dies away*; this its otherness has been taken back into itself; and its real existence is just this: that as a self-consciousness Now, as a real existence, it is *not* a real existence, and through this vanishing it *is* a real existence. This vanishing is thus itself at once its abiding; it is its own knowing of itself, and its knowing itself as a self that has passed over into another self that has been perceived and is universal (Ibid: 308-09).

Nothing has been lost or disappeared; whatever death has not taken away has been taken back again, resurrected in the concept of 'I', in the philosophical subjectivity because death itself has been preserved as work. The onto-theo-logical subject of philosophy is the worker of death who converts his anguish and his nothingness into the salvation of the concept. Hegel's system is realization of this work, the redemption of his suffering and his feigned tragedy in that he is already sure that nothing of his anguish will go waste; nothing would be lost without giving profit of meaning, namely, the knowledge of death itself. For the sake of this knowledge—Hegel's philosophy is only this knowledge of death—wherein lies surety and certainty of its salvation, the sensuous subject sacrifices itself, undergoes its death agony: such is the compromise that Hegel accomplished through his 'work'. The result is, as Bataille notes, not the 'sovereign anguish' but the servile existence of meaning, the very cowardly gesture of the slave who works for profit. 'Sovereign' experience remains something for Hegel that has eluded him, and which he sought to annul through his work of negativity. What remained of Hegel is the emptiness of the Notion:

> A comic little summery. Hegel, I imagine, touched upon the extreme limit. He was still young and believed himself to be going mad. I even imagine that he worked out the system in order to escape (each type of conquest is, no doubt, the deed of a man fleeing a threat). To conclude, Hegel attains *satisfaction*, turns his back on the extreme

> limit. *Supplication is dead within him.* Whether or not one seeks salvation, in any case, one continues to live, one can't be sure, one must continue to supplicate. While yet alive, Hegel won salvation, killed supplication, and *mutilated himself.* Of him, only the handle of a shovel remained, a modern man. But before mutilating himself, no doubt he touched upon the extreme limit, knew supplication: his memory brought him back to the perceived abyss, in order to annul it! The system is the annulment (Bataille 1997: 73-74).

In his 'Hegel, Death and Sacrifice', Bataille elabourates Hegel's failure to attain sovereignty of the limit-experience in the following way,

> If the attitude of the Sage (Hegel), is not, for its part, sovereign, at least things function in the opposite direction; Hegel did not distance himself and if he was unable to find authentic sovereignty, he came as near to it as he could...sovereignty in Hegel's attitude proceeds from a movement which *discourse* reveals and which, in the Sage's spirit, is never separated from its revelation. It can never, therefore, be fully *sovereign;* the Sage, in fact, cannot fail subordinate it to the goal of a wisdom which supposes the completion of discourse. Wisdom alone *will be* full autonomy, the sovereignty of being... at least it *would be* if we could find sovereignty by searching for it: and, in fact, if I search for it, I am undertaking the project of being sovereignly: but the *project* of being-sovereignly presupposes a servile being! What nonetheless assures the sovereignty of the moment described is the 'absolute dismemberment' of which Hegel speaks, the rupture, for a time, of discourse. But the rupture itself is not sovereign. In a sense it is an accident in the ascent. Although the two sovereignties, the naïve and the sage ones, are both sovereignties of death, beyond the difference between a decline at birth (between a gradual alteration and an imperfect manifestation), they differ on yet another precise point: on Hegel's part, it is precisely a question of an accident. It is not a stroke of fate, a piece of bad luck, which would be forever deprived of sense. Dismemberment is, on the contrary, full of meaning. ('*Spirit only attains its truth*', writes Hegel (but it is my emphasis) 'by finding itself in absolute dismemberment '.) But this meaning is unfortunate. It is what limited and improvised the revelation which the Sage drew from lingering in the regions where death reigns. He welcomed sovereignty as a weight, which he let go...(Ibid: 292-93).

What is at stake here towards which Bataille drives us? I would try to summarize in the following points,

(a) That what Hegel fell short of full sovereignty is the subordination of sovereign experience to the 'work of negativity'. In this way the singularity of experience is reduced to the generalized economy of the concept. I mean by this something different from what Bataille calls, 'general economy'. What I call here 'generalized economy of the concept' is what Bataille calls 'restrictive economy' : reduction of the 'general economy' to the exchange and productive value of the servile discourse of being. Thus 'general economy' is not what is generalized in the name of concept. What is insubordinate to the generalized concept and thus insubordinate to the meaning is called 'sovereign'. 'General economy' is sovereignty, the excess of work and meaning, of negativity that constitutes self-consciousness of the human. Hegel, thus, makes the sovereign anguish bearable by reducing that singularity of experience only to a negative moment of his discourse. Not only that way singularity of sovereign experience is effaced but that it is also reduced to the servile projection of being.

(b)This sovereign experience is irreducible to the meaning of being or to the profit of knowledge. The tragic experience is excessive; excess is tragic. Instead of being in the service of the production of the concept (which discourse reveals), instead of founding the abyssal experience in the *Aufhebung* (thereby realizing metaphysics to its utmost possibility), tragic experience exposes us to the groundless abyss of being. Without *cathartic* redemption, the tragic experience is an infinite expenditure of being without profit. The sovereign tragic experience puts into question metaphysical principle of onto-theo-logy itself. If tragic is joyful, it is not because it has re-discovered or re-conquered its lost ground, but that joy is essentially tragic and sovereign (which servile discourse of metaphysics quickly covers over so that meaning be preserved, and so that humanity be conserved, so that death be bearable and self-presence of being be grounded). Tragic is excess because it exceeds the restricted economy of the servile being, and exceeds the metaphysical closure of restricted *mimesis*. The question for us to show how what exceeds the restricted *mimesis* of onto-theo-logy is nothing but mimesis itself, the very mimesis which works to produce the meaning of being and the knowledge of death: it is this work of mimesis that unworks itself. In other words, it is mimesis which is tragic. Mimesis is tragic because it exceeds itself, because it exposes us to the breakdown of the subject (thereby opening us towards what exceeds the closure of the present, beyond the closure of the self-presence of the determinable 'here' and 'now' of negativity). This negativity is, what Bataille calls,' unemployed' (Ibid: 296), the remnant or the excess that is left outside the system, outside the totality of satisfied self-consciousness. What is left outside the system of absolute knowledge is nothing but representation itself; it is representation that cannot be recuperated once and for all, because it unworks in the very process of working. If tragic experience is excessive, it is because tragic experience is nothing but representation itself: Dionysian tragic joy always *disguises* in Apollonian form of *presentation;* behind the comedy of self-satisfied self-consciousness, the Dionysian tragic joy rends asunder the subject of the tragic, tears apart the very Apollonian subject of negativity! Dionysus always appears with a mask of Apollonian face and does not present itself in its self-presence of being but rather presents itself, disguises itself in the name of presence, and yet, in this very presentation, de-constitutes this very presentation, absenting itself in this presence: presence exposes itself to the vertiginous groundlessness! If Nietzsche desired madness, it is this absolute expenditure (of what has hitherto been conserved) that is meant. Madness for Nietzsche is tragic because it is absolute rupture, the impossible experience that cannot be recuperated in self-presence of being. Presentation, in re-presenting, absents itself from itself at the very summit of self-presence: such is excessive tragic experience of the sovereign being! Nietzsche's experience of eternal return is the impossible simulacra of feigned comedy behind which lurks the most abyssal thought of bottomless ground. Representation is feigned. Is it not what Plato reproached the poets for, and for which the poets have no place in the republic? If Plato depreciated the poets on the ground of morality, it is because all transgression of morality is essentially transgressive. Representation is excessive, and is dangerous. One can understand why more than any other poets it is the tragic poets who are denounced by Plato (but Aristophanes, the dramatist who wrote comedy, was Plato's friend). This is because representation, being excessive, is tragic. Representation is simulacra, an illusion and deception: with this determination of tragic mimesis as deception which is to be depreciated, there arise the whole Platonic metaphysical oppositions between 'reality' and 'fiction', 'truth' and 'simulacrum', 'apparent world' and the 'real world'. This is "how the 'real world' at last became a myth" (Nietzsche 1968a: 40). "The antithesis of a real and an apparent world is lacking here: there is only *one* world, and this is false, cruel, contradictory, seductive, without meaning—a world thus conquered is the real world. *We have need of lies* in order to conquer this reality, this "truth", that is, in order to live—that lies are necessary in order to live is itself part of the terrifying and questionable character of existence (Nietzsche 1968b: 451).

The whole of metaphysics resides in this necessity to lie (in order to live, in order for 'humanity' to be possible), and yet forgetting that it is nothing but a lie, it thinks itself as possessing the ontological grounding in its immanent becoming of 'truth'. What has come to be called real world is a lie which is added to the 'real world' of simulacra, while 'real world' has become now an apparent world. Metaphysics, the discourse of truth, forgets that it does not have its foundation in its immanent possibility which engenders itself and constitutes its *telos,* but rather this belief is a lie. The philosopher is 'genius in lying', an *artist* par excellence. This art—this secret most possibility of philosophy, and its foundationless foundation—is what is most dangerous and most abyssal, the most unthinkable excess of philosophy. Art is the seductive secret of philosophy and yet philosophy is incapable of this secret:

> Metaphysics, morality, religion, science—in this book these things merit consideration only as various forms of lies: with their help on can have faith in life. " Life ought to inspire confidence": the task thus imposed is tremendous. To solve it, man must be a liar by nature; he must be above all an artist. And he is one: metaphysics, religion, morality, science—all of them only products of his will to art, to lie, to flight from "truth", to negation of "truth". This ability itself, thanks to which he violates reality by means of lies, this artistic ability of man par-excellence—he has it in common with everything that is. He himself is after all a piece of reality, truth, nature: how should he not also be a piece of genius in lying! (Ibid: 451-52).

The metaphysics of truth is this servile escape not to confront the most "terrifying and questionable character of its existence" (Ibid): its will to lie, its escape from the seduction of its secret, which it cannot appropriate. The depreciation of *mimesis* and art in the name of morality is a self-preservative gesture of metaphysics in its inability to affirm deception. 'It is better to affirm nothing than to affirm the will to deception': so a nihilist says. From Plato to Hegel, it is this denial or saying 'no' to the will to deception, by either banishing the poets from republic or announcing 'the death of art' that constitutes the nihilism of metaphysics. If *mimesis* haunts from Plato to Hegel, it is because the logic of *mimesis* is not affirmed to the limit, and deception is not willed. If art is necessary, it is because this metaphysician's will to truth to be put into question by delivering and exposing it to its own secret, which means, to its own lies. "We possess *art* lest we *perish of the truth*"(Ibid: 435). It is necessary to will even the will to deception, the will to illusion and it is necessary to affirm even simulacrum, the seductive subtleties of mimesis of which Plato depreciated:

> The will to appearance, to illusion, to deception, to becoming and change (to objectified deception) here counts as more profound, primeval, "metaphysical" than the will to truth, to reality, to mere appearance: —the last is itself merely a form of the will to illusion. In the same way, pleasure counts as being more primeval than pain: pain only as conditioned, as a consequence of the will to pleasure (of the will to become, grow, shape, i.e., to *create* : in creation, however, destruction is included) . A highest state of affirmation of existence is conceived from which the highest degree of pain cannot be excluded: the *tragic—Dionysian* state (Ibid: 453).

Is it not this will to deception (this tragic-Dionysian affirmation of art so as not to perish in truth) the reversal of Platonism? : This is Heidegger's question. Heidegger's interpretation of Nietzsche being 'the last metaphysician' who has realized the utmost possibility of nihilism by reversing the metaphysics in question seems to be acceptable. Even the thought of eternal return is also extreme form of nihilism. Is it not what Nietzsche himself to say in *The Will to Power* as in the following?:

> Let us think this thought in its most terrible form: existence as it is, without meaning or aim, yet recurring inevitably without any finale of nothingness: "*the eternal recurrence*".
>
> This is the most extreme form of nihilism: the nothing (the "meaninglessness"), eternally" (Ibid: 35-36).

But is that all Nietzsche has to say? The thought of eternal return has two meanings: one nihilist and the other affirmative thought of the tragic; one pushes to the extreme the thought of the recurrence of the same and the other affirms difference, multiplicity, forgetting and the eternal joy in creation. Between one moment and the other, there is the abyssal transmutation or transfiguration of one into the other: transfiguration of nihilism into the affirmative tragic joy, the transmutation of the saying of 'no' into saying 'yes'. It is essentially necessary to be a nihilist and it is necessary even to will deception and simulacrum, it is necessary to reverse metaphysics so that nihilism can be transmuted into the most affirmative tragic joy in the eternal return, so that man and god can be overcome and overman be affirmed, so that with the abolition of the real world we can abolish the apparent world too':

> We have abolished the real world: what world is left? The apparent world perhaps?...But no! *With the real world we have also abolished the apparent world*!
>
> (Mid-day ; moment of the shortest shadow; end of the longest error; Zenith of mankind; INCIPIT ZARATHUSTRA.) (Nietzsche 1968a: 41).

Was Heidegger oblivious of this paragraph or rather he did not see it? Whatever it is, for Nietzsche, nihilism and reversal of metaphysics—which he accomplishes—is essentially only a necessary moment of exceeding metaphysics. One has to be nihilist; one must be the lion who annihilates: tragedy must, even for a certain moment, smell offensively Platonic and Hegelian, though in reverse mood so that nihilism can be exceeded. For the exceeding of metaphysics, and nihilism to be possible, it is essential to push the logic of deception and illusion, in other words the logic of mimesis, to the limit so that representation can itself transmute what is most nihilist into the affirmation of the eternal return, into the tragic joy of affirming what is most terrifying and strange, questionable and unthinkable. This is what Plato and Hegel refused to affirm: to push the logic of *mimesis* to its limit, to affirm deception itself to the limit, and to affirm the tragic joy in simulation and seduction. Instead Plato banished the poets from the republic in the name of morality, and Hegel announced the death of poetry. *Mimesis* is denied for it is seduction of thought to life (Nietzsche 1968b: 452): the excess of mourning for something that absolutely lost. and affirmation of this mourning itself to its limit. Excessive mourning, infinite mourning, and ceaseless mourning of death: this is what philosophy is incapable of thinking. Philosophy has never been, from Plato to Hegel, able to think the tragic. One can understand why Plato himself was absent when Socrates drank poison so that the narrator of the mourning be preserved, so that he can narrate Socrates' death; while the ceaseless mourning of women over Socrates' death is narrated (Plato 2001: 279-323). Plato would not want to be lost in infinite mourning over Socrates' death so that a discourse of it must be made possible, the significance of Socrates' absence would be meaningful (and moreover, the subject of mourning, that is Plato himself, would be preserved and conserved). Plato's discourse of Socrates' death, like Hegelian wisdom to constitute a discourse (in which to be narrated his own death and yet preserving the very subject of mourning, namely himself), is restricted economy of mourning, the servile discourse to preserve at all costs the very subject of mourning.

Mourning is excessive, and that's why Antigone has to be punished. Here once more Hegel takes tragic representation as the dialectical paradigm of speculative thought. The logic of Aufhebung is put into motion through the tragic spectacle of 'restricted economy' for the sake of conservation, negation and elevation of the sensuous, immediate, individual existence to the life of the universal through death of the individual. If the self-engendering of the subject of philosophy is the Aufhebung of the individual through death, which is put into work, then this Aufhebung should be present in the phenomenological-speculative consciousness; in other words, phenomenological consciousness should be able to re-present this work of death as experience. Representation is, therefore experiential: both the object of representation and the movement of representation! The constitution of the subject of philosophy, as Aufhebung of the individual which must appear as experience, is representation, and that this representation is exploited (yet what a comedy) as the tragic form in Hegelian philosophy. The philosophical knowledge of death and mourning, the experience of death and its anguish, needs a spectacle so that knowledge of this death be possible, and its experience must yield the profit of meaning. Such spectacle is none other than tragedy.

It is now that the role and the importance of Antigone which has preoccupied Hegel's thought from his school days onwards seems to be intelligible to us: it is because, for Hegel, Antigone serves as the very dialectical paradigm of the tragic representation of death; Antigone dramatizes the logic of Aufhebung of the individual life of sensuous, immediate existence into the universal life of philosophical knowledge (which the subject of philosophical subject has to undergo to achieve the cathartic knowledge: the resolution of the tragic contradictions). The very task of dialectical philosophy is at stake here: the logic of Aufhebung, the task of engendering of the philosophical subject as tragic subject! Therefore, though discussion of tragedy occupies so small a part in Hegel's work, it draws attention from later thinkers and commentators than any other sections.

In the next section we show how Hegel takes Antigone as the dialectical paradigm of representing infinite mourning (through Antigone's mourning for her brother) so that infinite mourning would at last be represented in the phenomenological-speculative consciousness of the dialectical subject; the excess of mourning would thereby be economized, and sublated into the universal world of the philosophical knowledge. Hegel, then, evades bringing his philosophical system to the limit of his logic: instead he brings his system to its completion by conceiving this death itself as the Aufhebung of the dialectical contradictions. Hegel would not push the anguish of death and its incessant mourning to the limit, the limit that would be transfigured into the affirmation of 'tragic joy'; this mourning would rather be recuperated, the system would be achieved and the knowledge of death be accomplished through this tragic spectacle itself. Antigone serves as the privileged spectacle of this thought. What Antigone learns or arrives at her tragic knowledge through her suffering is the resolution of the dialectical suffering, the acceptance of the work of reification of the universal (that effaces singulars in the name of Reason).

Is it not what Hegel's philosophy is all about, the very task of philosophy as he defines it, not to push philosophy to its limit but to bring the limit back into the closure of representation, to justify the tyranny of the anonymous work of Reason (which wages war on the singulars and founds its genesis and telos on the violence which Reason exercises)? Is it not legitimization of violence, a certain violence of Reason that founds the discourse of Reason itself, the universal community of the self-sufficient Being that encloses itself into itself and wages war whenever other presents itself as Other? If tragedy served as the dialectical representation of death and violence, it is because it seems to realize, for Hegel, this work of legitimization of the universal grounding of philosophical knowledge, and its onto-theological closure of representation. By seeking philosophical knowledge of death and making death and its anguish the dialectical paradigm of thought and source of all meaning, Hegel's discourse is already reduced to the servile discourse of a feigned comedy.

Reading Antigone

In *Phenomenology of Spirit*, Hegel's discussion of tragedy belongs to the chapter (VI) under the first section "The true Spirit: The ethical order". This section, along with the following two sections belongs to the larger heading, entitled " Spirit" which is preceded by " Reason", the first of the third part of *Phenomenology.* It means this: that the question concerning the ethical order is already an actualization of Reason and as actualized Reason, the truth of Reason is Spirit. In other words, the question concerning the turbulence of the ethical order, which is in question here, belong to the dialectical stage of *Spirit* which is *actuality* of substance inasmuch as substance is understood as the spiritual essence. Antigone's suffering is spiritual, and belongs to the ethical order, which is already that of universal realm of actualizing substance. Though it is the universality of the spiritual realm to which the ethical order belongs, the ethical order is not yet conscious of its substance, and hence, as in the previous shapes of Spirit, it is marked by the dialectical contradiction of individual and universal, in-itself and for itself, the finite and infinite, the resolution of which is sought in the synthetic moment. The simple spiritual substance is divided, rent asunder into human law as the universal law and divine law as individual law. As in Aristotle, this contradiction is that of the duality of 'actuality' which belongs to the universal realm of Spirit on the one hand, and 'potentiality' which is yet to be actualized, the individual realm of sensuous existence on the other; human law is actual inasmuch as it is universal, and the potential is what is yet to be sublated into the universal world of human law. One can see that this division is not in which both sides are equally recognized: man, who is the human law of universality has already actualized the potential which is to be seen in the real institutions in objective forms, the State and customs, and which takes the discursive form of law, the sovereign law of universality that has sublated what is the mere particular, animal existence of the individual through negativity, through *the act of his own death*. Man is one who has actualized his *humanity* through the negative-negating action by putting in animal existence in risk, by taking up death as task, and by putting his death into work, he produced himself as *Subject* of *his-tory*; he is the terror of the negative, the terror of the State who subsumes the individuals by waging war on them. As such, man is the worker who transforms the given animal existence to produce the universal order of Reason. By destroying his individual sensuous existence, through this death, man attains the universal status of 'citizen',

> The deed, then, which embraces the entire existence of the blood-relation, does not concern the citizen, for he does not belong to the family, nor the individual who is to become a citizen and will cease to counts this particular individual; it has as its object and content this particular individual who belongs to the family, but is taken as a universal being freed from his sensuous, i.e. individual, reality. The deed no longer concerns the living but the dead, the individual who, after a long succession of separate disconnected experiences, concentrates himself into a single completed shape, and has raised himself out of the unrest of the accidents of life into the calm of simple universality. But because it is only as citizen that he is actual and substantial, the individual, so far as he is not a citizen but belongs to the family, is only an unreal impotent shadow (Hegel 1998: 269-70).

The member of the State, the citizen, is universal who has sublated his animal, irrational existence which is his *work,* and this work is the work of the negative. The universal citizen is the *Aufhebung* of the disparate and unconnected particular existences into the self-present unity of Being. If man has been able to raise himself from "*the unrest of the accidents of life*", it is because he is one who has been able to take up death as task, and has been able put death into work. One can quickly point out the *phallogocentrism* figure of the onto-theological metaphysics in the figure of the worker: the onto-theo-logical figure of the worker is always a man, a slave who works and produces history by putting negativity into labour.

> This universality which the individual *as such* attains is *pure being, death*; it is a state which has been reached *immediately*, in the *course of Nature*, not the result of an action *consciously done*. The duty of the member of the family is on that account add this aspect, in order that the individual's ultimate being, too, shall not belong solely to Nature and remain something irrational, but shall be something *done,* and the right of consciousness be asserted in it ... death is the fulfilment and the supreme 'work' which the individual as such undertakes on its behalf (Ibid: 270).

It is Antigone's brother who fulfils the "supreme work" of death and not Antigone herself. She is one who is outside of the state while still being inside, the singularity of the 'remaining', the indifferent difference to the universal: the woman is the unconscious night of immediate existence, who is *yet* to sublate herself into the universal work of the state. Not being able to work, she is the unworking excess of the state, the remnant of the totality of significations, which constitutes historical discourse of the 'world'. Yet, she is also the one who performs the last duty of the universal, by burying the dead body of her brother so that his death would not be a natural death of the animals but through death, freed from his sensuous existence, he would a find a place in the community (Ibid: 271). She has "the highest intuitive awareness of what is ethical" (Ibid: 274) and yet she is not conscious of it. Woman, as such, is

> ...An internal enemy—womankind in general. Womankind—the everlasting irony [in the life] of the community—changes by intrigue

> the universal end of the government into a private end, transforms its universal activity into a work of some particular individual, and perverts the universal property of the state into a possession and ornament of the family. Woman in this way turns to ridicule the earnest wisdom of mature age which, indifferent to purely private pleasures and enjoyments, as well as to playing an active part, only thinks of and cares for the universal. She makes this wisdom an object of derision for raw and irresponsible youth and unworthy of their enthusiasm…The community, however can only maintain itself by suppressing this spirit of individualism, and, because it is an essential moment, all the same creates it and moreover, creates it by repressive attitude towards it as a hostile principle (Ibid: 288).

Woman is 'irony' because she is excessive in relation not only to the community in which individual finds his place through the negating action of death, community which she manipulates through her intrigue but also in relation to herself: she does not belong to the community because she does not belong to herself. Therefore it is she who poses the danger to the universality of the community, to the universal order of Reason: she is the excessive negativity that *unworks* the community, or any aspiration towards the formation of totality of significations. Woman is 'irony' because not only she empties out and undermines the ontological ground of the community and its fundamental structure but also that she is difference, the 'bad infinity' of forever deferring and differing excess. That's why 'irony' is dangerous; it delivers Reason to its own unworking in an unforeseeable manner; she is the ruse that undermines the very dialectical ontology itself, and brining disaster to it while pretending to fulfil its promise. Woman is dangerous because it is she who is deceptive, and who, through her cunning and ruse, secretly brings disaster to the work of the universal; she is dangerous because, unable to sublate herself into the 'human law' of the universal signification, yet she claims to fulfil the work of reason and truth. Is it not the same threat that the poets pose for the Plato's philosophical republic—representation that exceeds itself, and thereby exceeds and threaten to ruin the very philosophical foundation of the community (inasmuch as the philosophical discourse aspires to determine the fundamental structure of the community)? It is Antigone, then, who is a tragic figure, the "everlasting irony of the community", and the excess of meaning (meaning that the ethical community aspires to engender itself through the work of death). Irony is tragic because it is 'excess'; only 'excess' is tragic. Irony, subverting and threatening the very work of negativity, threatens to throw the community to its bottomless abyss, to the vertiginous groundlessness, delivering the work of death to its own unworking, and undermining in advance any aspiration of Reason to constitute itself as the universal order. The onto-theo-logical community finds itself in the figure of the worker, always male, the subject of community itself, but this subject of community always confronts the opponent in the figure of the woman, the irony that undermines the universal order of the faceless Reason. I cannot discuss here the tragic character of irony, what makes irony a 'hammer' for a tragic philosopher—one should be able to examine, in a sustained philosophical manner, how two great tragic philosophers (I am excluding Pascal), namely, Nietzsche and Kierkegaard, use irony that puts into question the very philosophical foundation of meaning and truth, of community and the universal work of Reason. What is important here is to notice that Hegel had a glimpse—he always had a glimpse in everything—of what is truly tragic, in the character of Antigone: her irreducible excess, her irony and the negativity that she represents, the unworking unconsciousness, the night that threatens to deliver all foundational gestures of Reason into a vertiginous abyss! Already foreshadowing Nietzsche's 'unconsciousness' as tragic, and the irony of the tragic philosopher, Hegel discovered Antigone as unconsciousness of the community itself, the surplus of the universal order, and the danger of the tragic as the unworking irony. In the figure of Antigone, it is 'tragic'—being excessive—which is dangerous. Like Plato, it is finally the tragic which seems to be the 'internal enemy' that must either be destroyed, or be subsumed at any cost so that the essence of community may be preserved, the meaning of the 'world' may be saved, and the work of negativity can pursue its movement to its utmost conclusion. For Hegel, it is *war* that subsumes this 'internal enemy',

> War is the Spirit and the form in which the essential moment of the ethical substance, the absolute freedom of the ethical *self* from every existential form, is present in its actual and authentic existence. While, on the one hand, war makes the individual *systems*

> of property and personal independence, as well as the *personality* of the individual himself, feel the power of the negative, on the other hand, the negativity is prominent in war as that which preserves the whole (Ibid: 288-89).

This war is the war to recuperate the excess of negativity: it is the recuperation of the tragic, and of the enemy of community, namely, woman. As always, Hegel gives a place to its own excess in his discourse of negativity, but this excess would not be pushed to the limit, is not affirmed to the limit, but only to the extent that it preserves the 'whole' all the more firmly, so that system is conserved from an excessive expenditure of mourning. Antigone's mourning over her brother would soon be cut short by waging a war against her 'irony', against her excess and subduing her singularity by the power of the negative. Here the speculative system closes up once again, and closure of its representation is once more achieved. Is it not precisely from Plato to Hegel through Aristotle that Western metaphysics seeks to accomplish, and that, through tragic representation, Hegel accomplishes its utmost conclusion? Antigone's tragic is nothing but a critique of philosophy itself, an opening to something other outside the closure of onto-theo-logical metaphysics. But it would soon be covered over: Antigone feels "the power of the negative", and subsumes herself to the universal, phallocentric order of Reason. This reconciliation with the universal order of Reason (that needs the subjugation of what is excessive, the feminine, and the tragic) takes the form of *tragic knowledge,* the cathartic knowledge that assumes the character of *Aufhebung.* Antigone acknowledges that she has erred, and this acknowledgement is her tragic wisdom,

> *Because we suffer we acknowledge that we have erred.*
>
> With this acknowledgment there is no longer any conflict between ethical purpose and actuality; it signifies the return to an ethical frame of mind, which knows that nothing counts but right. But the doer thereby surrenders his own *character* and the *reality* of his self, and has been ruined. His *being* consists in his belonging to his ethical law, as his substance; in acknowledging the opposite law, the other ceases to be for him his substance, and instead of attaining actuality it has become an unreality, a sentiment or disposition. The

> substance does appear, it is true, *in* the individuality as his 'pathos', and the individuality appears as that which animates the substance and hence stands above it; but the substance is a 'pathos' that is at the same time his character. The ethical individuality is directly and intrinsically one with this his universal aspect, exists in it alone, and is incapable of surviving the destruction of this ethical power by its opposite (Ibid: 284).

What appears as Antigone's tragic knowledge is the resolution of the dialectical contradiction in which the excess of negativity is recuperated again, and is reduced to the dialectical moment within totality: the whole of dialectical paradigm is this representation of negativity, the Aufhebung of the individual subject to the universal subject of philosophy, the Aufhebung of the feminine subject into the phallocentric subject of onto-theo-logy. The whole dialectical paradigm of tragic representation points towards this, and is centred on this Aufhebung: the development of contradiction, and restriction of this contradiction to the identity principle of self-presence. Even if synthetic principle must be able to unite both the moments, it is one of the moments—here the feminine—which must be able to renounce itself so that resolution is possible. This form of renunciation is, what Hegel calls, sacrifice. In other words, speculative philosophy constitutes itself as the philosophy of totality in the name of universal Reason only by sacrificing what is feminine: the singularity of excess that is always already left behind the system. Hegelian onto-theo-logy is, after all, metaphysics of sacrifice, and philosophy of representation of its violence. It recognizes that all the source of human meaning and all ideals of human truth, and the very foundation of human community is nothing but: the anguish of sacrifice and its sheer nothingness, the violence of sheer expenditure, the sheer loss of the subject, and the bottomless abyss that man is. But instead of pushing consciousness to its absolute limit so that man may be delivered over to this bottomless abyss (to this excess that founds human community) so that 'sovereign' experience of this nothing be possible, so that the depth intimacy with this anguish be attainable ('man is the Night', says Hegel himself), Hegel soon sought to convert this nothing in his absolute knowledge. What Hegel sought through Antigone to represent is this nothingness itself dialectically. He exploited tragedy speculatively to conserve what is sheer annihilation through the power of negative. At the end, tragedy has turned out to be only a comedy show, the sure return of the same through his feigned death and recuperation of the negativity. Hegelian speculative tragedy is only a pseudo-tragedy; it does not attain the sovereignty of anguish, which the tragic seeks. Sovereign tragic experience is not the constitution of the universal subject through loss, which would be recuperated, but the absolute loss of all foundation and thought, the unworking disaster that cannot be conserved or resurrected: tragic that doesn't have form of resolution through catharsis. Hegel fell short of it because he was afraid of the summit, and for the servile desire for profit, compromised his sovereignty. Not only the singularity of the sensible—and here appears in the figure of Antigone—is reduced to the individual moment of the discursive totality of universal Reason, this reduction is achieved only through the most violent means of war that defaces the face of the singular to sublate it to the anonymous, cold tyranny of the universal order represented by the State, the phallocentric order of 'humanity' and its infinite negativity. Speculative ontology builds upon tragedy as dialectical representation of the work of Aufhebung only by waging war against the singularity of justice, only through the logic of exclusion by leaving behind and constricting the 'excess' (which singulars present). In order for this justice—not Hegelian justice that takes the name of law—to be possible, it is necessary that the freedom, in the name of which Creon undertakes to exercise the work of law on the singulars, should be questioned. It is this freedom, which Antigone puts into question, but Hegel wanted resolution of the dialectical contradictions: soon the possibility of questioning and being dissent would be sublated into the consensual order of Reason. Antigone is made to acknowledge her error; the system is once more closed.

Sacrifice, representation and the sovereign anguish

The source of all human meaning (his self-consciousness which constitutes the very 'humanity' of man and the ground of 'community') is violence, the negativity which has the form of sacrifice; it is violence of sacrifice and its sheer nothingness which constitutes as the abyssal condition of possibility of 'humanity'. However, the philosophical discourse (that seeks to discover the ontological foundation of this humanity)—humanity which is nothing but this 'night, the empty nothing'—would like to make us believe that human existence has already in its service of preservation and conservation the ontological foundation of meaning. Man is already put into service of constituting this servile discourse so that the sovereign anguish is put at a bay; man is kept at a distance from the horror of the experience of the limit, and from the sovereign expenditure of time. If man is this anguish in the very abyss of his being—which constitutes the very humanity of him—he is not satisfied with this experience of anguish; he must also be able to be *conscious* of his anguish; he must *know* his death! Therefore, all servile discourses, such as philosophical discourse of Being and meaning, assume the form of consciousness. Hegelian philosophy has only pushed to the limit this servile discourse by releasing the thought of absolute knowledge. Henceforth (it has always been so. Was there a time when sacrifice presented itself to human experience in its immediate way the intolerable anguish of death?), the sovereign anguish of violent eruption is given the form of discourse, and is reduced to the forms of life and to its various possibilities that can be effectuated through the labour and project of consciousness (which assumes the discontinuity of the 'world' and 'time' as the very mode of its consciousness). The sovereign anguish is reduced to these 'possibilities' of life based upon the knowledge of death and consciousness of its anguish; what is 'sovereign' and its groundless abyss has been reduced to the calculative possibilities of metaphysical *economimesis*. Man becomes far away from the very depth intimacy of his night, his empty nothingness and the horror of his being, unable to push his anguish to the limit of the 'possible'. Yet death remains 'impasse' for philosophy.

Here Bataille's insight takes the form of questioning: is not death precisely the limit of the 'possible', the emptying out of all human meaning? If philosophy is a discourse that must know death, its sadness and pleasure, then, death is also the limit of possibility: the knowledge of death threatens to ruin the very possibility of the subject of philosophy. Death is 'impossible' because it ruins its own discourse, its own possibility; it is irreducible to any projection of knowledge or meaning. The philosophy of death has learnt is that—was not Hegel the wisest of all mortals, who has even achieved the absolute knowledge precisely with this knowledge? In order to have the knowledge of death, not only that death has to be present to the consciousness of the subject of philosophy but also that he has to be able to maintain himself in his ruin, to maintain himself in his "utter dismemberment". Representation—sacrificial representation and tragic mimesis—allows us not to only have a glimpse of our foundationless foundation of human consciousness, it also, through repetitive enactment of representation, make death all the more bearable. Death is put at a distance. Thus representation serves servile project of effectuating human freedom, and of the labour of constituting his world. In tragedy and in the ritual sacrifice, someone dies for the spectator while the spectator remains intact, maintaining himself in "utter dismemberment" while the head of the animal, or another human, is chopped off, and yet, having, in that terrible moment, the glimpse of our utter nothingness, the anguish of our abyssal emptiness. But is it not that this terrible anguish is too abyssal, the excess of which, at the summit of our possible, remains irrecuparable? If representation serves the work of servile discourse for the profit of meaning or knowledge (which is the project of history and 'world), it is likely that this very gesture also leads the project of absolute knowledge, this humanist discourse of servility, too far from itself. At the very summit of its possibilities, because it is the absolute possibility, leads to its own downfall, and the absolute knowledge, exceeding its absolute light, is lost absolutely in the absolute night, the night of excessive light. If representation is necessary for the production of knowledge and human meaning, it is necessary to push this representation to its limit of the possible so that the absolute knowledge—of that servile man of profit—may be delivered to the sovereign anguish (that cannot be recuperated into profit again). Man is delivered again to its depth intimacy of his abyssal horror. If representation produces knowledge—the tragic knowledge—it also, with this same gesture, ruins the absolute knowledge, and dissolves the very subject of philosophy: representation always exceeds itself, and transmutes its anguish into tragic joy, into the most affirming affirmation. The truly tragic is, then, to be understood as irreducible to the work of negative, as irreducible to the speculative synthesis of dialectical contradictions: tragedy transmutes what is most nihilist to the affirmation of existence. The truly tragic is not the work of negative but the most affirmative joy of transfiguration, the renting joy in destruction without the servile conservation of meaning.

Why such terrible anguish is also joy, or what we called earlier, the 'tragic joy'? It is because it is representation! Representation fascinates us to the point of throwing us outside of ourselves at the limit of our closure of being, exposing us to what is most questionable, what is most strange and terrible, of what is abyssal and monstrous. It is the excessive character of fascination that representation is, the ecstatic rupture of our being which such a 'fascination' transports us to: it is this excessive character of representation that Plato feared most about *mimesis*. Representation transfigures what is ugly, terrifying into what is beautiful and attractive, fascinating us with its seductive power, *simulating* us with its power of unreason and ruse, with its deception and untruth, and transporting us outside of ourselves, delivering us to most violent eruption of laughter and ecstasy. Therefore, Hegel calls woman 'everlasting irony'. *Woman is simulacra*, the deceptive power which ruins the project of being while pretending to fulfil its demand. Representation is fascinating because it is what is excessive; it marks, while unmarking, the limit of our being and of our possibilities, freeing us from our discursive enclosure to the infinite experience of the impossible, transfiguring and transforming our world of project and world, our world of negativity and the heavy burden of labour. Tragic experience is transfiguring, not because it gives us the ontological foundation of the world in the name of concept (transforming the given animal existence into the human world of discourse and meaning) but that transfiguration frees us towards the utmost possibilities of sovereign experience: not the possibility of being but the limitless becoming of being. If there is tragic joy, it's because of this: transfiguration of being, and its freeing us towards the limitless, innocent becoming of existence.

Thus, discourses are necessary, and Reason is not to be renounced, the labour of thought and its patience and suffering is rather to be pursued so that we can enter into that night which we enter when the day's work done and history gets over; yet it cannot be determined as *telos* of an onto-theo-logy. Is it not this uncertainty the condition of possibility of all the discourses of certainty and truth, of Reason and meaning? We need knowledge—and even absolute knowledge—so that knowledge be exceeded and brings its own dissolution, so that subject of philosophy brings its own ruin, and we are delivered over to the sovereign nothing that we are. Bataille expresses it beautifully,

> Once history's finished, the existence of man would enter animal night. Nothing is more uncertain than this. But would not the night need only this as its initial condition—that we remain unaware that its night? Night that knows its night wouldn't be night but would be the fall of day...(the human Odyssey ending up like *Aminabad*) (Bataille 1997: 58).

The whole of Bataille's thought can be summed up here. It is from Nietzsche that we learn that the formation of all human meaning—his 'world', his knowledge and his notion of human truth, in other words, his very 'humanity'—is fictional, a figurative artefact, a mimetic artefact, and that even the very foundation of human possibility is this most foundationless abyss. It is not Aristotle already had a glimpse of it when he defended poetry—what a servile defense!—In the name of mimesis, that all human knowledge is derived from representation? Is not thereby Aristotle showed that the foundation of human truth is figurative or fictional? Is it not Hegel too recognized the fictional character of the foundation when the uttered the most terrible thought that being is, can only be, what it represents itself to itself, that being is nothing but this: one who mimics, a mimicking being? Is it not Schopenhauer who recognized this very abyssal ungrounding of representation in his *Representation as Will and Idea?* Yet, from Plato to Schopenhauer through Kant and Hegel, *mimesis* still haunts the Western imagination as something threatening and destructive, something that needs to be domesticated, by giving it rule and norms. Philosophy assumes this role of master discourse that gives rules, and controls what is most abyssal and terrible. *Philosophy is fictional:* Hegel was aware of it when he thought the necessity of tragic spectacle and sacrificial enactment of death so that death be a 'possibility' or 'capacity', so that there can be knowledge of death and its negativity which constitutes the possibility of philosophy and humanity. Hegel knew this, and this knowledge saddened him. But he quickly renounced this for the sake of salvation; in other words, he sought the comfort of the slave. Fictional is abyssal, not because it has ontological possibilities but because it exceeds any recuperation. Philosophy, which always aspires to constitutes itself as philosophy of recuperation, is a refusal to confront the secret of its own possibility (and thus its impossibility), and thus to recognize its abyssal groundlessness, and its fictional foundation; instead, it always constitutes itself in this forgetting, and in this refusal of what is non-philosophy. In other words, this refusal to recognize its abyssal impossibility is the condition of possibility of the philosophical discourse itself; it leads us to believe that it has, at its possession, its necessary ontological ground. Therefore, philosophical discourse always appears as philosophy of negativity, the saying 'No' to the intimate abyss of its nothingness, the refusal of the tragic. That's why Nietzsche could say that metaphysics is based upon a lie, which a genealogical investigation should be able to reveal: philosophy is 'feigned comedy' (as Bataille remarks) but behind this Apollonian ground, there bursts forth, as violent eruption of erotic anguish, the tragic unconsciousness of Dionysian terror. As in sacrifice, which is supposed to lead us from unknown to the known, or even to the absolute knowledge through the ritual enactment of death (thereby allowing the spectator to have the experience of death, and which, in this very process, delivers us to the unknown that exceeds every system of the absolute), philosophy is always (through its own work of representation) delivered to the unknown. While for Hegel such an experience is only limited to a moment of his discourse (which he should be able to recuperate without any loss), the tragic philosopher, on the other hand, such an embarking into the perilous sea of the unknown and its icy solitude implies an absolute risk, an absolute loss that cannot be recuperated. Nietzsche's madness is this absolute loss and absolute risk: not in sight of absolute knowledge but the sovereign experience of finitude. This very experience of finitude—the finitude of philosophy and the finitude of God, the finitude of meaning and man—that Hegel, the phenomenologist, is afraid to look face to face, the experience not from unknown to the known but known to the unknown, to the becoming 'monster' and 'inhuman', of becoming 'woman' (Antigone, for example), of becoming ironist (but the irony of the theatrical man like Socrates). Unlike Hegelian phenomenologist, the tragic philosopher brings his own dissolution so that the experience of the limit, the experience of death of god be attained without seeking to sublate it to Being and meaning. Unlike Hegel, he would refuse to put this sovereign experience to the work. For Bataille, such a tragic philosopher is called 'atheistic mystic' whose negativity is never recuperated into speculative-dialectical knowledge of Being:

> The atheistic mystic, *self-conscious*, conscious of having to die and to disappear, would live, as Hegel *obviously said concerning himself*, 'in absolute dismemberment'; but, for him, it is only a matter of certain period: unlike Hegel, he would never come out of it, 'contemplating the Negative right in the face', but never being able to transpose it into being, refusing to do it and maintaining himself in ambiguity (Ibid: 294).

At the limit of this servile philosophical discourse, desire and poetry, laughter and ecstasy lead us from the known to the perilous sea of the unknown, to the excessive expenditure of time that has never been taken up, which empties the Notion of its content, and which, instead of synthesizing Being and Nothing, (as Hegel attempted to achieve in his *Logic*), rather delivers us to its excess, to the inexhaustible ecstasy of laughter and poetry, to the ever beginning time of irreducible desire. Such sovereign experience is, what Bataille calls, '*inner experience*': the impossibility of the Subject, its dissolution and de-constitution:

> Action introduces the known (the manufactured); then understanding, which is linked to it, related the non-manufactured, unknown elements, one after the other, to the known. But desire, poetry, laughter, unceasingly cause life to slip in the opposite direction, moving from the known to the unknown. Existence in the end discloses the blind spot of understanding and right away becomes completely absorbed in it. It could not be otherwise unless a possibility for rest were to present itself at a certain point. But nothing of the kind takes place: what alone remains is circular agitation—which does not exhaust itself in ecstasy and begins again from it (Bataille 1988: 111).

We are already far away from Hegelian atmosphere of speculative representation. Instead of being remained in the closure of history and its work of negativity (which converts even non-being into being), already far from the speculative logic of *Aufhebung*, and far from the metaphysical logic of action and production (that in producing knowledge/ history/ discourse, also produces the subject of knowledge itself), representation pushes this *economimesis* to its limit, and produces its own surplus which cannot be subsumed into the totality of the historical world of 'humanity' . Bataille names this surplus, in a letter to Alexander Kojeve, "unemployed negativity": negativity which is left outside the system when the work of history is over, and totality (granted it has been achieved) achieved: the remnant, the surplus that cannot be assumed, negativity which cannot be 'employed' in the production of self-consciousness for the profit of knowledge, that which remains irrecuparable into the self-presence of the Same. Tragic experience is this "*unemployment negativity*": the sovereign anguish and the sadness of death which is pushed to the limit so that it overturns the *economimesis* altogether, bringing a halt to the dialectical movement of the labour, delivering us to the depth intimacy of the sacred experience, to the horror of nothing that we are through its very representation. Such is the experience of the limit, the tragic experience: the dissolution of the subject of philosophy at the very limit of its possible and its 'utter dismemberment', which it cannot recover. Unlike Hegelian onto-theo-logical figure of the worker who always maintains himself even in his own disaster, tragic experience is the impossibility to maintain oneself: it is the rupture of the philosophical discourse of totality; the rupture of the very subjectivity of the worker, the slave that produces meaning and assumes the discontinuity of time. Now the question comes: what happens to him who remains 'unemployed' when the work of history is over, and nothing is left to do, for whom death is not a 'possibility', he for whom the ability to say 'I' has disappeared, he whose anguish cannot assume the form of *Aufhebung* in the name of the concept? What happens to him who cannot interiorize through memory the suffering of destiny so that the very ontological ground of his being works and unworks in the same process, thereby delivering over to his nothingness?

> If action ('doing') is—as Hegel says—negativity, the question arises as to whether the negativity of one who has 'nothing more to do' disappears or remains in a state of 'unemployed negativity'. Personally, I can only decide in one way, being myself precisely this 'unemployed negativity' (I would not be able to define myself more precisely). I don't mind Hegel's having foreseen this possibility; at least he did not situate it at the conclusion of the processes he described. I imagine

> that my life—or, better yet, its aborting, the open would that is my life—constitutes all by itself the refutation of Hegel's closed system (Bataille 1997: 296).

One wonders what Hegel would have answered to this complaint. Would he bring another arbitrary concept which is dialectically in contradiction to this experience of the limit? Would not he thereby bring, once more, his utter ruin, his disaster so that his closed system would open up once more, that means infinitely? May be at the end of history, as Bataille remarked, we would once more enter into the night, not the night where 'all cows are black' but which is dark with excessive brightness; maybe he who has embarked in this perilous sea without any hope of return (wherein his very humanity is at stake) would enter into the unforeseen, unpredictable non-humanity, the inhuman who has lost his humanity precisely because he has realized it through history. One can ask, whether with the death of god, we also announced the death of man, or in Hegelian terms, whether subject could survive substance? Neither having subjectivity within us, nor substance, neither having our humanity within us nor having divinity, what ethical thoughts be possible at the limit of philosophy wherein (which is no site at all) we are abandoned? What ethical thoughts are possible that are irreducible to the facile humanism of closed system? This is the question a tragic philosopher—if he still wants to call himself a philosopher—asks in this abandoned time when man is abandoned to the most abyssal void which the death of god and man has left us with. By this tragic, we don't understand not the Hegelian onto-theo-logical tragic of Aufhebung: the representation of death and its labour to achieve the closure of the system so that philosophy can be ontologically grounded. We rather understand by this tragic that we are in abandoned time, without subjectivity and humanity remained intact but thrown over to an abyss where all foundation empties itself: system that is opened once more towards an infinite other of the outside. Tragic question is the one—if that is still a question—that is asked at the end of philosophy, and at the end of history when the god is dead and the absence of god throws us into the void which god's absence leaves us with. It is no longer a question concerning the task of uniting the dialectical contradictions of finite and infinite through the tragic resolution of synthesis, no longer a question how to put into work the negativity of death and through which to achieve the subject of philosophy. It is rather a question of thinking of opening for a future to come, thought of promise of a rupture exceeding any speculative closure of Being. Therefore, the tragic philosopher, such as Nietzsche, always appears as the philosopher of the future, 'the untimely philosopher': what is tragic is not the Aufhebung of memory and interiorization of the past, not the closure of the system and reification of the subject but the tragic forgetting—the immemorial! Tragic thought is thought of opening towards the time to come, not the time understood as 'presence' (which speculative ontology recognizes as the synthetic negativity because we live in a time where time has emptied out its synthetic meaning). Hegelian tragic dialectic is only at best a pseudo-tragic, or, if we can use Bataille's terms, 'restricted' tragic. To open up such tragic closure, to exceed this 'restricted economy' of the tragic towards something entirely other, it is necessary that such experience of the tragic should be pushed to its utmost limit, to open up to what is tragic of absolute loss, to another vision of tragic where meaning is not that of conservation. Using Bataille's concept of inner experience and Nietzsche's sense of tragic, we attempted to open up towards this irreducible thought of tragic, beyond the speculative closure of tragic representation.

The tragic

The tragic and the question of value

The question of tragic is a question of value or morality. Before Nietzsche the problem of value has never been put in relation to the question of tragic. It is Nietzsche's contribution to philosophy to introduce, as Deleuze puts it, "the concepts of sense and value into philosophy" (1983: 1). The concept of tragic is a critique of the value of values from which all values derive. Here comes Nietzsche's reproach of Kant: Kant's critique has failed to introduce the problem of value and sense into philosophy, which 'critique' must be all about, that 'critique' must be able to put into question our innermost beliefs in the most unquestioned metaphysical principles that seem to constitute our 'world'. Instead, Kant remained stuck in his *Critique of Pure Reason* answering the question, 'is metaphysics possible?' With Hegel, metaphysics is sought to be realized as onto-theo-logy where Kant seems to have failed (as Hegel claims); the question of value and sense, however, has never been introduced. The problem of tragic, as Nietzsche thought, is a question of value, and forms a critique: neither to determine the condition of possibility of knowledge, nor how to determine the self-engendering fundamental structure of our thought and being as in Hegel, but this: a genealogy, the art of evaluation and interpretation. Against the self-preservative logic of *Aufhebung,* of the interiorization of pain through memory (which the onto-theological figure of the worker conserves for the profit of meaning without loss), against the metaphysical principles of negative, of the saying 'No' to life and against the burden of values (such a work of negativity assumes), against such a philosophy of the negative (which Hegel seeks to realize its utmost possibility in his dialectic), against such a slave morality: Nietzsche conceives his tragic philosophy. Philosophy of tragic should be critique of morality. Hegelian refusal to put into question the value of all values (which constitutes *resentment*, *bad conscience* and *ascetic ideals*: the three typological elements of reactive forces), his refusal to affirm the tragic joy of destruction and joy (that pushes the fundamental structures of our reified culture to its abyssal unworking), his refusal to affirm the new possibilities for the 'future to come' (rather than the reification of the various shapes of the Spirit which in its becoming preserves its past): all these amount to Hegel's refusal to affirm the 'tragic', to affirm and create new forms of life through destruction of all ontological ground. Instead what Hegel affirms is the 'yea' saying of the ass, of the slave who says 'yes' to the burden of values on his back. Hegel's morality is slave morality, the logic of interiorization and reproduction of the pain of labour so that life can be denied, depreciated in the name of the 'suffering' of the labour, and so that what is active, powerful and beautiful can be separated from what the active can do, what the affirmative can affirm, and what the powerful can assert. Saying 'no' to life, the subtlest intrigue to triumph over the active forces through the dialectical 'ruse of reason' of which Odyssey is expert: such are the principles of Hegelian dialectics of negativity. Therefore, dialectic always appears as the philosophy of negative, whether in Socrates or in Hegel. Guided by the slave morality of *resentment* and *bad conscience*, dialectic metaphysics is a refusal to confront and affirm what is most terrifying, strange and tragic about human existence.

Difference, forgetting

What the tragic affirms is difference. Affirmation is difference. Affirmation affirms difference and difference affirms affirmation (Ibid: 36). Difference is tragic because difference is abyssal, irreducible to the conservation of meaning, or to interiority of the concept; it is rather that brings rupture to the very interiority of the subject, a tear that opens up the system to the vertiginous abyss of its impossibility, a freeing of time from the constrains of the constrictive principle of memory (memory that allows the simultaneousness of various 'nows' to sublate into the homogeneity of 'Now'). In other words, tragic experience is affirmation of difference and forgetting. Forgetting: the fissured (hence differential) time of heterogeneity (which cannot be conserved into the interiority of the philosophical consciousness as memory)! Forgetting is abyssal because it does not allow the conservation of sense through the synthetic principle of *a priori unity of apperception* (that accompanies all representations, and through memory gathers in its presence all its representations). *Protention* and anticipation (Husserl 1981: 277-88) are the various modes of presence (thus the condition of possibility of memory) that allows the synthetic recollecting of various 'nows' into the homogeneous self-presence of being. Memory as the reactive principle of slave morality—the principle of revenge and resentment—constricts the abyssal unworking of forgetting into the homogeneous reification of presence (by converting the nonbeing into being through the dialectical logic of *Aufhebung*). The abyssal difference is held at bay, or is reduced to the work of memory, memory that gives 'depth' (pregnant with the meaning of past, heavy with burden of values and suffering with the most interiorized pain. *Aufhebung* is this form of cure, the pathological discharge through the tragic contradictions of infinite and finite). Is it not the whole of *Phenomenology* nothing but this work of memory, the constitution of the interiority of the subjectivity of the historical worker that transforms the world through negative action, the depth of his subjectivity deepened by the pain of the negative and who traverses through the 'highway of despair'? The worker—the Subject of history—assumes discontinuity that marks time, and through memory gathers into itself the sameness of itself in difference (which also defines the ontology of the produced object of consciousness as historical product). Therefore, the philosophy of the negative always appears as philosophy of memory, as the conservation of past traces; through the retracing of the recuperative work of remembrance, it seeks to rediscover and re-conquer that self-sameness that is present in various 'nows'. Through memory, the Subject installs and re-installs itself on its immanent ground. Therefore, it is the installation and constitution of the Subject that is at stake here: dialectical negativity is the philosophy of the Subject, of the Same, which constitutes itself through the work of memory. Therefore, we see that at the end of *Phenomenology*, Hegel sums up the whole movement of Spirit as an act of remembrance.

> But the other side of its Becoming, *History* is a *conscious*, self-*mediating* process—Spirit emptied out into Time; but this externalization, this kenosis, is equally an externalization of itself; the negative is the negative of itself. This Becoming presents a slow-moving succession of Spirits, a gallery of images, each of which, endowed with riches of Spirit, moves thus slowly just because the Self has to penetrate and digest this entire wealth of its substance. As its fulfilment consists in perfectly *knowing* what it is, in knowing its substance, this knowing is its *withdrawal into itself* in which it abandons its outer existence and gives its existential shape over to recollection...the *goal*, the Absolute Knowing, or Spirit that knows itself as Spirit, has for its path the recollection of Spirits as they are in themselves and as they accomplish the organization of their realm. Their preservation, regarded from the side of their free existence appearing in the form of contingency, is *History*... (Hegel 1998: 492-93).

We wonder whether this work of memory, which constitutes history, excludes, and excludes by constricting forgetting because it is forgetting that constitutes the condition of (im) possibility of memory (and not vice versa). The condition of possibility of history is that which history cannot remember: the condition belongs to an immemorial past that cannot be recuperated. Because memory is marked by finitude, the subject of memory (the subject of history, the self-conscious man) must confront its own finitude, its limit and its necessary loss, its absolute forgetting. It is this abyssal loss of Being in the limitless forgetting of itself that de-constitutes the work of memory (so it incessantly postpones to close time into itself once and for all. Yet, it is this very forgetting that bestows time to memory and memory to time to be conserved and produced, effectuated and known in the historical subject of self-consciousness. Memory does not constitute the condition of possibility of forgetting: forgetting cannot kept, preserved and recollected, cannot be maintained and effectuated through the historical labour of the concept; it is rather memory that delivers itself forgetting. It is this unworking (while working) and delivering (while gathering into itself) is what we call *experience of the limit. Experience of the limit* means: the delivering of memory of itself to its own dissolution, the delivering of its project to the unworking of forgetting. In contrast to Hegelian onto-theo-logic maintenance of memory of resentment and internalization of the pain, tragic is delivering of itself to forgetting, the innocent delivering of its project to the most unforeseen fate. To affirm fate and to affirm forgetting, to affirm the unburdening of the heaviness of values, and to affirm play rather than the seriousness work: this is secret of the tragic joy, which the Greeks were capable of. Hence is Nietzsche's motto: *amor fati* (Nietzsche 1968b: 536)—not the resignation of life but the affirmation of what is terrifying and questionable in existence (Ibid: 434-35). To affirm destiny, chance, play and joy in the most innocent becoming of existence, to affirm life despite sufferings: this is what the theatrical man, the slave, the dialectician does not know. Unlike the tragic thinker, he is the gloomy and sad man, carrying the labour of the negative and the burden of project and responsible work, the most serious ascetic whose patience and suffering is internalized into the most reactive denial of existence. The dialectician, the slave and the ass (in *Zarathustra* who carries the burden of values) is cannot be tragic. "Can an *ass* be tragic?—To be crushed by a burden one can neither bear nor throw off…The case of the philosopher" (Nietzsche 1968a: 23). To affirm future (Nietzsche 1968b: 224), and for the sake of the coming of 'overman' to renounce meaning, and to displace the most arbitrarily imagined anthropogenetic subjectivity: such is the untimely tragic thought. The tragic philosopher affirms forgetting; he affirms active forgetting, passing through the bottomless abyss of devaluation of all values, to confront the strange and perilous sea of nihilism. Thus speaks Zarathustra,

> Where do the highest mountains come from? Thus I once inquired. Then I learned that they come out of the sea. The evidence is written into the rocks and into the walls of their peaks. It is out of the deepest depth that the highest must come to its height (Nietzsche 1995: 226).

The tragic philosopher affirms even the most abysmal nihilism, pushing nihilism to the limit so that nihilism overcomes itself, turns back against itself so that time of open future be opened up from the constriction of slavish memory and pain to the most innocent joy of eternal play. Therefore, the death of god, the most abysmal nihilist thought, is a precondition for the freedom towards the promise of the future to come. Therefore, this most abyssal thought can also be the meaning of our joy, our tragic cheerfulness:

> Indeed we philosophers and "free spirits" feel when we hear the news that "the old god is dead" as if a new dawn shone on us; our heart overflows with gratitude, amazement, premonitions and expectation. At long last the horizon appears free to us again, even if it should not be bright; at long last our ships may venture out again, venture out to face any danger; all the daring of the lover of knowledge is permitted again; the sea, our sea lies open again; perhaps there has never yet been such an "open sea"—(Nietzsche 1974: 280).

The tragic joy comes out of this self-overcoming of nihilism: devaluation of all values must be pushed to the limit, but this extreme form of nihilism should not remain at a mere 'No', or halt at a will to negation. This negation, which is the reactive will to power, itself must be negated again. But this double negation should not be confused with Hegelian negation of negation that returns to the positivity of the Same. Here we find the most intricate of Nietzsche's deconstructive strategy: negation negates itself but the affirmation that comes out of this double negation is not positivity of the Same, but the eternal return of becoming (which affirms difference and forgetting). In other words, Nietzsche's question is: can there not be non-positive affirmation which is not the positivity of the circular return of the same (because the positivity of the double negation must remain mere philosophy of negation)? Therefore, it is not for nothing that Hegel still understands double negation as "infinite negativity". Non-positive affirmation: the tragic thought! Hegelian thought remains the thought of negativity and pseudo-tragic affirmation: the donkey that appears in Zarathustra that says 'yea' to everything because it lacks the courage of the lion that destroys. Nietzsche's deconstructive strategy consists in showing that nihilism, at the limit of its possibility, must annihilate itself and affirms affirmation: the completion of nihilism is also self-destruction of nihilism, the crisis of nihilism and reversal towards the most affirmative teaching of the eternal return. But for that, the thought of nihilism must be pushed to the utmost possibility, and the death of god be affirmed without compromise. Hegel's pseudo tragic thought sacrificed God in the figure of Christ only to reconcile and resurrect the finitude of the human, sensuous figure of Christ into the universal god of infinite: the death of God is immediately compromised once again for the sake of the life of Concept. If there is death of God in Hegel, it is only a negativity of the concept: the concept itself, which is itself nihilistic, would not be put into question. As such, the thought of nihilism is not pushed to the limit of itself to the point of transmuting and transfiguring nihilism itself to the tragic joy. What Hegel calls *transfiguration* is only this reconciliation, this form of resurrection, displacement of one value with another; it is not the devaluation of all values; it is not the affirmation of the death in its utmost limit. Thus Hegel remarks about the death of God and transfiguration as reconciliation:

> The *death* of the divine man, *as death*, is *abstract* negativity, the immediate result of the movement which ends only in *natural* universality. Death loses thus natural meaning in spiritual self-consciousness, i.e. it comes to be its just stated Notion; death becomes transfigured from its immediate meaning, viz. the non-being of this *particular* individuality, into the *universality* of the Spirit who dwells in His community, dies in it every day, and is daily resurrected. (Hegel 1998: 475).

Here with Hegelian death of God, it is not a question of overcoming metaphysics: the death of God does not overcome metaphysics but seeks its utmost realization. *Aufhebung* takes here the most spiritual form of reactive forces: *resurrection* and *transfiguration* of the death of God from particular being-in-itself to the universal life of concept is memory that recaptures and recuperates. Resurrection is memory that is recaptured; death that is not lost in forgetting but through remembrance, is brought back again. Is it not the speculative philosophy all about—the releasing of the night that would be recuperated, releasing of death that would be represented, sacrifice that would not be released without drawing meaning from it? With Hegelian Christian-speculative form of *Aufhebung*—the death of God and his *resurrection* and *reconciliation* with the infinite—the Platonic metaphysics of *anamnesis* is not put into questioned but is reified all the more firmly into its onto-theo-logical foundation. *Aufhebung* is the act of memory inasmuch as it allows the preservation of the dead, and elevation of it into the self-presence of its ground: could the onto-theo-logical metaphysics know any other thought? Memory, the conservation of all the past values and *Aufhebung* of the traces, images through which shapes of Spirit has passed (*history is the gallery of images*, Hegel says): this act of memory is not pushed to *infinity.* This is because Hegel was conscious of finitude, which defines 'humanity', and therefore he needed a *telos* and *arche* of his narrative.

Hegel sought above all to preserve and conserve 'man' despite his pretensions to overcome him. The result is re-installation of metaphysics in human terms: it is now man who becomes God! Otherwise Hegel would have known that memory which, when stretched towards infinity, reverses its possibility, and is drowned in irrecuparable abyss of forgetting. This is the time of reversal of values that Nietzsche calls 'transfiguration', which is the essence of the tragic; it is not the Hegelian transfiguration of the death of God resurrected in the universality of the concept. This is what we mean by tragic in relation to the death of God (which Zarathustra affirms): an opening to the strange sea of future; the moment of transmutation and transfiguration of all values; the reversal from the reactive will to power of negativity to the most affirmative thought saying 'yea' to life. For this 'God' and his successor 'man'—both have to be put to death without resurrection, without *Aufhebung*. If our contemporary world, marked by the absence of God and by the death of man, can be called 'tragic', it is because our experience, our laughter and anguish, our joy and abyssal sufferings is marked by an experience of finitude, of God and his successor. This finitude is not the sublated death of Hegelian negativity that would be recuperated in the world, which is constitutive of the world: it is the limit of the 'world', the world marked by time and assumed by labour of memory, but this limit itself cannot be taken up by the labour of negativity, and by the act of memory. If death can be said to put a limit to the 'world', to human project and signification, it is not the dialectical negativity for which death is a capacity or human 'possibility'; it is rather that death drowns the 'world' into most meaningless abyss from which new affirmation must be created. As in *Thus Spoke Zarathustra*, the lion is to be followed, and not preceded by the child and the poet. Hegel did not know this tragic thought or perhaps, refused to know this. His own desperate attempt of not to be mad is only one of the examples.

The Experience of the Limit–II

> ...How the spirit who bears the heaviest fate, a fatality of a task, can nevertheless be the lightest and most transcendent—Zarathustra is a dancer—how he that has the hardest, most terrible insight into reality, that has thought the "most abysmal idea", nevertheless does not consider it an objection to existence, not even to its eternal recurrence—but rather one reason more for being himself the eternal Yes to all things, "the tremendous, unbounded Yes and Amen."—"Into all abysses I still carry the blessings of my saying Yes "—But this is the concept of Dionysus once again.
>
> —Friedrich Nietzsche (1989a: 306)

Signification of madness in the history of philosophy

For a long time in the history metaphysics, Being is determined as identical to thought; the reality of thought, hence the being of thought, would thus be determined as identical to itself in its self-determination. In other words, the beingness of being lies in its 'capacity' or 'possibility' of thought. This relationship which is the founding principle of metaphysics can be called adaequatio: thought must be adequate to the Being of the thinker that thinks inasmuch as the beingness of being lies in its capacity to be identical to the thought it thinks. With this thought of being or thought of beingness of thought as identity, metaphysics inaugurates its history. In other words, the foundational gesture of metaphysics is based on two fundamental principles:

1. The principle of reality (the ontological principle that is expressed in its will to truth by excluding itself from the will to illusion,

from simulacrum which is the fictive reproduction of the world in its asynthetic disjunction that only simulates what it pretends to reproduce).

2. The principle of identity (the ontological principle that is expressed in its constriction of difference through repetition as it is realized in its utmost possibility in the circular reappropriation of the Same).

What happens when we would rather say that the will to truth is nothing but will to error, and consequently, the principle of reality (on the basis of which this will to truth manifests itself as truth, as other than simulacrum), is nothing but this will to error, the very fiction it tries to disengage from? What happens if the principle of identity of being and thought always produces what it cannot recuperate into itself again, something that exceeds its limit of possibility, and hence, remains either more or less than its adaequatio?: thought that exceeds itself, and brings dissolution the very Subject of thought! This is precisely what Nietzsche affirms: the impossibility of thought, being as fable and thought as excess, being of thought as excess, or thought of being as fable: "Parmenides said, 'one cannot think of what is not';—we are at the other extreme, and say, 'what can be thought of must certainly be a fiction'" (Ibid: 1968b: 291).

With this affirmation, Nietzsche at once seeks to deconstruct the whole Western metaphysics: that for Nietzsche, the relationship of being and thought is not that of 'possibility' but that of its limits, of difference and becoming. With this gesture, Nietzsche at once displaces the two principles that hitherto guaranteed the Western metaphysics its foundation and possibilities. If Philosophy is nothing but thinking of thought, then philosophy cannot avoid avoiding this limit and its impossibility (cannot avoid avoiding fiction and simulacrum), and yet, this impossibility of avoiding would ruin the very thought of metaphysics: the impossibility that ineluctably exceeds the closure of being, the impossibility of simulacra which truth introduces at the very heart of being. Thought produces its own simulacrum, and yet, it cannot *own* its simulacrum: hence is its madness! Thought produces its own monstrosity (its own fiction), and yet it cannot recuperate this other: hence is its madness!

Around the beginning of the nineteenth century, 'thought' is determined by various philosophies (which emanate from Critical philosophy and German Idealism) as identity in the name of the self-presence of Being (see Hegel 1971: 129,154,224); this self-presence is understood in turn as *the* interiority *of* self-consciousness (or as 'facts of consciousness') that sublates through memory every form of experience. Nietzsche, instead, indicates towards the limit-experience of thought as pure exteriority, in a voice and language as uncanny as that of a madman. Therefore, it is not surprising that for Nietzsche the thought of eternal return—which he considered as the thought of thought—must have appeared to him as a delirious and abyssal vision whose lucidity exceeds the very 'possibility' for him: in other words, in the thought of eternal return—and Nietzsche himself, the very subject of thinking—disappears so that exteriority itself appears as simulacrum: simulating silvery voice of the sirens that presents itself to itself in absence, and in presenting itself, absents itself thereby, leaving only the hollow sounds of the caves where incessantly murmurs the echo of the absence itself, the emptiness resounding interminably. Nietzsche's thought of the eternal return is this very abyssal experience of thought: the limit-experience of thought whose impossibility unworks and displaces the subject of thinking. Such limit-experience could only take a form as lucid as madness, a lucidity from which the subject of thinking must turn away in terror: Nietzsche could not bear such a thought, and terror seized him! Such experience, instead of reinstating the subject of thought as interior consciousness (maintained intact by the synthetic act of memory), pushes the subject to such limit that it does not return to its sovereign self-sameness. Madness would be the name of this limit-experience of thought: traversal to the limit that unworks the work of Reason; the limit that cannot be limited once more by a dialectical ruse; the limit that unworks the unity of the subject by emptying out all its attributes and predicates. And there, at this limit (exceeding the absolute knowledge of absolute spirit), we are delivered over to the absolute Night (not the night where 'all cows are black'): to the empty space of the absent God! It is this thought, the most abyssal of thought, that Nietzsche's thought of eternal return indicates at the end of nineteenth century: the death of God, the end of history, displacement of metaphysics, the thought of being which hitherto has given meaning to human existence (its sense of value, or value of sense); it also indicates the possibility of another thought, the other of thought, the thought of the exteriority as affirmative thought (that transfigures even the most abyssal death of god into a willing this very emptiness itself). In other words, that such thought is both abyssal (nihilistic) and affirmative: it pushes to the limit, and displaces thereby, all foundational attributes of being from which all sense of truth were derived. This includes what Hegel comes to call 'Reason' and 'Absolute Subject'. Nietzsche thereby unleashes open the limitless limit, the spaceless space, and 'there' points towards an affirmation: the thought of the outside (outside the closure of Being or subject, in other words, outside the closure of metaphysics)! Such is the ineluctable necessity: the thought of eternal return can only be a mad thought, the most abyssal thought, the thought of thought, the very thought of philosophy! With this madness, philosophy itself is displaced by displacing the subject of philosophy.

Nietzsche's philosophy puts into question philosophy itself; Nietzsche's thought is put into question by thought itself. Anyone who undertakes to think this thought of thought, must also think, or will his own impossibility! This is the impasse of thought that the thinker cannot assimilate into his subjectivity: the impossibility of thought, this sheer madness and infinite anguish! Hence is Hegel's own anguish and his fear of going mad (which he sought to evade by compromising with it, by enacting his monumental System and therein lies the cowardly and what a comic gesture of Hegel), Kant's depression and Hume's thinking of himself as becoming 'monster'. Hence is Nietzsche's madness and his mad thought of eternal return which he could not avoid avoiding, and yet nothing but must seek to avoid at all cost (hence, his desire to communicate his thought of eternal return to his friends and Lou Salome, and his desperate attempts to make it seem like doctrine by providing with scientific proof, his desire to write the Book which he could not write)! It all points towards this impossible thought that philosophy is a limit-experience: experience that cannot be lived without becoming a 'monster' thereby; the experience of becoming other at the edge of history! Is not this very experience of thought that is the impossibility of thought, which Plato alludes when he says, "it is through madness that the good things came to Greece "(see the quotation below from Nietzsche)? Yet, is it not madness that presented itself as the greatest danger to philosophy itself?: something that must be avoided at all costs, an invincible and invisible adversary, as uncanny and innocent as the very becoming of the world against which one fight with all one's power! Is not the whole history of philosophy anything but a history of this fight? What essential relationship madness entails with thought that it has to be such an ineluctable necessity, and yet, whose avoidance is equally ineluctably necessary in order for thinking to be possible at all? How Nietzsche's limit-experience of the eternal return, the mad thought, puts philosophy itself into question by pushing philosophy to the limit where philosophy can no longer maintain itself but rather, confronting its impossibility, ceaselessly affirms what cannot be affirmed: namely, the death of god and the eternal return of this ceaseless death? Henceforth, philosophy would eternally affirm what it cannot affirm: its own limit and its own impossibility. This is, then, the name of Nietzsche's thought of the eternal return: the unnamable name for the eternal murmur of its impossibility; the unforeseen unworking of thought in the very process of working; the undoing of what it seeks to constitute as the condition of its possibility; the unproductive 'worklessness' that accompanies in the very suffering and patience of the concept; the unconscious forgetting that ruins every attempt of total signification! Nietzsche's eternal return as such a limit-experience at the limit of philosophy that opens up the closure of philosophy to something exceeding its totality: towards an exteriority that never belongs to any immanence of self-presence. Madness is the name of that abyssal limit-experience: the very thought of thought! What relationship madness entails with thought in such a way that it gives thought to thought, and yet, giving thought to thought, exceeds itself in this very giving so that thought be at once possible and in this very gesture impossible?:

> Almost everywhere it was madness which prepared the way for the new idea, which broke the spell of a venerated usage and superstition. Do you understand why it had to be madness which did this? Something in voice and bearing as uncanny and incalculable as the demonic moods of the weather and the sea and therefore worthy of a similar awe and observation? Something that bore so visibly the

> sign of total unfreedom as the convulsions and froth of the epileptic, which seemed to mark the madman as the mask and speaking–trumpet of a divinity? Something that awoke in the bearer of a new idea himself reverence for and dread of himself and no longer pangs of conscience and drove him to become the prophet and martyr of his idea?—While it is constantly suggested to us today that, instead of a grain of salt, a grain of the spice of madness is joined to genius, all the earlier people found it much more likely that wherever there is madness there is also a grain of genius and wisdom—something "divine", as one whispered to oneself. Or rather: as one said aloud forcefully enough. "It is through madness that the greatest good things have come to Greece", Plato said, in concert with all ancient mankind (Nietzsche 1982: 14-16).

Why has it to be madness that prepares the way for the new idea, 'which breaks the spell of a venerated usage and superstition'? The following follows the lines quoted above,

> ...All superior men who are irresistibly drawn to throw off the yoke of any kind of morality and to frame new laws had, if they were not actually mad, no alternative but to make themselves or pretend to be mad... " How can one make oneself mad when one is not mad and does not dare to appear so?"—Almost all significant men of ancient civilization have pursued this train of thought...who would venture to take a look into the wilderness of the bitterest and most superfluous agonies of soul, in which probably the most fruitful men of all times have languished! To listen to the sighs of these solitary and agitated minds: "Ah, give me madness, you heavenly powers! Madness, that I may at last believe in myself! Give deliriums and convulsions, sudden lights and darkness, terrify me with frost and fire such as no mortal has ever felt, with deafening din and prowling figures, make me howl and whine and crawl like a beast: so that I may only come to believe in myself! I am consumed by doubt, I have killed the law, the law anguishes me as a corpse does a living man. The new spirit which is in me, whence is it if it is not from you? Prove to me that I am yours; madness alone can prove it" (*Ibid*).

According to Nietzsche, the history of morality is constituted as the history of a certain forms of rationality; the throwing off their 'venerated usages' and creation of new values through 'revaluation of all values hitherto', thus, amounts to a philosophical form of madness. Hence, the question posed by Nietzsche—an impossible question because the answer evades to be communicated in the 'venerated usages' which constitutes the values of the time, and of the self-preservation of the species—is this: how to be mad when one is not? And hence, it is not surprising that madness—here we are concerned with the philosophical form of madness—should be the greatest danger for the humanity, that erupting unreason which sweeps away in its vertiginous gesture of all the foundations of thought and meaning, of truth and reason that constitute the 'humanity' of mankind:

> The greatest danger.—If the majority of men had not always considered the discipline of their minds—their "rationality"—a matter pride, an obligation, and a virtue, feeling insulted or embarrassed by all fantasies and debaucheries of thought because they saw themselves as friends of "healthy common sense," humanity would have perished long ago. The greatest danger that always hovered over humanity and still hovers over it is the eruption of madness—which means the eruption of arbitrariness in feeling, seeing and hearing, the enjoyment of the mind's lack of discipline, the joy in human unreason. Not truth and certainty are the opposite of the world of the madman, but the universality and the universal binding force of a faith; in sum, the non-arbitrary character of judgments. And man's greatest labour so far has been to reach agreement about very many things and to submit to a law of agreement—regardless of whether these things are true or false. This is the discipline of mind that mankind has received; but the contrary impulses are still so powerful that at bottom we cannot speak of the future of mankind with much confidence.... continually, precisely the most select spirits bristle at this universal binding force—the explorers of truth above all. Continually this faith, as everybody's faith, arouses nausea and a new lust in subtler minds...it is in these impatient spirits that a veritable delight in madness erupts because madness has such a cheerful tempo. Thus the virtuous intellects are needed—oh, let me use the most unambiguous word—what is needed is virtuous stupidity, stolid metronomes for the slow spirit, to make sure that the faithful of the great shared faith stay together and continue their dance. It is a first rate need that commands and demands this. We others are the exception and the danger—and we need eternally to be defended (Nietzsche 1974: 130-31).

If philosophy has hitherto been concerned about the discipline of the mind—'their rationality'—it is because 'Reason' for them serves the gregarious principle for the preservation of certain species, namely, of the decadent type that seeks nothing but the law of faith agreeable to the conditions under which it survives. It is to this metaphysical need for a universally binding law (an agreeable law—in other words, morality) that Nietzsche looks for the genealogy of 'Reason'. Before going further with this question, I would like to make the following remarks:

1. Here it is a question of the genealogy of Reason. Reason is no longer for Nietzsche the self-engendering Subject (as in Hegelian speculative ontology) that its own *arche* and *telos* within it; Nietzsche traces its genesis further back to entirely another origin: to the immemorial unconsciousness of originary impulses, the inscrutable origin of Reason that cannot traced back without being drown! Hence Reason can never be autochthonous and aboriginal: it is only derivative; it forgets its own origin; it exists only through a process of constriction of those impulses that are not agreeable to its self-preservation. Thus Reason is only 'fictive', a figural construction, which forgets its own fictional character; it thus presents itself as 'reality', a 'truth' or 'fact'. Here is the genesis of the 'reality principle', which we mentioned earlier: at origin of Reason lies this 'reality principle'. That something is 'real' and something is 'apparent': this very distinction is metaphysical one that serves as the self-preservative principle of the most decadent type, the gregarious at the expense of what is singular, the 'sick' and the 'weary' at the expense of what is 'healthy' and powerful.[1] At the

1. In a note published in *The Will to Power*, Nietzsche remarks: "The aberration of philosophy is that, instead of seeing in logic and the categories of reason means towards the adjustment of the world of utilitarian ends (basically, towards an expedient *falsification)*, one believed one possessed in them the criterion of truth and *reality*. The "criterion of truth " was in fact merely the biological utility of such a system of systematic falsification; and since a species of animals knows nothing more important than its own preservation, one might indeed be permitted to speak here of "truth". The naiveté was to take an anthropocentric idiosyncrasy as the *measure of things*, as the rule for determining "real" and "unreal": in short, to make absolute something conditioned. And behold, suddenly the world fell apart into a "true" world and an "apparent" world: and precisely the world that man's reason that devised for him to live and settle in was discredited. Instead of employing the forms as a tool for making the world manageable and calculable, the madness of philosophers divined that in

origin of the fiction of Reason lies the problem of value: if Reason is considered as 'valuable' (and consequently 'moral') in the history of humanity, it is because of its utility for the most decadent type. Hence the relationship of the most intricate accord of philosophy (that makes possible for thinking the sovereign Reason) and morality (as the universal binding law of shared fate, as is expressed in Kant's famous 'practical reason'): both have their genesis in the reality principle of the most decadent type: the self-preservation of the sick and weary! Therefore, both philosophy and morality (along with religion) are decadence forms, which have their counter movement in art: "our religion, morality and philosophy are decadence forms of man", says Nietzsche, "The counter movement: art" (Ibid: 418).

2. Here reemerges the ancient quarrel between poetry and philosophy once more. Poetry: the will to illusion that dissimulates the very will to truth, the simulating simulacra that erupts amidst the enduring faith, the erupting excess that threatens to exceed every limit of the universally binding law of Reason and morality. Is not this erupting madness, this excess of Reason and seductive world of simulacra (that brings dissolution to the very thing it imitates: differing and deferring simulation) that has posed the greatest danger for humanity (if 'humanity' is nothing but the universalization of the most gregarious type which must be overcome)? Man is something

---

these categories is presented the concept of that world to which the one in which man lives does not correspond—the means were misunderstood as measures of value, even as a condemnation of their real intention…This is the greatest error that has ever been committed, the essential fatality of error on earth: one believed one possessed a criterion of reality in the forms of reason—while in fact one possessed them in order to become master of reality, in order to misunderstand reality in a shrewd manner… (Nietzsche 1968b: 314-15).

In another note, Nietzsche says: "I believe that this and that is so as essence of "truth". In valuations are expressed conditions of preservation and growth. All our organs of knowledge and our senses are developed only with regard to conditions of preservation and growth. Trust in reason and its categories, in dialectic therefore the valuation of logic, proves only their usefulness for life, proved by experience—not that something is true. . "The real and the apparent world "—I have traced this antithesis back to value relations. We have projected the conditions of our preservation as predicates of being in general. Because we have to be stable in our beliefs if we are to prosper, we have made the "real world" a world not of change and becoming, but one of being (Ibid: 275-276).

to be overcome; 'humanity' must be overcome. Hence we must push this humanity itself to its limit whose negativity must be transfigured into something affirmative 'Yes'. But for that aesthetic justification and transfiguration of existence to be possible, it is necessary that we be seduced to life; we must be seduced to becoming whose innocent character is far more profound than the will to truth (the latter determining the reality principle as the gregarious principle of Reason and morality); therefore—and this is important here to note—the aesthetic justification and transfiguration of existence must be a "veritable delight in madness", the will to deception and arbitrariness of feeling and seeing: "The will to appearance, to illusion, to deception, to becoming and change (to objectified deception) here counts as more profound, primeval, "metaphysical" than the will to truth, to reality to mere appearance: —the last is itself merely a form of the will to illusion…A highest state of affirmation of existence is conceived from which the highest degree of pain cannot be excluded: the tragic-Dionysian state" (Ibid: 453).

The limit-experience of madness for Nietzsche is an aesthetic one at the limit of philosophy (philosophy, according to Nietzsche, along with morality and religion, are the decadence forms of mankind). If madness as limit-experience is affirmative, it is because it is aesthetic justification and transfiguration of existence from the most nihilist one to the utmost 'amor fati', this 'Yes' to life, to the innocence becoming of the world. The 'veritable delight' in the erupting madness is the tragic joy in destruction: tragic joy is the limit-experience at the limit of all foundational and gregarious discourses of decadence:

> Saying Yes to life even in its strangest and hardest problems; the will to life rejoicing over its own inexhaustibility even in the very sacrifice of its highest types –that is what I called Dionysian, that is what I understood as the bridge to the psychology of the tragic poet. Not in order to get rid of terror and pity, not in order to purge oneself of a dangerous affect by its vehement discharge—Aristotle misunderstood it that way—but in order to be oneself the eternal joy of becoming, beyond all terror and pity—that joy which includes even joy in destroying (1979: 273).

From the lines quoted above, it is clear that Nietzsche thought of his vision of eternal return—the lived experience of which can only present itself as limit-experience that de-constitutes the very being of the thinker—as the experience of tragic that dismantles the tradition of metaphysics at the expense of the dissolution of his (Nietzsche's) own subjectivity. His experience of eternal return, the experience which seized Nietzsche with such terror and ecstasy, is not the purgation of self-consciousness through tragic knowledge (that gives the tragic consciousness the satisfaction of return to its self-same home). Here we see Nietzsche's decisive confrontation with Aristotle and Hegel. In the previous chapter we have seen how Hegel's speculative phenomenology exploited tragedy as the dialectical paradigm for the re-installation of the sovereign Subject by putting death itself into work. All these things come with full force here: Nietzsche's thought of tragic, this most abysmal tragic thought of eternal return, is not the return of the sovereign Subject to its self-identity and self-presence through purgation; the exigency of the eternal return claims, with an ineluctable necessity, the dissolution of this sovereign Subject; that the eternal return is rather the "unworking" (that unworks the labour of the concept) of the self-consciousness that gives fictive sense of unity to itself through the most gregarious use of language in its grammatical form of 'I'; that the eternal return demands the dispersal of the synthetic principle of reality and identity; and along with it demands dissimulation of memory and representation which give us the interiority of self-consciousness. The ecstatic character of the experience of the eternal return lies in its aesthetic redemption, and liberation of the slavish consciousness (or, the gregarious character of our existence) through the rupture such an experience introduces into being, the rupture that opens us to which has been repressed through constrictive acts of memory and representation; in other words, it rejuvenates forces of unconscious impulses. With this a decisive and the most unsettling displacement of the whole tradition of metaphysics occurs: if metaphysics realizes its utmost possibility in this ontological principle of identity of Being and thought (which Hegel realizes by transforming this ontological principle into the identity of the Subject of thought), then Nietzsche's displacement of the self-conscious Subject (by showing that thought has its genesis in far more profound, simulating non-foundational, non-ontological unconscious impulses) signifies the displacement of the tradition of metaphysics itself. With the displacement of consciousness (as that which is the mediative identity of reflection), and the phenomenological notion of 'experience'—as we have seen that it determines the whole movement of Hegel's *Phenomenology of Spirit*—the philosophical experience of thought is no longer seen as the self-positing act of the Subject, but as the vertiginous experience of the unworking of consciousness. Hence is the libidinal character of the experience of thought, its unconscious forces interrupting the self-consciousness of Reason.

It is at this point; we would like to make the following remarks—

1. With this displacement of the 'phenomenological consciousness', the metaphysical determination of Being on the basis of the ontological principle of identity of thought and Being (here 'consciousness') is displaced. Thinking is no longer thought as the self-unfolding act of a phenomenological consciousness (that posits itself), but only as derived and secondary (even arbitrary) phenomenon whose genesis lies somewhere else, in some remote forgotten past.
2. Since there is no such thing called 'consciousness' (which is a mere fiction, a grammatical illusion which the gregarious invents for the sake of their metaphysical comfort), the genesis of thought cannot be determined through consciousness qua consciousness (Nietzsche 1968b: 375-377): thinking is rather the 'excess' of consciousness; it is the limit-experience which consciousness cannot maintain but must dissimulates itself: such is the delirium of thought, its sheer eruption whose threatening aspects terrify 'humanity' itself, and which poses the greatest danger to human history. For a long time we have been associating thinking with 'rationality', 'interiority' and 'consciousness' on the basis of the metaphysical notion of truth as *adaequatio,* and on the basis of the gregarious principles of reality and identity. Nietzsche, on the other hand, made thought the stuttering voice of the perilous sea, the voice of tempests and of the most questionable existence: thought is not *adaequatio* of subject and the predicate, but an excess of pure exteriority, the voice of the other shore whose shattering waves cannot be translated into the language

of the concept (since it dissimulates the very identity principle through which concept recognizes itself to be such); thought is not the voice of reason (there is no such thing called 'inner voice' which the Christian priests made so much use of. Is not this very voice, in an entirely different language Kant too evokes as his 'practical reason'?) and of 'consciousness', but resonance of unconscious forces of libidinal impulses whose eruption destabilizes the mimetic logic of speculative economics; thought is not the recuperative purgation of self-consciousness through memory but forgetting that would be lost forever. Nietzsche does not associate thinking with the decadent form of 'rationality' but as experience of the 'excess': the 'veritable delight' in the eruption of repressed impulses that enhance to the utmost the joyous affirmation of the innocent becoming of existence. As such, thought takes up what it cannot master on the basis of its 'capacity' or 'possibility': it is its own excess; it is its own 'veritable delight' in its own eruption without the Subject.

3. What happens to the question concerning the ground of philosophy when the very ontological principle (that guarantees its ground is displaced), and when the metaphysical notion of the Subject is so violently displaced (and is shown to be a mere fiction, a grammatical illusion which the decadent and the sick needs for its self-preservation)? Since thought does not belong to itself but rather is its very excess (which it cannot recuperate), thought cannot ground itself ontologically. Rather thinking is the most abysmal ungrounding from which mankind would be perished one day. Thought does not produce Being (that would constitute as the source of meaning, truth and knowledge); it ceaselessly produces simulacra that incessantly unwork any attempt for self-grounding. Thinking introduces the movement that differs and defers any possible point of closure of absolute knowledge: it repeats this closure, and through this repetition, opens up unforeseeable difference that thought cannot take up. What exceeds the closure would not be grounded, for, repetition does not cease becoming, thinking does not cease exceeding itself, and does not cease reproducing its own simulacrum. Thought as simulacrum: with this thought the relationship between poetry and philosophy blurs indefinitely.

4. The problem of madness is the most disconcerting one, the classic problem in philosophy: it raises the most terrifying question concerning the very possibility of philosophy—its ground and its legitimacy; it raises the most dangerous and abysmal question concerning the possibility of meaning, truth or knowledge; and, even the question concerning the possibility of 'humanity' itself. If thinking cannot be dissociated from the aesthetic seduction of simulacrum, then thinking that (being 'rational') is supposed to guarantee 'humanity', would rather bring destruction to 'humanity'. Is it not this danger that led Plato to banish the poets from the republic (for the poets are those that simulate us in most insidious way, that what they produce is nothing but mere simulacrum)? If poetry is dangerous for 'humanity', it is because it simulates the reality principle by reproducing only simulacra. Is it not the very cause of the eruption of the most arbitrariness of feeling and seeing that is called 'madness'? That thinking itself—and if philosophy is nothing but thought of thought—has the most intricate and dangerous relationship with madness (and with poetry and to its simulacrum): is it not what Plato was dangerously close to assert in *Phaedrus* when he associated both poetry and philosophy as different manifestations of madness? Is it not precisely this madness which afflicted Hegel to the point of drowning of his whole existence, and from which he sought escape by the most ingenuous means by constructing the most ambitious system of thought? Is it not precisely this madness of thought which seized him when Nietzsche received in his vision the thought of eternal return (and which un-worked his very humanity, to the point of the dissolution of his subjectivity)? Yet, this is precisely what Nietzsche desired: "Give me madness…", because he refused to compromise with the gregarious, with what is decadent and sick, with the slavish principles of reality and identity; this is what, seeking salvation of his soul and desperately trying to escape from madness, Hegel compromised. Therefore, Hegel needed to reinstate once more firmly the gregarious principle of identity coming down from Parmenides that thought and Being are same. Hegel sided with the decadent, with the slave, with the

life-negating principle of negativity and memory, with the sick consciousness of resentment that needs 'pain' and 'memory' (See Nietzsche 1989a: 60-61& 84-85). Hegel wanted to be sane, to be rational, and with this the singularity of the healthy is compromised once more; and at the expense of the powerful and healthy, the most decadent type of self-preservative mankind is asserted once more.

Madness of the subject

At stake here is the question of the subject of philosophy. In fact, this dissertation in a certain way concerns with nothing but this: what is at stake when one poses the question of the subject of philosophy? Let's reformulate this problematic once more: that the question concerning the subject of philosophy is a question of the very genesis and structure, the very possibility and ground of philosophy itself. In the first chapter we discussed how in Hegel's onto-theo-logical constitution of metaphysics the question concerning the genesis and structure, the possibility and ground of philosophy, becomes the problematic of the installation of the subject of philosophy (inasmuch as this subject of philosophy is determined speculatively on the basis of the ontological principle of the identity of thought and Being, and dialectically as the phenomenological consciousness which reconciles the sundering moments of its own difference). That this onto-theo-logic subject of philosophy should also be phenomenological, that was far from unclear there and I can only repeat again what has already been said: if the 'facts of consciousness' not merely be of 'possible experience' (as in Immanuel Kant's 'transcendental unity of apperception' as the synthetic principle of a priori judgment) but of actual and self-posited experience (as constitutive of internal self-consciousness), movement must be introduced in Being (so that time is not merely 'form'/'formless form' in which experience is given but the very becoming of experience: here is Hegel's departure from Kantian formalism). So the question is no longer that of either remaining mere formal, or that of privileging 'content', but rather is the resolution of this dualism of 'form' and 'content'. It is a familiar story that already in Kant, with Descartes' behind him, the question concerning the genesis and structure of philosophy rests upon this question of the 'facts of consciousness' (hence, Kant's famous question: is metaphysics possible?, is inseparable from the question of 'consciousness'. The whole post-Kantian philosophy had to struggle with this question). Hegel, who introduces movement (or, 'becoming') into thought and Being: the 'facts of consciousness', therefore, no longer is mere as 'possible (or, formal) experience', but, being a process, is also 'actual' experience. Thus, it is on the possibility of the Subject of philosophy there rests the whole question of the possibility and ground of philosophy itself. Therefore, for Nietzsche, displacement of this Subject of philosophy amounts to the displacement of the very ancient program of metaphysics: displacement of the ontological principle of identity of thought and Being that grounds philosophy itself; and displacement of the epistemological principle of reality that grounds any possibility of knowledge. All the metaphysical concepts such as 'substance', 'truth', and 'reality' are seen to arise out of our firm belief in the 'subject' and not the reverse:

> The concept of substance is a consequence of the concept of the subject: not the reverse! If we relinquish the soul, "the subject", the precondition for "substance" in general disappears. . The subject: this is the term for our belief in a unity underlying all the different impulses of the highest feeling of reality: we understand this belief as the effect of one cause –we believe so firmly in our belief that for its sake we imagine "truth", "reality", "substantiality" in general.—"The subject" is the fiction that many similar states in us are the effect of one substratum: but it is we first created the "similarity of these states; our adjusting them and making them similar is the fact, not their similarity (—which ought rather to be denied—)(Nietzsche 1968b: 268-69).

And in another note,

> When one has grasped that the "subject" is not something that creates effects, but only a fiction, much follows.
>
> It is only after the model of the subject that we have invented the reality of things and projected them into the medley of sensations. If we no longer believe in the effective subject, then belief also disappears in effective things, in reciprocation, cause and effect between those phenomena we call things.

> There also disappears, of course, the world of effective atoms: the assumption of which always depended on the supposition that one needed subjects.
>
> At last the "thing-in-itself" also disappears, because this is fundamentally the conception of a "subject-in-itself". But we have grasped that the subject is a fiction. The antithesis "thing-in-itself" and "appearance" is untenable; with that, however, the concept "appearance" also disappears (Ibid: 297-98).

To put the question in another way: what happens when time is introduced into Being and thought (in other words, to put it in Hegel's terminology, it is no longer a question of 'substance' but rather that of the Subject)? Hegel introduces temporality—movement and becoming—so that the gathering of manifold of experiences, and of the differential multiplicity of sensations into the self-presence is not a dead 'thing' but a living process. This is why Nietzsche calls the Hegelian subject as 'effective subject': the subject effectuates, and produces what it is, the subject of thought; the subject as the gathering unity of the manifold; the subject who initiates the process of becoming which levels (thus constricting difference of the manifold) off the fluctuating intensity of thoughts and reduces them to 'similar states' by arbitrarily constituting a causal chain (there arises the causality of thoughts that serves the ontological principle of identity); the subject which reduces the differential multiplicity of 'nows' into the self-same presence of the 'Now'. In the first chapter we have tried to show how 'memory' serves this process of sublation and effectuation (the work of recuperation and anticipation) and 'constricts' the differential multiplicity of incommensurable 'nows'. It means this: if thought has served being, then thought must be determined metaphysically as essentially recuperative and effective/effectuating. This is what Hegel seeks to do by introducing time into thought and Being. This onto-theo-logical delimitation of thought brings two problematic to our notice:

1. The problematic of the relationship between memory and thought—the onto-theo-logical determination of thought as memory and memory as thought.

2. The problematic relationship between work and thought—the onto-theo-logical determination of thought as work and work as thought.

They amount to the single problematic: the (dis) installation of the Subject as the ground and possibility of thought in which what is to be grounded must be identical to the ground. Would not thought thereby affirm, being freed from work and its essential negativity, the necessity of play and chance: being as play—becoming itself—that aesthetically justifies and redeems, transfigures and transforms existence by willing this eternal return once more (that means infinite times)? Thought would, then, be affirmative, and not 'negativity' (Hegel determines thought as 'negativity'). This affirmation would be possible only as much as, being freed from memory, it forgets its own affirmation. In other words, eternal return forgets its own affirmation, and thereby affirms nothing but its own forgetting: such is the 'impossibility' of the thought of eternal return, the thought of the limit that affirms itself only in its inability to affirm itself. With this, the thought of eternal return does not belong to the 'realm of possibility' that defines self-consciousness; the thought of the eternal return is the impossible, the limit thought of the possible because it must affirm what cannot be affirmed, that is, its own forgetting and unworking. The 'subject' must disappear in order to affirm its own disappearance; it must bring its own dissolution and its identity. Yet this is what Hegel was afraid of when he complained of his 'going mad': the shipwreck of his 'subjectivity' and the loss of identity, which it entails. Thought is monstrous, and the philosopher must pay his own 'humanity' for its sake.

In the following section, I ask the following: how thought is onto-theo-logically determined as memory and as work, and how in these determinations lies Hegelian desire to install the Subject as the very ground and possibility of thought? How Nietzsche puts these determinations into question, and thereby displacing the onto-theo-logical constitution of metaphysics? Only through this detour we will be able to arrive at Nietzsche's thought of eternal return, and to the understanding of what it entails, that is: the problematic of the de-constitution of the Subject, and displacement of metaphysics itself.

Work and pain

If, as Heidegger rightly brings to our notice, 'work' and 'logos' are the two conditions that determine metaphysics as history of Being, then it should be obvious for us that Hegelian onto-theo-logy, with its determination of 'Being' and 'thought' as 'work' and "Reason' (*logos*: hence Hegelian ontology, which is that of his *Logic*, is called 'onto-theo-logy') is the utmost realization of the tradition of metaphysics. In fact, and this is not difficult to show, that the two are inseparable or even, in Hegelian onto-theo-logical determination, are the same: both point toward the possibility of the most interior, or the most intimate gathering into unity; in other words, the possibility of 'installation' (that means, 'representation'—here it is the problem of 'mimesis') of the Subject. If one thinks this question of Being as Subject in relation to 'thought', then these two onto-theo-logical conditions make possible the most 'interior' and most ' intimate' gathering into unity. In other words, they point toward the possibility of the installation of the 'Absolute Concept'. That means, thought is determined, speculatively, in sight of the possibility of sublating (that means 'negating') into the Concept (that means the concept of the concept). Therefore, Hegel determines the essence of Being, and thought as 'absolute negativity'. In what sense negativity is the most 'interior' and most 'intimate' gathering into unity if not because of the pain of its work? If the essence of thought is 'absolute negativity', it is the negativity of 'work'—'the labour of the concept'—whose essence lies in the most intimate pain of labour. Therefore could Hegel say that philosophy is "the seriousness, the suffering, the patience and the labour of the negative" (Hegel 1998: 10); that philosophy is "the way of despair" (Ibid: 49), and that as the work of negativity, "consciousness suffers this violence at its own hands" (Ibid: 51). Therefore, the metaphysics of 'work' and 'logos' is inseparable from 'pain': the most violent sundering of consciousness at its own hands! Yet, it is this very violence that, at the same time, points toward the very possibility of the most intimate gathering of the Subject—through its most intimate pain—of its own experiences (such is the dialectical ruse of pain) into its self-present 'interiority'; in other words, into the very possibility of 'self-consciousness'. Hegelian phenomenology is the becoming of this self-consciousness, becoming of the subject of experience. As such, the phenomenological pathway of consciousness is the pathway of pain. With this phenomenology of pain, the whole Western metaphysics gathers into its utmost interiority—the most intimate gathering of thought—, and hence, the most intimate possibility of the installation of the Subject. The essence of thought as work and its pain produces the most intimate self-consciousness of the Subject. Heidegger says the same thing about Hegel when he remarks,

> In order to be able to delineate more clearly the relations which carry the connection between "work" and "pain" nothing less would be necessary than to think through the basic fundamental structure of Hegel's metaphysics, the uniting unity of the Phenomenology of the Mind and of the Science of Logic. The fundamental character is "absolute negativity" as the eternal force of reality, that is, of the "existing concept". In the same (but not the equal) belonging to the negation of the negation, work and pain manifest their innermost metaphysical relationship ...if anyone, indeed, dare to think through the relationship between "work" as the basic feature of being and "pain" via Hegel's Logic, then the Greek word for pain, namely algos, first becomes articulate for us. Presumably algos is related to alego, which as an intensive of lego signifies intimate gathering. Then pain would be the most intimate of gatherings. Hegel's concept of the "concept" and its properly understood "tension" say the same thing on the transformed level of the absolute metaphysics of subjectivity (Heidegger 1959: 70-71).

Conceptual thought is the work of the negative. With these two metaphysical conditions, 'work' and 'logos' can said to be the same, insofar as their intimate relations point toward the installation of the Subject. There this strange connection between 'logos' (Reason), 'algos' (pain) and 'lego' (gathering) becomes clear: 'pain' 'gathers' the manifold into its inmost intimacy, which installs 'logos' as the Subject. With this the determination of the essence of thought as 'work' and 'negativity', as 'experience' of 'pain' that gathers, the onto-theo-logy accomplishes the metaphysics of subjectivity as the last stage of dialectical becoming.

What has happened here? By transforming thought as possible experience into the phenomenological experience (that is, becoming actual), thought itself has become, in Hegel's philosophy, none other than this very work of actualization: thought has come to be determined as work. The pain of this work produces the 'interiority' or 'depth' of the Subject: this is the consequence of determining, onto-theo-logically, thought as 'work': that is, the grounding of metaphysics, securing the identity of thought and Being with which metaphysics begins and with which metaphysics accomplishes its destiny . The figure of the 'worker' becomes the Subject who is transformed into the figure of 'humanity' itself: Heidegger points this out in his debate with Ernst Jünger. The figure of the worker belongs to the metaphysics of extreme subjectivity. Heidegger names it as En-framing (*Gestalt*), which is the "source of bestowing of meaning" (Ibid: 53).

In light of this problematic—that of metaphysics of "pain" constitutive of the "subjectivity" of—Nietzsche's constant engagement with the question of 'pain' becomes all the more abysmal problematic. What is the relationship of pain and thought? This question has already been decisive for philosophy from its very inception: pain already seems to Plato (one can only have to go through his *Apology*) to mark the limit of thought, that ruins in advance, or that brings disaster to the ontological foundation of the community. Does not this excessive mourning, which is supposed to be the cause of hysteria of women, mark the limit of all thought and unsettles thereby the ontological foundation of community? Therefore, when Hegel addresses the question of bringing together pain and work, and thereby sublating 'pain into the very constitutive possibility of consciousness, it is this problematic of madness and mourning the decisive issue here. Hegel thus seeks to 'cure' this 'madness' through dialectical ruse of conversion of the disease into remedy. In other words, by transforming the very disease itself into the work of remedy, Hegel evades not only his own madness, but also has made sure the ontological foundation of the community is firmly established.

When Nietzsche transforms his madness into the destinal experience of philosophical thought, it is this question of the limit that is at stake. What if, suffering of thought or philosophical experience of mourning, while destined towards work, must always already points to its own dissolution? Commenting on Nietzsche, Blanchot says:

> One may wonder why the writers and artists (strange names, always already anachronistic) who have borne such questions in a privilege

> manner and forced others to become attentive to them. The response is at first almost easy. "Madness" is the absence of work, while artist is one who is preeminently destined to a work –but also one whose concern for the work in the experience of that which in advance always ruins the work and always draws it into the empty depth of worklessness, where nothing is ever made of being (Blanchot 1993: 200).

What if the experience of thought already always ruins itself in advance, and thereby brings disaster to the work of consciousness? Would it not thereby mark the limit of this consciousness itself, consciousness that hopes to subsume pain by interiorizing into its immanent depth? Pain will thereby push consciousness itself to the limit of its possibility, and rend asunder the coherency the subjectivity of the thinker himself. Therefore, suffering seems to be indissociable from the very experience of thought for Nietzsche because it marks the limit of philosophy itself. The philosopher is the monster through whom the eruption of madness marks the limit of the measure of time and limit of the measure of possibility. Nietzsche's limit experience cannot be dissociated from the abysmal experience of thought which is irreducible to the 'acts of consciousness. Thought, thus, seems irreducible to consciousness and singular in every moment of thinking, excessive in relation to the very process of actualization of thought, to the principle of identity. Thought is suffering; thought suffers in not being able to be actualized, and yet, therein lays the sheer ecstatic madness of thought that marks the limit of possibility for the thinker. Pierre Klossowski, whose study on Nietzsche is attentive to this limit–experience of thought, brings this point to our notice,

> The act of thinking became identical with suffering, and suffering with thinking. From this fact, Nietzsche posited the coincidence of thought with suffering and asked what a thought would be that was deprived of suffering –as the impossibility of suffering—then came to be experienced by Nietzsche as the highest joy. But thought really have the power to actualize itself without itself suffering, without reconstituting its own suffering? Does thought itself suffer from its own inability to actualize itself? (Klossowski 1997: 23).

Passivity excess to every measure of time: pain in its not-being-able-to-be-actualized in the language of communication; the irremissible solitude that refuses to be included into the universal order of anonymous Reason! Mourning cannot be sublated into the interiority of the concept through memory; it rather marks the limit of anamnesis, and delivers subjectivity of the thinker to the monstrosity of forgetting. If there still something like communication takes place, it is only through the tonal affectivity of gestures that pushes to the limit the order of universal signification. Mourning does not gather together in the intimate ground of our interiority the manifold representations, but rather, not being able to gather together, suffering delivers subjectivity to its own dissolution, to its violent sundering apart which no work of synthesis can represent and sublate. Not being able to represent to itself its own suffering, it remains without its own name, and hence simulates every name, disinstalls every name which it simulates to name.

Art and fiction

Here Nietzsche's bringing up the question of art becomes more articulate for us. The question itself is classic one. It is the haunting aporia of the problematic of mimesis that always defers and differs the possibility of grounding philosophy on a firm foundation once and for all. This most unsettling question is this: what happens, if the rift between the installation of the figure of the worker and what it must leave behind in order for the work of installation to be possible (the rift which this very installation must presuppose in order to be what it is, must remain undecidable and indeterminate, unlocalizable non-space whose impossibility no category of Reason could ever supply, simply because the categories of Reason would be this side of the rift (yet the rift itself exceeds this line always already)? How can we, if we don't possess categories to distinguish between the 'simulacrum' and 'reality', distinguish between 'true' world and 'apparent' world? "We possess no categories" says Nietzsche, "by which we can distinguish a true from an apparent world. (There might only be an apparent world, but not our apparent world.)" (Nietzsche 1968b: 313).

Is not the very question of grounding philosophy on some firm ontological foundation at stake here, the foundation that must be able to provide the determination and decision concerning the distinction between reality or truth on the one hand, and simulation (simulacrum) of this reality on the other: a necessary distinction whose impossibility of determination and decision puts into question philosophy itself? This is what Plato was afraid of. This fear has, from Plato onwards, forever haunted any foundational discourse of philosophy. Thus it is not the problematic of the unavailability of the distinction between 'proper' and 'improper' but the undecidability and indeterminability (and hence, the non-proper) of the rift: this is where lies the abyss and the danger, the non-appropriability and the madness of simulacrum.

Yet this very problematic of the non-proper, which Nietzsche problematizes(and that threatens the displace metaphysical grounding), that Heidegger's thought of Being is not attuned to when he considers Nietzsche's 'reversal of metaphysics'. But things are not as simple to say that Nietzsche's 'reversal of metaphysics' simply belongs to metaphysics. It is not the reversal of the 'reality' into 'apparent', 'proper' into 'improper' but the aporia of the non-proper, exceeding the 'proper' and 'improper' that Nietzsche calls 'fable' or 'fiction':

> It is in the nature of thinking that it thinks of and invents the unconditioned as an adjunct to the conditioned; just as it thought of and invented the "ego" as an adjunct to the multiplicity of its processes; it measures the world according to magnitudes posited by itself—such fundamental fiction as "the unconditional", "the ends and means", "things", 'substances" logical laws, numbers and forms.
>
> There would be nothing that could be called knowledge if thought did not first re-form the world in this way into "things", into what is self-identical. Only because there is thought is there untruth (Ibid: 309).

Thus 'figuration' in the sense of *Gestalt* has its origin in the far more unconscious abyss of fiction: fiction itself cannot be grounded (hence its abyssal character); its non-properness always defers and differs to any appropriation (which any installation of ground demands); 'fiction' is disinstallation itself. But is not installation, onto-theo-logically determined, is the work of negativity (of thought)? 'Fiction' itself would then-- disinstallation of any installation—be undoing or unworking of the work of the negative, the dispersal of what it installs. The fable of thought is disinstallation of the ontological foundation of metaphysics: thought disinstalls not because it is false as opposed to the truth, but because it is the vicious simulacra of the truth. Therein lies the danger and abyssal character of fiction: that it 'seems' 'everything' while it is 'nothing', that its non-propriety and non-property is not appropriable, that it is unidentifiable because it simulates identity. It thereby ruins the very identity that it simulates; it un-appropriates what it simulates to appropriate. It assumes every identity because it has none and hence, it cannot be assumed by any identity; it assumes every depth or interiority of consciousness because it is unconsciousness, the bottomless, ungrounding that defers any constitution of self-consciousness; it only simulates grounding and never ceased simulating. It is to this 'fictionalization', to this abyssal exteriority, that the origin of the very 'figuration' must be traced: trace that erases itself, because, it is itself without origin and presence. If thought is called 'fiction', Nietzsche means that there is something inactive about 'thought' and its inactivity lies in its simulating character of 'activity'. The danger and the abyss of thought lays in its 'mimetic' disinstallation, in its dissolution of 'identity' and 'reality' (the two principles that determines the onto-theo-logical determination of 'work' and 'logos'). This is what Plato calls 'madness' of the poet: the abyssal character of *mimesis*, which is 'fiction'; that undoes the labour of the concept by simulating to 'do' it; the deconstitution of the foundational constitution of identity and reality while simulating to constitute it. Simulacrum is abyssal (because it simulates every form of identity while bringing dissolution to identity) and mad. Poetry, which is nothing but fiction, is constantly solicitated to madness. If 'Reason', 'Subject' and 'thought' (understood metaphysically as concept) emerge out of this abyssal fiction—out of this simulacra of thought (or simulacra as thought) which is unreason—then philosophy itself (which attempts to constitute its foundation in the name of 'Reason', 'subject' or 'concept') would not have in its possession the categories that should be able to determine its own origin and *telos*: it would not be able to determine the location of this very rift, the very "line", the disjunction, the very difference of Reason and unreason, truth and the apparition. Yet this is the very question that has ever-haunted philosophy, which it could not answer once and for all:

> In almost all respects, philosophical problems today are formulated as they were two thousand years ago: how can something arise from its opposite—for example, reason from unreason, sensation from the lifeless, logic from the illogical, disinterested contemplation from covetous desire, altruism from egoism, truth from error? Until now, metaphysical philosophy has overcome this difficulty by denying the origin of one from the other and by assuming for the more highly valued things some miraculous origin, directly from out of the heart and the essence of the "thing-in-itself". Historical philosophy, on the other hand, the very youngest of all philosophical methods, which can no longer be even conceived of as separate from the natural sciences has determined in isolated cases (and will probably conclude in all of them) that they are not opposites, only exaggerated to be so by the popular or metaphysical view and that this opposition is based on an error of reason...
>
> All we need ...is a chemistry of moral, religious, aesthetic ideas and feelings...what, if this chemistry might end with the conclusion that even here, the most glorious colors are extracted from base, even despised substances? Are there many who want to pursue such investigations? Mankind loves to put the questions of origins and beginnings out of mind: must one not be almost inhuman to feel in himself the opposite inclination? (Nietzsche 1994: 13-14).

What, if Reason arises from unreason? But is this (supposedly) antithetical character if only a provisional model of questioning for Nietzsche. What if this very oppositional relationship itself has its origin in something that is nothing but 'fiction' (which this opposition cannot ground)? Are not these names ('Subject', Reason', 'Concept') name anything other than the unifying principle of identity which is nothing but fiction (that means production of 'similarity' wherein lies difference)? If that is so, it means that 'Reason' or 'Subject' is only fictional production of the 'similarity': simulated production of 'identity' which simulates the 'ground' out of what is an abysmal unground! It means that 'Reason' or 'Subject' is only simulacrum that brings to dissolution its own identity (because simulacrum is its very dissolution, because simulacrum is non-proper and does not belong to itself), ungrounds itself and affirms its own ungrounding differential multiplicity, which disjoints any causal closure. Disjointing from the closure of causal chain, and exceeding the *arche* and *telos* of the temporal closure, thought is this eternal return of the differential multiplicity of simulacrum that makes the return of the identical impossible. This is because the Subject itself is only this simulacrum: this impossibility of 'identity' with itself, its incessant deconstitution of 'reality'. This is what Nietzsche's thought of the eternal return means. Not the eternal return of the self-same Subject, but the eternal exceeding of this temporal closure (because it is without origin and *telos*) which affirms the differential multiplicity of simulacrum. The Subject is the multiple and differential (hence it is dissolution of its own identity) because it is its own simulacrum; it is its non-proper which it cannot appropriate. "My hypotheses", writes Nietzsche, subject as multiplicity" (1968b: 270). With this is affirmed the eternal joy in eternal becoming of the world, of becoming multiple and becoming of the other. With the death of God, the world becomes joyous: dancing Gods with light feet!; there is now the transfiguration of existence from saying 'no' to the affirming of the joy of becoming: existence as play and dance, of becoming multiple!

It is now more articulate for us why Nietzsche considered the question: "how can one make oneself mad when one is not mad?" as the most significant question in the history of morality. "To make oneself mad when one is not mad', to simulate madness when one is not: with this Nietzsche affirms nothing but simulacrum of thought, simulacrum of Reason so as to push the gregarious value to its limit so as to affirm what cannot be affirmed: the impossibility of the subject of affirmation and dissolution of its identity. Nietzsche's will to madness ('give me madness') is this willing of the simulacrum of thought (simulacrum is madness. It disinstalls all foundation of 'subjectivity' and work of consciousness), affirmation of the abyss into which all affirmation must be carried to the limit of the possible: affirmation to be affirmed eternally, this willing of nothing but the eternal return of this willing (hence 'the eternal return of the same') once more (that means infinite times). It is in this sense Nietzsche's thought of eternal return is thought of the limit (that it must affirm the 'impossible'; that it must affirm the rupture of all foundations of the 'human' subject): such is the madness of the eternal return! If the thought of eternal return of the same is inseparable from delirium of thought, it is because the eternal return affirms the absence of work, the destruction of the identity of the thinker, the dissolution of 'consciousness'; it presupposes this dissolution of Reason to open thought to the infinite outside, beyond the circular closure of the Subject. Maurice Blanchot brings out this point in the following way,

> …The relation of the delirium to the thought of the Eternal Return that the delirium communicates …the "delirium" is the form of absence in which Nietzsche's identity destroys itself—that Nietzsche who, formulating the everything returns, thus opens the circle, makes its point of singularity (point at which the non-circularity of the circle would be defined) by means of which closure and rupture coincide). (Blanchot 1993: 278).

The eternal return

'Disinstallation' of the ground of philosophy is possible only as simulation that must (where comes this exigency if not from this very simulating character of repetition?) repeat the simulation of the ground repeatedly, that means, eternally. Only by infinitely repeating the ground, the grounding would be ungrounded eternally; for, ground itself arises from an abysmal freedom—which is the "groundless grounding of a ground", in Heidegger's words, that is, its 'fictional' character—that gives itself the possibility of a ground but itself is groundless. Heidegger remarks about this freedom in this following way,

Original commanding and being able to command always arise only from freedom and are themselves fundamental forms of true being free. Freedom—in the simple and profound sense that Kant understood its essence—is in itself poetizing: the groundless grounding of a ground, in such a way that it grants itself the law of its essence. But commanding means nothing other than this (Heidegger 1991: 119).

'Freedom' is fictional; the figural forming which itself is 'groundless'. Repetition of this ground is this will to 'simulacrum' of the ground that ungrounds itself: eternal return is the infinite proliferation of simulacrum infinitely repeating itself, ungrounding itself; the vertigo of the eternal difference of repetition and eternal repetition of difference. It is this vertigo that would seize Nietzsche on a certain day, on a certain evening walk in Sils Maria when the vision of the eternal return occurs to him. The 'necessity' of the eternal return, the destinal thinking of Being itself, arises out of the freedom whose abyssal character lies in the 'play' or 'chance' character of this vision: joyous free play of the differential multiplicity of the intensive states give itself out of its groundless grounding. Hence is the experience of euphoria at the experience of eternal return. With this joyous affirmation, both the 'necessity' and 'chance' are affirmed together, infinitely echoing each other, as the joyous affirmation of their disjunction from which the deepest pain is not excluded. Nietzsche calls this 'the Dionysian joy': an experience of the limit that pushes to the limit all possible works of 'synthesis' which the negative work of 'memory' and 'pain' gathers into the innermost intimacy of the Subject. That the disjunctive synthesis of the necessity and chance itself should arise from the groundless grounding: this is at once the tearing asunder of the thinker with abysmal pain, and the overwhelming joy at the impossibility of the thought's own possibility of thinking. Only Kant's experience of the sublime allows such a glimpse of the limit-experience of the impossible. After the few days when the vision of the eternal return occurs to him, Nietzsche writes to Peter Gast from Sils Maria, on 14 August, 1881,

> Well, my dear good friend! The August sun is overhead, the year passes on, the mountains and forests become more quite and peaceful. On my horizon, thoughts have arisen such as I have never seen before—I will not speak of them, but will keep my unshakable peace. I really shall have to live a few more years! Ah, my friend, sometimes the idea runs through my head that I am living an extremely dangerous life, for I am one of those machines which can explode. The intensities of my feeling make me shudder and laugh; several times I could not leave my room for the ridiculous reason that my eyes are inflamed—from what? Each time I had wept too much on my previous day's walk, not sentimental tears but tears of joy; I sang and talked nonsense, filled with a glimpse of things which put me in advance of all other men (Nietzsche 1969: 178).

One month later, in a letter to Franz Overbeck, Nietzsche complains of the "pain vanquishing his life and will",

> ...I am desperate. Pain is vanquishing my life and my will. What months, what summer I have had! My physical agonies were as many and various as the changes I have seen in the sky. In every cloud there is some form of electric charge which grips me suddenly and reduces me to complete misery. Five times I have called for Doctor Death, and yesterday I hoped it was the end—in vain. Where is there on earth that perpetually serene sky, which is my sky? Farewell, friend (Ibid: 179).

It is here in this intense and heightened state when the ability of saying 'I' disappears so that something exceeding take place: it is when the accumulating and the intimate gathering work of negativity is disinstalled and dispersed; when, exceeding the labour of the concept and exceeding the subjectivity of the Subject (that collects the manifold through memory and pain) there occurs the rupture of this very subjectivity of the Subject. It is in this intense state there may occur the highest affirmation of thought that transfigures our whole existence, and thereby redeeming our otherwise 'miserable limitations' of our ordinary existence. This is—painful such a limit experience is, for the highest affirmation does not exclude the most intense pain—what Nietzsche always desires. Very early in his life, Nietzsche was aware of what is at stake in his destiny, and what it entails, what will happen through him and what will occur: hence, his transformation of himself into 'destiny' of mankind. In the following writing of his early life, Nietzsche refers to such a limit-experience, which is 'destinal', the transfigurative-thought of highest affirmation,

> To further the production of the philosopher, of the artist and of the saint within us and outside us, and thereby to work at the consummation of nature...there are moments and, as it were, sparks of the brightest fire of love in the light of which we no longer understand the word "I"; beyond our being there lies something which in these moments becomes a here-and- now, and therefore we desire from the bottom of our hearts to bridge this distance. In our usual state we can admittedly contribute nothing to the production of the redeeming man; therefore we hate ourselves in this state. This hatred is the root of that pessimism which Schopenhauer has to re-teach our age but which is as old as the longing for culture itself. Hatred is the root but not its flower [...]: for at the same time or other we

> must learn to hate something more general than our individuality with its miserable limitations and restless flux. In that heightened state we shall also love somewhat differently than we do now. Only when we, in our coming and present incarnation, are ourselves taken into that exalted order of philosophers, artists and saints will a new goal of our love and hate be set before us (Nietzsche 1965: 56-58).

That for the transfigurative thought of highest affirmation of existence to occur (whose destinal character transforms one to the 'destiny': for this, the metaphysics of subjectivity of the subject has to be dissolved and disinstalled; that for this, one must suffer shipwreck and ruin and thereby become a monster; that one must push to the limit all the works of negativity which memory binds and pain gathers into intimacy to constitute the subjectivity of the onto-theo-logical subject. Nietzsche gave this process of de-subjectivization the name "depersonalization". I quote Nietzsche,

> Almost everything that I do now is a "drawing–the-line under everything ". The vehemence of my inner pulsation has been terrifying, all through these past years; now that I must make the transition to a new and more intense form, I need, above all, a new estrangement, a still more intense depersonalization. So it is of the greatest importance what and who still remains to me (Nietzsche 1969: 280).

Only out of this abyss of de-subjectivization, the 'yes' saying of the eternal return must be carried on; for, the eternal return does not make the 'subject' return in its self-same presence in the manner of, as in Hegelian phenomenology, the circular re-appropriation of difference. Eternal return is rather the eternal yawning of the abyss; it is the opening of the caesura wherein is affirmed the eternal difference, which cannot be recuperated once more: that means, only difference is affirmed, difference whose eternal abyss making affirmation itself possible; or rather, affirmation itself must be the abyss wherein difference affirms affirmation. One who wills this eternal affirmation must affirm one's eternal impossibility, for, in that must vanish the onto-theo-logical Subject. This is what Nietzsche alludes in a letter to Erwin Rohde, with a lucidity and preciseness. When he says, for example,

> It [Thus Spoke Zarathustra] is a sort of abyss of the future—something to make one shudder, especially the joy in it. Everything in it is my own, without model, kindred precursor; a person who has lived in it will return to the world seeing things differently (Ibid: 220-21).

What is at stake when the onto-theo-logical Subject disappears: the Subject of all subjects and naming of all names, the name that names all names which is constitutive of History, the name in the name of which all meaning and possibility of 'thought'/ 'meaning' "Reason' is conceived hitherto, the name of the unnamable supreme Being whose 'infinite negativity' unfolds its own genesis and telos, which causes itself and effects itself! What the eternal return affirms is the eternal return of this disappearing itself, the interminable death of the figure of God and the ceaseless dying of its god's successor—the onto-theo-logical Subject who is not afraid of death but maintains itself in "its utter dismemberment". But this death, the death that never stops dying, is the death of the phenomenological Subject of History. In Nietzsche's dissolution of his 'subjectivity', this death itself appears with its all-terrifying abyss. With the dissolution of this name called the 'Subject'—the subject that names everything because it names itself—it assumes what it cannot assume otherwise: all the names of history itself. In other words, it becomes multiplicity ("My hypotheses: subject is multiplicity", says Nietzsche); it becomes every name because it does not have a (proper) name; or, rather, it is the impropriety of all names that gives name to names. With the dispersal of the name—whether God or onto-theo-logical name of "subject"—names become the eternal simulacrum of their names, eternally assuming every names of History because it is simulacrum that grounds to all names, ground that absents itself in naming (in other words, presencing), ungrounds its ground thereby, all time, eternally.

Let us read a few letters Nietzsche wrote during his most lucid years,

To Jacob Burckhardt

> ... The unpleasant thing, and one that nags my modesty, is that at root every name in history is I; also as regards the children I have brought to the world, it is the case of my considering with some

distrust whether all of those who enter the" kingdom of God" do not also come out of God. This autumn, as lightly clad as possible, I twice attended my funeral, first as Count Robilant (no, he is my son, insofar as I am Carlo Alberto, my nature below), but I was Antoneli myself. Dear Professor, you should see this construction; since I have no experience if the things I create, you may be as critical as you wish; I shall be grateful, without promising I shall make any use of it. We artists are unteachable. Today I saw an operetta—Moorish, of genius—and on this occasion have observed to my pleasure that Moscow nowadays and Rome also are grandiose matters. Look, for landscape too my talent is not denied. Think it over...

I go everywhere in my student overcoat; slap someone or other on the shoulder and say: siamo contenti? Son dio, ha fatto questa caricatura ...

Tomorrow my son Umberto is coming with the charming Margherita whom I receive, however, here too in my shirtsleeves.

The rest is for Frau Cosima...Ariadne...From time to time we practice magic...

I have had Caiaphas put in chains; I too was crucified at great length last year by the German doctors. Wilhelm Bismarck and all anti-Semites done away with.

You can make any use of this letter which does not make the people of Basel think less highly of me. (Ibid: 347-48)

To Peter Gast [Postmarked Turin, January 4,1889]

To my maestro Pietro.
Sing me a new song: the world is transfigured and all the heavens rejoice.

The Crucified

To George Brandes [Postmarked Turin, January 4, 1889]

To my friend George! Once you discovered me, it was no great feat to find me: the difficulty now is to lose me...

The Crucified

To Cosima Wagner [Beginning of January 1889]

Ariadne, I love you

Dionysus (Ibid: 345-48)

With the affirmation of the multiplicity which now assumes all the names of History—including even Christ the crucified—the unifying ground of metaphysics is dispersed and displaced. With this affirmation of the death of God and death of the onto-theo-logical subject of history "the world is transfigured and all the heavens rejoice". This is the transfiguring moment of the eternal return, the aesthetically redeeming and justifying of existence whose precondition is affirmation of the abyss from where 'yes' saying must be carried on. Therefore, the eternal return is the abyssal thought, for it must affirm the death of god itself, wherein lays the limit of our possibility, our very impossibility to be able to say 'I'. With the dispersal of history, with the dispersal of the 'origin' and 'end' which makes history possible, the eternal return would affirm itself without origin and end, eternally opening towards an infinite future whose end cannot be conceived in the name of the self-engendering dialectical principle of identity. Hence, what is stake here is the opening of the closure of history to an infinite Other who is without origin and end, the displacement of the metaphysics of the subjectivity wherein history seeks its reason of being: henceforth, history would be delivered to its own openness once more, that means, infinite times. Would the name of this openness be writing, writing that opens itself towards its infinity when, supposing the Book of history has achieved its closure and at that limit, opens itself to writing? This is what Maurice Blanchot ponders: writing the opening, the opening of writing,

> The thought of eternal return at the end of history—the end of the Book and the beginning of writing: "let us suppose that, supposing the end of history, we were to suppose all these categories not abolished, certainly, but realized, comprehended and included, affirmed in the coherence of a discourse from now on absolute. The book now closed again, all questioned answered and all answered organized in the whole of a sufficient or founding speech—now, writing, there would no longer be any reason or place for writing, except to endure the

> worklessness of this now, the mark of an interruption or a break there where discourse falters, in order, perhaps, to receive the affirmation of the Eternal Return (Blanchot 1993: 272).

The thought of eternal return is the mark of this interruption at the closure of history and yet an infinite openness that names writing, that eternally affirms the faltering of a discourse repeating itself interminably. Is this not the question that is now to be asked at the limit of philosophy?

Thus we ask: what happens when the closure of history once more remains open like a yawning mouth, a wound or an abyss whose rupture marks the limit of time itself, and yet, opens time itself to its limitless eternal return that cannot be recapitulated once more? Would not time itself, now disjointed from both archeological and teleological principles, must become eternally differing and deferring because it would push to the limit any metaphysical determination of 'presence' to its own dissolution? That means, 'becoming'—as Nietzsche gives this unnamable name to this eternal disjunction of synthesis that must affirm the differential multiplicity—'becoming' here is not the onto-theo-logical synthetic principle of non-being passing into being and being passing into non-being; it is rather the limit of this principle itself; it is the disjunction of this eternal rupture. This eternally splitting apart of itself of every 'nows' would deliver every 'now' to its own forgetting, to its own unconsciousness which no work of memory can retrieve without further leaving something else to forgetting again.

Here the very metaphysical determination of time as 'presence' is at stake. As we have seen that in Hegelian determination of Being, Being is already always presupposed, metaphysically, as 'presence': Being presents itself to itself. It means, Being is identical to itself because of its self-presence; it determines itself temporarily (in temporal relation) as its own *arche* and *telos*: with this, the closure of Being is achieved. Hegel understands this closure as synthesis: Being is determined as 'synthetic' where 'synthesis' is understood as simultaneity of the simultaneous and non-simultaneous. Given that, we can ask, for example: how the thought of the eternal return is to be thought in (non) relation to the onto-theo-logical determination of Being as presence? The eternal return is to be thought as the interruptive non-simultaneity of thought; the eternal return, as the eternal return of the interruption, is non-simultaneous, and therefore is irreducible to its self-presence. Hence Nietzsche—the name through which we think the eternal return—is forever non-simultaneous or non-coincidence in relation to Hegel: Nietzsche is either too late to come with Hegel (therefore he can come only after Hegel, coming at the end of History when everything has already happened. The task remains, therefore, for Hegel the phenomenologist, only to recount infinitely this end of History itself. Since the thought of eternal return can be thought only at the end of History, which Hegel announces, Nietzsche comes only after Hegel) or too early (always already to have come, who is already unworking, in advance, Hegel's work of the negative. History, in order to constitute its beginning with the principle of identity, therefore always already must defer and differ and hence, it has already been its own undoing). Nietzsche is non-simultaneous, or non-self-presence, and non-presence to Hegel. Maurice Blanchot thus writes:

> Nietzsche (if his name serves to name the law of the Eternal Return) and Hegel (if his name invites us to think presence as all and all as presence) allows us to sketch a mythology: Nietzsche can only come after Hegel, but it is always before and always after Hegel that he comes and comes again. Before: since, even if it thought as the absolute, presence has never gathered in itself the realized totality of knowledge; presence knows itself to be absolute, but its knowledge remains a relative knowledge, because it has not realized itself practically, and thus it knows itself only as a present unsatisfied practically, unreconciled with presence as all; thus, is not Hegel, only a pseudo-Hegel? And Nietzsche always comes after, because the law he brings supposes the completion of time as present and in this completion its absolute destruction, such that the Eternal Return, affirming the future and the past as the only temporal authorities, authorities identical and unrelated, freeing the future of any present and past of any presence, shatters thought up to this infinite affirmation: in the future will return infinitely what could in no form and never be present, in the same way that in the past that which, in the past, never belong to any form to the present, has returned. Therefore, from that point on, for Nietzsche, the demand to live and to think (Blanchot 1992: 22).

What happens to 'presence' when the eternal return is only this eternal return of the rupture of 'presence' (of the self-presence of Being)? The eternal return, recurring eternally, brings its own impossibility eternally: its presence always already exhausts itself (it is its own past which cannot be retrieved in presence) and yet, because of its deferring and differing (not being able to be actualized in any presence) of its presence, its self-presence eternally absents itself from itself. 'Presence' here is thought as abyss: an immeasurable emptiness that marks (mark that erases itself in marking) the absence of time's presence; the abyss that eternally separates the beginning and end point of the circle and differs (and defers) their coincidence eternally. The beginning—*arche*—never meets its *telos*. The eternal return is, thus, not the accomplishment of the circular reappropriation of the same once and for all, but rather the impossibility of the circle. The 'Abyss'—'eternality' itself—separates, interrupts the meeting point of the beginning and the end of the circle. Deprived of presence, the simultaneity of 'nows'—the *hama*—would forever remain in abeyance: the suspended time of hiatus, a non-sublatable caesura! The series consisting the non-being of being (which is past) and being of non-being (which is future) would carry their impossibility of simultaneity to the nth affirmation; bereft of presence that alone makes simultaneity of the series possible, this rift itself—the time without time --is transfigured into 'eternity'. The moment when everything that must have already happened, and yet would never happen, must be thought together (this is the moment of 'eternity' itself) in the impossibility of their co-belonging. If the thought of eternal return is thought in relation to madness, if it marks madness --it is because of this: the eternal return itself is this abyss (of thought) which Nietzsche calls 'eternity' (or 'eternal'). Yet—here the ambiguity of the eternal return is more articulate for us—from this abyss itself, the 'yea' saying must be carried on henceforth. Hence, Nietzsche's saying—which we quoted as epigraph of this chapter:

> How the spirit who bears the heaviest fate, a fatality of a task, can nevertheless be the lightest and most transcendent—Zarathustra is a dancer—how he that has the hardest, most terrible insight into reality, that has thought the 'most abysmal idea', nevertheless does not consider it an objection to existence, not even to its eternal recurrence—but rather one reason more for being himself the eternal Yes to all things,'

> the tremendous, unbounded saying Yes and Amen"—" Into all abysses I still carry the blessings of my saying Yes."—But this is the concept of Dionysus once again (Nietzsche 1989a: 306).

Affirmation is possible only when negativity is pushed to the limit, when the closure affirms its own impossibility,and when the patience of labour (of the concept)—no longer able to work—delivers itself to the limitless 'worklessness', to the immeasurable mourning of thought, to infinite forgetting of itself. The 'Abyss'—what Nietzsche calls 'eternity'—is itself this forgetting that affirms the impossibility of the recollection of its origin, from which this 'yes' saying must be carried.

Let us dwell with this question of forgetting once more. What happens, if we ask, when this metaphysically grounding principle of synthesis itself is given its possibility by that which cannot be grounded in principle? This is because eternity would mark the limit of the very time that inscribes, and because eternity would not be less than time, because forgetting would not be less than memory. What happens when it could be shown that memory, in the basis of which the whole metaphysics is based (the Platonic ideal of anamnesis), is marked by finitude and can only recapture/recuperate what is already similar to itself, which already constricts difference-in-itself to the representation of difference ? Since forgetting marks the limit of finitude—the irrecuparable difference that is destined to transform itself to its own simulacra—would it not thereby mark the very limit of memory itself? 'Memory', which is the synthetic principle of gathering of the manifold, is itself only a fiction that seems to give us the feeling of identical (because it can only be in the case where identical cases exist): this is possible only inasmuch as various 'nows' is determined, contractedly, as 'hama'. If there is 'memory', it is not because sensations are indeed identical but that one affirms the eternal return, which is eternal forgetting; that is, only by forgetting this forgetting (that is eternal return). In other words, the eternal return to occur, one must defer and differ always this eternal return that means, one must not be able to remember. Only by this forgetting memory is possible. Every time 'I' remember, 'I' must always already have forgotten something else to be able to remember anything at all. That means that 'I' remembers only as forgetting. 'I' must not be able to remember everything, otherwise eternal return would not be possible at all, since the eternal return marks the very limits of my memory. In this sense, the eternal return is the experience of my limit of all possibilities; or, rather, it does not belong to any realm of possibilities that defines the onto-theo-logical subjectivity of Hegel. Thus, the Dionysian world is not history which self-consciousness makes possible through the work of the negative. Rather, the Dionysian world is the eternal forgetting that marks the limit of the phenomenological self-consciousness itself, ruptures history at the very moment of its closure, and transforms its infinite negativity into the affirmation of the eternal recurrence of the world, beyond good and evil. Such an eternal recurrence cannot occur within self-consciousness because its radical exteriority would eternally exceed memory all the time, eternally affirming its own difference and deference, irreducible to any metaphysical principle of identity:

> This world: a monster of energy, without beginning, without end; a firm, iron magnitude of force that does not grow bigger or smaller, that does not expend itself but only transforms itself; ...a play of forces and waves of forces, at the same time one and many, increasing here and at the same time decreasing there; a sea of forces flowing and rushing together, eternally changing, eternally flooding back, with tremendous years of recurrence, with an ebb and a flood of its forms; out of the simplest forms striving toward the most complex, out of the stillest, most rigid, coldest forms toward the hottest, most turbulent,most self-contradictory,and then again returning home to the simple out of the abundance, out of the play of contradictions back to the joy of concord,still affirming itself in this uniformity of its courses and its years, blessing itself as that which must return eternally, as a becoming that knows no satiety,no disgust, no weariness: this, my Dionysian world of eternally self-creating, the eternally self-destroying,this mystery world of the twofold voluptuous delight,my "beyond good and evil",without goal, unless the joy of the circle is itself the goal; without will, unless a ring feels good toward itself –do you want a name for this world? (1968b: 549).

What is affirmed here? Not the mnemotechnics whose work can be determined by a logical (or onto-theo-logical) principle of becoming, but becoming whose necessity is chance to the highest affirmation. Chance (that is outside time, outside presence) displaces that law of identity (law that assumes time and installs its rule in the name of necessity, universality and rationality) but this transgression cannot be once and for all accomplished. It is because the transgression of every law installs higher law, always other law (never the same one), which again would be transgressed by affirming chance (always in other form, other shape and so on eternally recurring). Eternal return is this never-ending return of affirming chance and negating the law of necessity. Willing the eternal return is both that of affirmation (of chance) and negation (of the law). Thus the eternal return has these two moments of affirmation that must be affirmed together in their discordance. Therefore, the thought of the eternal return—because it unhinges 'memory' (therefore from the burden of 'past') and frees time from the closure of 'presence' (thereby it does not become 'timeless')—can be thought as opening towards a future whose diachrony is already prepared by the dissolution of the God, and his successor, the human subject. That this highest affirmative thought, this transfiguring and transformative thought can also be of such abysmal thought—to the point of Nietzsche's own dissolution—should not be the thought of despair but an affirmation of our limit, and at the limit, an opening towards the limitless possibilities which the thought of eternal return affirms.

'Tarrying with the Negative'?

> Spirit is this power only by looking the negative in the face, and tarrying with it. This tarrying with the negative is the magical power that converts it into being.
>
> —Hegel (1998: 19)

Introduction

The problem dealt here is as old as philosophy's claim of its beginning. When philosophy announces itself, or, claims for itself to provide the ontological, and hence the foundational structure of community, from that on this question persists in a perseverance and in all its irresolvable ambiguity, namely: where is the place, the location or space—inasmuch as it is a question of installing the ontological and foundational structure of community- of literature/art in a community that must ground itself ontologically (in this way, 'community' is always already determined as 'philosophical')? We know that this is the question that bothers Plato in the *Republic* (and in certain other texts), the question to which Plato gives a negative answer (that literature does not have, or, rather must not have a space or a location in community: this has led Plato to banish literature from the Republic, from the philosophical community of discourse. Here an essential decision—a decision that set the whole metaphysical tradition in motion, and has determined ever since all other metaphysical decisions—has been reached. Whoever may have said whatever for and against Plato—many of them have written apology of poetry since then and some defended Plato—one must admit Plato's insight here, a tragic insight (it is 'tragic' because this knowledge has proved fatal for philosophy itself, and would bring disaster to any philosophical pretensions to found ontologically the foundational structure of community): that literature does not have 'space' or 'location' of its own, and therefore, it traverses every space and every location. Here lies the danger from literature: since literature does not have space of its own, being deprived of 'being', bereft of 'propriety' and 'property' that defines the proper, it invades, contaminates and vitiates every space and every form, every location and every name. Here lies the source of all lies and seductive deceptions, the immorality (because it exceeds every discourse of morality) and the terror of literature: the non-space of the space of literature, the non-being of the being of literature, the non-form of the form of literature—neither 'this' nor 'that' merely but exceeding all 'this' or 'that' (thus from all *ontical* determinations), exceeding even 'what' (thus exceeding the *ontological* determination of it). If this distinction—'this' and 'that' on the one hand and 'what' on the other—is metaphysical one, or, rather, if this distinction determines the very movement of metaphysics, then literature exceeds somehow philosophy itself. It is this that terrified Plato: that the question of literature is a question concerning the very limit of philosophy, and it is a question against which philosophy must measure its own possibility and ground. From then on– since philosophy has always been haunted by this question—philosophy tries to cure of this 'disease': from Plato to Hegel, it is this question that has never stopped haunting philosophers. Therefore, when Hegel announces 'the passing away of poetry', this announcement has already been decided from the very inception of philosophy. Therefore, this announcement can be seen as the philosophical exigency of the most self-preservative type: how to save philosophy from poetry! But Hegel's announcement has also been guided by the same tragic insight that Plato had about literature; therefore, one would be mistaken if he thinks that Hegel was simply mistaken about literature (for, one can ask: but literature is still written and perhaps more than ever? But that is not Hegel's point). Hegel's announcement of the passing away of literature is not the result of applying some arbitrary laws or principles which permitted him to draw such disastrous conclusion; he is rather guided by an essential metaphysical insight. What he did simply to apply the logic of literature to itself and to draw out the necessary consequence of this logic. And we know what this consequence is: literature's essential finitude, its ineluctable disappearance, its overcoming of itself, its exceeding of itself (because literature is this very 'excess' because it does not belong to itself. It belongs to itself only by exceeding this very belonging. Thrown outside of itself, literature empties itself out, empties out its own foundation and ground. Hence it calls upon itself its own disaster and death). Yet, Hegel did not push this logic to the utmost affirmation. The essential finitude of literature is affirmed only to the extent—and this is our complaint—and *only inasmuch as* or only in sight of *Aufhebung* literature into philosophy, inasmuch as the finitude of literature would assert the sovereignty of philosophical grounding. Here Hegel was doing nothing new but to respond to the philosophical exigency of constituting its immanent ground: the Platonic metaphysics is asserted anew through this ruse of reason.

What we attempt here nothing is other than pushing Hegelian logic itself to the utmost limit—the logic of negativity and *Aufhebung*, the non-proper of literature and its finitude—and at that limit, when everything is done and said, to show that Hegelian logic, when pushed to the limit, turns against the onto-theo-logical determination of metaphysics. Thus the logic of the non-proper of literature and its finitude, instead of reinstating the sovereign discourse of his onto-theo-logy through this disappearance of literature, would rather affirm the finitude of this onto-theo-logy itself which exceeds, in an indeterminable fashion, the very Hegelian closure of absolute knowledge. If literature would then be said as the excess of absolute knowledge, it is not because literature would somehow survive (would be alive) Hegel's announcement of the disappearance of literature (thereby to prove his mistake), but rather because Hegel did not know how much he was right about literature: literature's infinite disappearing, outside and beyond all dialectical-speculative closure. The disappearing of literature, since it is not posited absolutely as concept, is a non-posited disappearing, lengthened to an ancient past outside any determinable beginning, outside any recuperable memory, and to a future overflows the dialectical-historical re-presentation, since the future of the coming does not coincide with any speculative anticipatory representation of time. If this disappearing is not given to literature, nor to philosophy as 'possibility' and 'property', this impossibility belongs neither to philosophy and literature but to the outside; it is not a dialectical synthesis of being and not-being, for the relationship between the two languages is not dialectical either: literature, disappearing—disappearing that is not simply a 'capacity'—never takes the form of *Aufhebung*: it remains un-sublated into philosophical concepts; it never constitutes the dialectical-speculative closure of history; and thus it forever exceeds the absolute knowledge that puts into work the labour of the concept. Hence, this infinite finitude is never terminated; it never teleologically fulfils the satisfaction of absolute knowledge, despite Hegel's desire and despite the rigor with which Hegel pushes his logic to its utmost conclusion. Disappearing or 'death' if we call it, remains the impasse for the philosophical discourse: death that in dialectical–speculative philosophy is invested for condition of possibility of its ground, remains something *outside* all closures: an excess, a remnant that *remains* to be sublated, and which, not being sublated absolutely, never assumes the form of absolute knowledge; it refuses the subjective form of interiority by drawing one to the outside of oneself.

It is towards this thought of exteriority, and towards the remainder of the process of Aufhebung—this remaining outside of itself, and its ceaseless murmuring outside the closure of absolute knowledge—that Maurice Blanchot's writing point towards, calling us to respond to this outside, and to affirm this response: infinite responsibility, a responsibility impossible to affirm each time, and yet to be affirmed all the time. But this affirmation must proceed only by 'tarrying with the negativity' itself, the negativity that this responsibility to respond—responsibility that writing affirms—exceeds. Literature is this unnamable name of the excess that 'tarries with the negative' and yet exceeds it thereby.

Disappearing of literature

The exigency of the dialectical-speculative thought as the last philosophy—which is the onto-theo-logical fulfillment of the metaphysics of presence—demands that poetry must be a *mere* moment of absolute knowledge, and hence is to be sublated into the infinite negativity of Concept. If the Concept—the Concept of concepts: the infinite form of absolute knowledge—is determined as 'absolute negativity', it must have an immanent and intricate relationship with what it sublates: with poetry itself, which means that the poetic language must, on its own account, move towards its very negation. With this dialectical ruse of reason Hegel points towards the dialectical resolution of the famous "quarrel between poetry and philosophy" that haunts philosophical discourse from Plato onwards. The following is, then, Hegel's dialectical resolution: poetry must not be banished, poetry being a necessary and ineluctable moment in the destinal becoming of the concept through which the ontological structure of the historical community is made possible. Since this necessary moment of the appearance of poetry at its most affirmative possibility must also be its impossibility—because poetry cannot maintain itself in the face of death, lacking its 'essence' as identical with itself, poetry that defers and differs from itself—poetry must disappear. This is the (philosophical) truth or (philosophical) Sense of poetry. With the emergence of the Sense in its self-presence that guarantees Being with its Sense—for Sense is always sense of Being, for Being presents to itself as Sense—poetry, being not yet (absolute) Sense (or absolute concept) must disappear in its referring to this Sense: Sense (to be Sense) that negates 'not yet Sense', and thus sublates poetry to the fully self-present concept of speculative knowledge. The accomplished labour of the concept is nothing other than the essential truth of poetry, the truth of negativity as sense, sense in which poetry disappears while appearing in its utmost possibility: this is why, though it seems ironical, Hegel could pronounce 'the disappearing of art' at the very moment when Hegel himself saw in romantic literature the utmost fulfilment of art's affirmation, when literature becomes self-reflective and self-consciousness of its own becoming, which is none but its own disappearing. If it is true as Blanchot writes "A philosopher who would write as a poet would be aiming for his own destruction" (Blanchot 1995a: 63), so inversely, *the poet who would write as philosopher must aim his own destruction*, the poet whose poetry has become none but the quest of its own source and origin. It is the gaze of Orpheus that must not look back, and yet cannot avoid looking back, and cannot avoid looking towards its own abyss of origin so as to reach the blinding lucidity of self-consciousness and self-knowledge. Henceforth the question of the Absolute for literature is inseparable from its abyss and its self-destruction; the question of its possibility and origin is inseparable from the ineluctable necessity of disappearing and its ruin. Poetry brings its own disaster because its origin is outside its possibility, and its end does not end *within* itself: without either origin or end within itself, poetry only murmurs its own impossibility; it ceaselessly laments it's disappearing. This persistence of infinite dying remains to be recounted by the absolute negativity of the concept, which seeks to recount everything so as to constitute itself as absolute recounting not only of reading and writing, but its own recounting itself. The infinite dying remains un-recounted at the very moment of absolute knowledge recounting absolutely; it would remain unreadable at the very moment of the possibility of an absolute reading: the labour of the concept recounts once more. It recounts once more its mourning and in recounting it mourns once more.

The question that literature poses for philosophy is, thus, essentially one of mourning. What remains as remainder of the dialectical historical closure is a mourning un-sublated, a mourning for a past that is not within the immanent process of dialectical historical process of the Concept. Already in the very moment of beginning, the beginning falls outside it; already in the very positing of its presence, the presence is lapsed without return. It is the abyss of the origin, the unfathomable dark night which is the very source of the time that the dialectical-historical process presupposes; it is the night that Orpheus gazes into and loses his beloved.

Language and death

The Platonic question: what is the (non) space or (non) location of literature in the founding ontological structure of the human community, becomes for Hegel: when/what is the (non) space, (non) location of literature (or art) in the historical becoming of Spirit, which is absolute negativity? If the historical becoming of Spirit can be seen as the becoming of the fully constituted/fully satisfied sense of Being or Being of sense that must be able to present to itself in its self-presence, inasmuch as *sense* is already determined as *presence,* and if this self-engendering of sense must be the accomplished as the work of death which has form of *Aufhebung* as concept (concept would then be fully self-present Sense), then for Hegel the question is: where is the (non) space of literature in this becoming of sense inasmuch as this (non) space of literature must refer to this sense ? As one can see that whereas for Plato it is a matter of knowing and determining the (non) space of literature in the ontological foundation of human community, for Hegel this foundational structure of human community is that of the *ontology of sense* which is historical and processual. In both ways, it is matter of determining the (non) space of literature in the foundational structure of community, whether this structure is determined in the transcendental manner of thinking Being as essence (as in Plato), or, in the immanent-historical-ontological manner of thinking sense (as in Hegel). If history, as Hegel determines it, is the accomplishment of sense through the labour of negativity which must appropriate into its self-presence what it posits as non-sense, then (so Hegel asks): how is (non) space of literature be determined in this historical labour of becoming sense? It is in this context the question of literature would be posed in Hegel's recounting of the historical becoming of sense as absolute negativity. If sense is the accomplishment of the work of death whose infinite negativity makes possible history, then literature must disappear in this accomplishment of sense: it is because literature, which is *sensible* representation of idea, must give way to *sense* as its *Aufhebung*. Such is the negativity of language wherein Being announces its self-presence by sublating sensible into the sense of the concept: with the emergence of *sense*, the *sensible* must disappear. This is here, where it is a question of the appearing of sense and disappearance of sensible, that the problem of language-- as we will see soon that it is also the question of reading and writing—comes to announce itself: it is this that determines the disastrous Hegelian conclusion of the death of literature. Since literature is a sensible representation of ideas, and since this representation must always refer to sense—that means, its own self-consciousness—it negates this very sensible, and makes this sensible disappear so as to sublate this sensible to the fully constituted sense. Language is death whose work of negativity makes possible history as sense (or sense as history); or, rather, language *presents* itself as the negative labour of time (for history is this time itself). One can also say, in the same way, that this temporal labour of negativity accomplishes what constitutes sense as presence that *sublates* sensible. How the work of negativity (inasmuch as negativity is time) presents itself in language in sublating sensible into sense, according to Hegelian semiology? Here we will take up again what has already been discussed, in somewhat detail manner, of Hegel's determination of language as negativity in relation to time inasmuch time has already been determined, speculative-phenomenologically, as presence. This determination, as we have seen, doesn't anyway shake or interrogate the tradition of the metaphysics of presence but rather seeks to confirm on an unshakeable foundation. If temporality is introduced, in Hegelian phenomenology, into language as pointing towards the possibility of sense, it is so only *in sight of* this metaphysical determination of Being as presence. Language would be determined in such a way so that presence is secured in its self-presence: this is done precisely at that point in *Phenomenology of Spirit* when the problematic of time is posed, the problematic of determining the aporetic 'nows'. This is the very first chapter with the title: "Sense-Certainty: Or the 'This' and 'Meaning' [Meinen]" of the first part (entitled "Consciousness") of the three parts that constitutes *Phenomenology*. Why the problematic of language or the question of sense is treated in relation to the determination of time as presence? What is the relation of language and temporality, and how this relationship determines the movement of phenomenology (not merely of the book called by that name, but also what the book names, in which case both would be inseparable in their becoming identical)? Therefore it is the question of the Book—not merely the book consisting of black letters on white papers enclosed by the covers that gives it the sense of unity for the reader who is going to read or has already read—*but the Book as system, as discursive system of sense or totality of signification:* it is this question that Hegel poses here, which is also the problematic of reading and writing that must set the movement of the Book in motion (to write for Hegel and for us to read). It is this temporal movement—the becoming of the Book—that labours to sublate sensible into sense, it is this process that fulfils the possibility of the Book as fully satisfied system of signification. The language of time (or, the time of language) is that of negativity that sublates sensible into sense; language is this *passage* from sensible to sense, which is the temporal passage. This passage is nothing but death, and its work assumes mastery through the terrible force of the negative that makes history possible: history as the space where sovereignty of humanity must affirm itself by transforming nature into history. Language is, thus, determined in Hegelian phenomenology as the most powerful work of death that, through its work of negativity, destroys the given natural condition, which is thought here as sensible (here is not the brute nature of trees and wilderness 'out' there but animal nature that we are as 'sensible', contingent being) and through this negation, transforms it into the spiritual life of sense (which is self-consciousness that defines the 'humanity' of man). It is because of this, the problem of language is posed precisely at that point when it is a matter of sublating sense-certainty of sensible existence from the immediate 'this' or 'now' into the universal signification that will have the characteristics of "*Being in general*" (Hegel 1998: 60).

Let us go to the chapter under discussion. Hegel's point here is to show that sense-certainty of 'this' or 'now' cannot maintain itself its truth as truth (the sense-certainty of 'this' and 'now' whose essence is nothing but non-essence of incessant coming and going, appearing and vanishing), and therefore must sublate itself into the universality of sense, which is 'Now' as presence that maintains itself as continuous and simultaneous 'Now' in the very passing and vanishing of all non-simultaneous and non-continuous 'nows'. But how this 'Now' of sense could be determined as presence (because each 'now' does not presents itself to the other 'now' or even to itself as presence, that means the 'nows' can only be—that don't have being—non-continuous and non-simultaneous), for only as presence (as continuity and simultaneity in various nows) can there be sense (of 'now' as 'Now')? It is here—as to the question 'what is Now?'—the problem of language and writing occurs. Here is Hegel's statement of the problem,

> To the question: what is Now?, let is answer, e.g. 'Now is Night'. In order to test the truth of this sense-certainty a simple experiment will suffice. We write down this truth; a truth cannot lose anything by being written down, any more than it can lose anything through our preserving it. If now, this noon, we look again at the written truth we shall have to say that it has become stale (Ibid).

What has become stale when we look at this written truth that writes 'Now is Night'? It is 'now' itself which has already disappeared, having appeared—since it is nothing but this very appearing and disappearing—and yet '*Now that is Night*' is preserved, having written down the truth, which would continue to be 'Now' in all appearing and disappearing 'nows', ever present and continuous with itself, forever identical and simultaneous with itself: hence 'Now' that is presence itself as sense, because being sublated into the universality of sense, it will have the characteristics of *"Being in general"*. Hegel says,

> The Now that is Night is *preserved*, i.e. it is treated as what it professes to be, as something that *is*; but it proves itself to be, on the contrary, something that is *not.* The Now does indeed preserve itself, but as something that is *not* Night; equally, it preserves itself in the face of the Day that it now is, as something that also is not Day, in other words, as a *negative* in general. This self-preserving Now is, therefore, not immediate but mediated; for it is determined as a permanent and self–preserving Now *through* the fact that something else, viz. Day and Night, is *not.* As so determined, it is still just as simply Now as before, and in this simplicity is indifferent to what happens in it; just as little as Night and Day are its being, just as much as also is it Day and Night; it is not in the least affected by this its other-being. A simple thing of this kind which *is* through negation, which is neither This nor That, *a not-This,* and is with equal indifference This as well as That—such a thing we call a *universal* (Ibid).

How this self-preservative 'Now' can be determined as possibility for sense or sense as possibility if language itself, the written truth that preserves the truth, doesn't have the capacity/possibility of sublating, as the very act of negativity, of sensible nows into the 'Now' of sense as presence? Hegel thus goes on to say,

> It is as a universal too that we *utter* what the sensuous [content] is. What we say is: 'This'; or, the *universal* This; or, 'it is', i.e. *Being in general.* Of course, we do not *envisage* the universal This or Being in general, but we *utter* the universal; in other words, we do not strictly say what in this sense certainty we *mean* to say. But language, as we see, is the more truthful; in it, we ourselves directly refute what we *mean* to say, an since the universal is the true [content] of sense-certainty and language expresses the this true [content] alone, it is just not possible for us to ever to say, or express in words, a sensuous being that we *mean* (Ibid).

Thus the temporality of language—which is the work of negativity itself—serves as *Aufhebung* of space: this temporality of sense is, as we have noticed, already determined as presence that has characteristics of Being in general. "Language", says Hegel in *Philosophical Propadeutik*, "is the disappearance of the sensuous world in its immediate presence, the suppression of this world, henceforth transformed into a presence which is a call apt to waken an echo in every essence capable of representation" (Quoted by Derrida 1982: 87). To say that the appearing of sense is *Aufhebung* of the sensible is to say that temporality of sense (or time is sense) is the *Aufhebung* the spatiality of the sensible (that is given, natural and sensuous existence). Elsewhere Hegel says,

> The intuition—in its natural phase a something given and given in space—acquires, when employed as a sign, the peculiar characteristics of existing only as superseded and sublimated [*aufgehobene*]. Such is the negativity of intelligence; and thus the truer phase of the intuition used as a sign is existence in *time* (but its existence vanishes in the moment of being), and if we consider the rest of its external psychical quality, its institution by intelligence, but as institution growing out of its (anthropological) own naturalness (Hegel 1971: 213-14).

The 'Now' of presence which the temporality of writing constitutes itself as sense, is the self-preservative—and hence *Mnemosyne*—act that makes possible the unification of various 'nows' as synthesis; writing conserves the lost presence of sensible 'nows' and recuperates it, through the synthetic act of memory, into the sense 'Now'. Thus only by this writing 'Now' in *Phenomenology*—which is supposed to conserve 'nows' through the recuperative and the synthetic act of memory (sense is this memory itself, the interiorization of the 'nows')—that the unity of the Book of history or the whole idea of the History takes the form of the Book is rendered possible: writing inscribes the lost as retrievable presence, and through this inscription, the lost presence can be recuperated. However, it is only on the condition that the temporality of writing is already determined as presence, an essential inscription that conserves the sensible. Writing, then, would be determined as 'event', that happens in a determinable 'presence' whose inscription bears witness the possibility of the Book (the system). In that way, writing would be determined not only as that which inscribes, it is also something that is inscribed. If Hegel takes seriously the possibility of the Book (or system) as the very process of becoming Book itself, in other words the temporality of inscribing that assumes the form of writing, then the philosophical exigency of the Book not only demands that writing inscribes but that writing itself must be inscribed, or, arrested, so as not to allow writing itself to exceed the Book: it is because writing always already exceeds books, exceeds the book of all books, the Book itself. Hence the violent demand of philosophy—of which Hegel's philosophy bears witness—to arrest writing itself which otherwise makes itself fetish of itself, to circumscribe writing itself by determining writing as labour of the negative. Writing, which constantly unworks, must be held at bay by making writing itself work to accomplish the presence of being as sense, and hence writing or language is determined as the labour of negativity. Writing, then, for the Hegelian philosophy of negativity, is akin to death: writing is death that assumes time's labour which, through its act of negation and annihilation, transforms nature into self-consciousness; writing opens up the space of history as discursive system that closes itself up by gathering, into its self-presence, all 'nows' into the signification 'Now'. Writing assumes death; or, even better, death assumes writing in order to make secure the possibility of the Book, to preserve writing from other writing that never writes in presence as presence, to preserve death from dying that never presents itself as labour of negativity, to preserve 'Now' from 'nows' that have gone by and irremediably lost without return. Death is, then, for Hegel is the master over dying (dying that refuses to take form of 'event' in any determinable time of presence in the becoming of History); (Hegelian) writing is, then, the master over the other writing that never inscribes but erases itself in the very process of writing (and interminably and incessantly exceeds the Book). Death and writing (both have to do with time) is determined only as presence in Hegelian philosophy. This presence, accomplishing this presence, must be the work of death and writing. If in this way death and writing is onto-theo-logically determined as work, it is only in sight of this presence, whether this presence is determined as 'sense', 'Subject', 'concept', or, 'idea'. Writing is death because it negates nature; death is writing because it seeks to arrest dying itself (as writing is supposed to arrest the appearing and disappearing of 'nows' into the 'Now') by writing 'Now', 'This', 'Death'. Thus writing and death in their kinship are forces that must produce the 'world', the discursive world of the Book: only in sight of this Book there takes place writing in Hegel's book, and death inscribes its presence as sense. The accomplishment of the Book and the end of writing: this is the dream that Hegelian discourse nurtures for whose sake the labour of concepts will announce their role in his book.

When, or, at what instant of presence does Hegel recount the very temporality of writing? When the time of writing takes place (we would like to ask Hegel) and when, at what point of phenomenology, this time is recounted if nowhere but outside the Book, that means, in an unrecountable presence, exceeding presence altogether? That means the time of writing itself would never be recounted, since it exceeds all recounting and exceeds its own presence in any recounting. Between the written 'Now' and 'now' (which would have been written), *the time of writing itself has imperceptibly slipped away without recounting in the Book or the Book recounting.* Perhaps Hegel has forgotten to recount it (as if Hegel forgets anything)! As if Hegel, in the very act of remembering, has forgotten this forgetting itself: time of writing outside presence, this infinitude of dying in every moment of writing, the incessant dying that inserts itself between sensible 'now' and sense 'Now', the time-between which is no longer time but its abyss. Rupture, hiatus, and caesura: that breaks the series in-between, inoperation of the work of death, the non-presence of the cleft in the sense of the 'Now'! Hegel has forgotten to recount this absence of time-between—could it have been otherwise?—time that has never inscribes: non-inscription or exscription—of trace! The whole of Hegelian Book, the Book that is Whole to the extent that it must remember everything (therefore it assumes the discourse of History that remembers everything, that means, itself) and inscribe everything, has its condition of possibility outside it: in the forgetting and ex-scription, in the dying of writing and its infinite fatigue. The abyss of forgetting, that has already always rendered vain the power of the negative to conserve, is the perpetual flight from itself, from any inscription of self-presence by erasing itself; it presents itself only as erasing, and thus, belongs neither to the sensible 'now' nor to the sense 'Now', neither belongs to the absolute Night where 'all cows are black' nor to absolute Day where reason is rendered visible in its own manifestation. Hence the impossibility of dying is writing that belongs neither to the Night as absolute 'possibility' (because *Nothing is same as Being* in Hegelian onto-theo-logy), nor to the Day as absolute 'possibility': not being able to be inscribed in death's possibility of self-presenting, writing eludes the very possibility of death as possibility of the Day, the Day when the Book manifests its freedom and reason. Not being able to be Day, the infinitude of dying which is writing, persists its murmuring and mourning in this hither side of the Book, on this side of the Day, and yet, it gives philosophy its mid-day dream of arresting time as presence, of making death a power of the negative. Writing, which is neither 'instance' (it never presents itself in any 'now') nor an 'event' (it doesn't leave trace and hence cannot located at any moment through any recuperation), while throwing outside of itself because it is already exiled, it also throws itself outside the Book, and yet, calling forth the exigency of another book, other books in its trail (to enclose it), because it has not yet reached its closure (and would not be reached): in this way it infinitely defers and differs any possible closures, never being contemporary with itself in any presence. Writing is the deferral and difference of the Book because it never takes place in any 'here' and 'now', because it is never simultaneous and never contemporary with the written-negative form of 'Now'. Writing doesn't have time, would not have time: if the closure of the Book implies the relationship of the Book with the presence of writing that makes the Book possible, then the closure of the Book can only be its own absence: the end of the Book and the incessant-never-began beginning of writing! Writing can only begin incessantly, and interrupt the Book incessantly (that means the beginning of writing is forever beginningless, it has never time to begin, having already began somewhere, elsewhere) because the Book never ends 'here' and 'now' (hence it must end unendingly, it must die unaccomplished and all the time): the incessant cessation of the Book and the never-began (already begun) beginning of writing. But this incessant ending of the Book, and the incessant beginning of writing itself cannot assume the form of the Book, because the diachrony of both end of the Book and the beginning of writing exceeds the Book itself, the system of the Book, the Book as system.

It is towards this thought of the end of the Book and the incessant beginning of writing (that incessantly interrupts the presence of the

Book)—there, towards the worklessness of writing which ruins the very erotic of onto-theo-logy, that Maurice Blanchot's writing and thinking takes us in a movement other than the movement which negativity assumes. If philosophy always assumes the form of the Book—and Hegelian onto-theo-logy is the utmost possibility of this thought—writing, at the very heart of its labour of this Book, introduces rupture in this Book by introducing another language and another time: not the temporal language of negativity and labour where death would announce its presence as sense (where death would be determined as 'possibility', but another language, not of death but of dying, writing that is the infinite patience of time's absence; not of labour but interminable undoing of itself; an infinite opening of writing beyond the Book. If in Hegel's philosophical work death is constantly at work where death assumes the sovereign mastery of the human 'possibility' (where language itself, by the same measure, assumes the power of the negative to make appear what disappears through its power to name everything), there also occurs, every time such a possibility appears, the necessity not to disappear in dying: a dying without return and without profit, dying whose anguish no concept can represent in its self-presence. If Hegel could not avoid seeking the discursive totality of signification in the form of the Book, it is thus so as not to confront the eternal abyss of writing; if Hegel could not avoid seeking the historical totality of absolute negativity by seeking death a *possibility* by employing this possibility of annihilation (concept is death, murder of the thing that makes possible *Sense*), it is so because dying itself, its *impossibility* and its abysmal anguish and solitude must not be approached. This is what brings halt to the entire movement of the dialectical negativity, its 'blind spot' (Bataille who was aware of this. This phrase is his) that would haunt this movement, as if something that 'rings false' in this process. As Maurice Blanchot remarks,

> Yes, let us remember the earliest Hegel. He too, even prior to his "early" philosophy, considered that the two deaths were indissociable, and that the only act of confronting death—not merely of facing it or of exposing oneself to its danger (which is the distinguishing feature of heroic courage), but of entering into space, of undergoing it as infinite death and also as mere death, "natural death" –could found the sovereignty of masterhood: the mind and its prerogatives .The

> result was perhaps, absurdly, that the experience which initiates the movement of the dialectic—the experience which none experiences,the experience of death—stopped it right away, and that the entire subsequent process retained a sort of memory of this halt,as if of an aporia which always had still to be accounted for. I will not go into detail about the way in which, from Hegel's early philosophy onward, and through the prodigious enrichment of his thought, the difficulty was surmounted. This is well known. It remains, however, that if death, murder, suicide are put to work, and if death loses its sting by becoming powerless power and then negativity, there is, each time one advances with the help of *possible* death, the necessity not to advance any further, not to approach the death without expression, death without any name, the death outside the concept—the *impossibility* itself (Blanchot 1995a: 68).

Nothingness of infinite dying—writing that refuses sense and is outside the concept, nothingness that cannot be negated once again more and therefore would not assume the form of *Aufhebung*—this nothingness of dying that would not, thus, be a moment of negativity, and would not be a 'possibility': such is the writing of disaster, writing as disaster, disaster that writes—outside the Book, outside presence, outside Sense. If philosophy of the Book, the Book of sense, seeks, by the most violent and yet with what cunning, the Right to death, the Right to murder and annihilate, and assumes the sovereign power of the Negative—literature, or, writing, with its infinite patience and its most unforeseen powerlessness, delivers the Book and its Right of death to disaster and ruin, to the infinite dying and its eternal anguish. The terror of the negative and Hegel's tarrying with this negative (which wants to look death in its face and not be afraid of it), would, then, be delivered over to that dying without concept and without possibility, dying that cannot be tarried with, 'the impossibility of every possibility':

> But what would the difference be between death by suicide and death by any other cause (if there is such a thing)? The difference is that the first, by entrusting itself to the dialectic (entirely founded upon the *possibility* of death, upon the ruse of death as power) is the obscure oracle which we don't decipher, but thanks to which we sense, and ceaselessly forget, that he who has been all the way to the end of the

> desire of death, invoking his right to death and exerting over himself a power of death, he who opens, as Heidegger said, *the possibility of impossibility*—or again, he who believes himself to be master of un-mastery—lets himself get caught in a sort of trap and halts eternally (halts, obviously, just an instant) at that point where,ceasing to be a subject,losing his stubborn liberty,and becoming other than himself,he comes up against death as that which doesn't happen, or as that which reverses itself (betraying, as though demented, the mendacity of the dialectic by bringing it to its conclusion)—reverses the possibility of impossibility into *the impossibility of every possibility* (Ibid: 70) .

'*The impossibility of every possibility*': with this is realized the Book's extreme possibility and death's utmost realization—that of the end of the Book and incessant beginning of writing. With this is affirmed the affirmation of the future and the future of every affirmation. If writing has any relation with the future whose affirmation writing seeks to affirm, it is only because the presence of the Book, its self-presence is realized—which becomes the absence of the Book, the impossibility of its possibility, and the impossibility of death's possibility; it is because the closure of the Book is at once the impossibility of its closure (because closure would be forever deferred, closure that would not have time to close, because it never happens 'here' and 'now') and an opening to the future of writing which, having already begun, would affirm it. If writing has this essential relationship with dying—but not with death and its possibility—it is because it exceeds itself, bringing disaster not only to the Book of sense but its own sense, its own *sense* of disaster (there, thus, cannot be sense of disaster, but there is disaster of sense). Writing of disaster is disaster of sense and not the sense of disaster; like writing, disaster exceeds sense while bringing sense to its realization:

> Like writing (and in the same way that the quick of life has always already exceeded life), the cry tends to exceed all language, even if it lends itself to recuperation as language effect. It is both sudden and patient; it has the suddenness of the interminable torment which is always over already. The patience of the cry: it does not simply come to a halt, reduced to non-sense, yet it does remain outside of sense—a meaning infinitely suspended, decried, decipherable-indecipherable (Ibid: 51).

In the following section we will discuss in detail the relationship of writing and Blanchot's thinking of disaster: the problematic of the relationship of writing, dying and disaster as Blanchot thinks, and how writing of disaster can be seen to affirm itself at the end of the Book of sense—of which Hegel's system would be the example here—in which case writing would be seen to affirm incessantly, the disaster of the Book itself. Writing interrupts the labour of the Book, and yet interruption itself cannot labour: workless and fatigued, inoperative and unavowable.

The absence of the Book

Can one "read" Hegel without already been read by him? Is not every reading of Hegel always already belongs to his jurisdiction and occurs under his authority? In The Writing of the Disaster, Maurice Blanchot ponders on the impossibility of reading Hegel, or, even the impossibility of not reading Hegel, on the impossibility of this 'reading' itself:

> One cannot "read" Hegel, except by not reading him. To read, not to read him—to understand, to misunderstand him, to reject him—all this falls under the authority of Hegel or does not take place at all. Only the intensity of this non-occurrence, in the impossibility that there be such a thing, prepares us for a death—the death of reading, the death of writing –, which leaves Hegel living: the living travesty of completed meaning. (Hegel the imposture: this is what makes him invincible, mad with his seriousness, counterfeiter of truth: "putting one over" to the point of becoming, all unbeknownst to him, master of irony –Sylviane Agacinski). (Ibid: 47).

"Reading" Hegel is impossible if reading implies the anticipation of reading of that which is not "yet read"; for, Hegel's philosophy, being the last philosophy that must include or that already has included what has happened "already", and also includes, being the philosophy that assumes the "total" philosophy or the form of the Book, the "not yet" of all reading that comes after Hegel. That means, Hegel's philosophy, which is the last philosophy, must include in its totality what not only preceded him but also philosophy after Hegel: only in this sense Hegel's philosophy is the total accomplishment of all the labour of negativity, the Book wherein all the labour of signification has assumed the form of *sense*. Therefore any attempt to read Hegel finds itself already read by him, already finds itself within the *system* of reading and writing, of sense and signification, and already finds itself inscribed within the totality of its labour. Therefore, any reading, that must begin with the 'not yet' of reading (the future of reading), finds itself already nullified, negated, or, to use Hegel's phrase, "sublated" into the Book because it has been already read by Hegel. It means, in other words, this: reading has a relationship with future, future that is "not yet" of the system, of the Book but this "not yet", according the Hegelian speculative reading, *is* only to the extent that it is anticipated that it would occur or come to pass. Therefore thinking the *difference* of future (future that is difference itself), the *difference* of reading (because difference is reading, the reading of "not yet")—the difference between the Book (Hegel's Book) and its reading—is thought, through the dialectical ruse of reason in Hegel, *only to the extent* that this difference would be sublated into the identity of reading and what is to be read. The "not yet" would then be passed into the reading that presents itself in its self-presence; the reading would again assure, by the very means of its difference, the identity of the Book with itself, the identity of the Book and the hermeneutic of its reading. The "reading" would be rendered impossible; or, reading is allowed its possibility only to the extent that it becomes its impossibility *a priori* (yet this *a priori* can be fully comprehensible only *a posteriori)*. To read the Book is already to have read it, and yet not knowing that one has read the Book. Only at the moment of completed reading, through recollection that one knows that one has already read it. Therefore, the Book always takes memory seriously, that it assumes its form of discourse as History). Werner Hamacher notices this impossibility of reading Hegel when he writes,

> And thus every new reading of Hegel's writings finds itself confronted by the dilemma of inevitably figuring at a place already appointed for it within the text it seeks to locate, of already being grasped by what it struggles to grasp, of already belonging in advance to what it would appropriate understanding for itself. It finds itself already read by what it seeks to read. And every attempt to understand the structure of the speculative-dialectical system, every attempt to analysis

> it critically, even every attempt to ignore it and turn to something more important, must be prepared to recognize—if indeed the object of understanding, of analysis, of marginalization in general is specifically determined as a system of dialectic—that in searching to identify this determined object, it has already been discovered by the system, already been caught up within its circling coils (Hamacher 1998: 1).

And therefore, Hamacher proceeds,

> Rather that the dialectic of cognitive processes also obeyed by the exposition and critique of this philosophy threatens to become the very same dialectic which is articulated by the texts themselves. That the absolute philosophy and its philosopher, therefore, cannot be disturbed in its 'circle of circles' because every disturbance would already be an element of the circle or, at the very least, one of its tangents (Ibid: 2).

It is in this sense, as Maurice Blanchot notes, to read or not to read Hegel is under the authority of Hegel, because all reading that has not yet occurred, the difference that is outside the circle of the Book, that is at the threshold of the Book—*would come to pass* (because the non-being of the "not yet" cannot maintain its identity and must pass over into identity of the self-presence of Being. While discussing the problematic of time in the chapters 1 and 2, we have shown this in Hegelian dialectic treatment of time), would *occur*, in which case "not yet" of reading would not be able to persist, and reading that claims to be outside of the Book would be sublated into the Book itself (see Hamacher 1998: 4). Here—as in his *Logic* where Hegel demonstrates the passing of difference into contradiction and in his treatment of time in both *Philosophy of Nature* and *Phenomenology* wherein Hegel demonstrates the passing of the non-being of 'not yet' into the self-presence of Being—the "not yet" of reading is thought only in relation to the *occurrence*, in other words, as 'possibility'. The future of reading that would not occur, that does not take place and would not come to pass, future that is infinitely future, the Other of all presence and of its dialectical absence, reading as difference that would forever hesitate before the Book, arriving too late or too early but never being contemporary with the Book, difference that exceeds the very closure of the Book by opening once more to the possibility of reading: this impossibility, which is reading itself, would remain unread by Hegel himself . Since the Book must be infinitely, repetitively open to reading –without which the name of the Book, or, its Sense would be a mere fetish, in which case the discourse would be only a discourse, a pure saying and nothing to do with human experience—the Book also must, with the same gesture, introduce ceaselessly the infinite deferral of the delay of reading: it must ceaselessly open itself to the "not yet" of reading. This infinite "not yet" that would not come to pass, that would infinitely keep the Book open to "not yet"—the "not yet" that does not have the characteristics of "once and for all", the non-occurrence that infinitely exceeds the "possibility" to be actualized—it is this non-occurrence of the reading (Blanchot also calls it 'impossibility'), if there is such a thing, that Maurice Blanchot invites us to think. Blanchot's thinking of disaster—disaster as reading and disaster as writing and vice versa—points towards this absence of the Book which speculative reading and writing inevitably refers to.

We wonder here, with Blanchot, what the Book would *be* or the *sense* of the Book, supposing that the labour of the Book is accomplished (its absolute sense achieved, since that is its work and accomplishment)? For if the Book constitutes itself only to avoid fetish—that the absolute as sense, or name as this absolute sense must not be confused with any particular, sensible 'this' and 'now'—it avoids this fetish inherent in *sensible* (therefore also fetish that remains as remnant in 'art' or 'literature') by the work of negativity, by showing that sensible must itself negates itself and sublates itself into *sense*. Suppose the name "Hegel": Hegel the philosopher is the death of the Hegel who drinks, shits and looks at pretty girls (in his youth he liked looking at pretty girls!). Reading and writing "Hegel" would thus be the murder of this Hegel who is *sensible* (Since *concept* in murder itself): but this is, this vulnerability of Hegel in "my" (the reader's) hand who allows himself to be killed or murdered, only to make living Hegel the philosopher, who through this very reading by the reader (by me) by allowing himself to be destroyed by this reading, avoids the danger of making himself fetish. Hegel dies in "my" hand (in my reading) but so as not to be destroyed: he lives or finds resurrection in his own destruction and discovers his truth in his "utter dismemberment". Through his destruction in his reader's reading, he discovers his "life of spirit" renewed, and thus avoids the reduction of his death being a mere fetish—the reduction of death to "mere" death, fixed and lifeless. Thus destruction or death is necessary. Hegel here plays the role of imposture, allowing his sheer annihilation in the reader's reading: this is his *irony*, his trick through which he avoids his own death as fetish, this is only to make himself living once more so as not to be lifeless, fixed immobility of grammatical proposition (see Hegel 1998: 36-41).

Thus one sees that the reader—who wants to open the Book to reading, to open to its future, to what is outside the Book by introducing another time ("not yet" of reading) and difference of its inevitable delay, a hesitation before birth—ends by reducing himself an impostor, an instrument in the hands of Hegel the impostor who by allowing the reader this opening, this difference and outside, merely serves his own purpose by serving his own end: the closure of the Book by once more reading through the reader, thus avoiding being fetish of inert, fixed death .

But the question, however, remains. What happens, suppose the Book has accomplished its labour—supposing the work of negativity has avoided, by accomplishing sense, itself to be the fetish at being reduced to the sensible of the particular? What would be the sense of presence which has successfully (supposing that such a thing to be possible) sublated the non-being of what has already happened, and 'yet to be', and thereby, sense that has avoided being the fetish at being reduced to the sensible? Or, what would be the sense of 'Now' that has sublated all 'nows', and thus has avoided being the fetish at being reduced to 'now' of already gone or the 'now' of the 'not yet'? 'The Book', 'Sense', 'Presence': in not being able to say anything other than itself (since it must have sublated all that says of 'this' or 'now'), must henceforth only say itself—a pure discourse, a pure saying that says nothing, or a presence that effaces itself. The work of negativity that has accomplished this discourse—which is free from the fetish of all sensuality and sensibility, free from all the unreality of 'nows' that come and go—itself becomes its fetish which takes upon itself the claim to say everything, which in fact says nothing at all. Not being able to say anything 'this' or 'that', it would only murmur this impossibility itself: of its own effacement in its very presenting, of its reduction of itself into nothing but a mere discourse which claimed to recount the totality of human experience. The work of the Book that wanted to accomplish this—to show the effectuation of meaning in concrete human existence through human experience—ends by unworking itself, by producing the Book that effaces itself, that murmurs its own impossibility and its sheer absence from itself, the silence of all sayings, the silence of all meaning and all presences. This is what would eternally, infinitely halt the progression of the movement of dialectical negativity:

> Something rings false in the dialectic, but only the dialectical process, in its inexhaustible demand, in its ever-maintained completion, allows us to think what is excluded from it—not on account of weakness or because it is unacceptable, but in the course of the process's functioning and in order that this functioning be interminably pursued all the way to its term. All the way, that is to the end of history: the world completely known and totality transformed, in the unity of the knowledge which knows itself (and this is to say that the world has forever *become*, or that it is *dead*, like man, who was its temporary representation, like the Subject whose sage identity is no longer anything but indifference to life, life's immobile vacancy). At that point, where it is given us on the rare occasion –albeit fictively and by the most dangerous stratagem –to convey ourselves, we are by no means freed from the dialectic, but it becomes pure Discourse: that which speaks, utters itself and says nothing, the Book which destroys by constructing itself, the work of the "No" in its multiple forms behind which reading and writing, prepare for the advent of a "Yes" both unique and ever reiterated in the circularity where there is no longer any first and last affirmation (Blanchot 1995a: 72-73).

In other words, the Book announces, or says its own disaster, its sheer inoperation and unworking: the Book is delivered by itself to its impossibility; the work of negativity delivers the Book to the 'unemployed negativity' (as Bataille remarks). This excess, which is also its utter destitution, would not be a moment of the Book once more: a loss, expenditure without profit of sense! Avoiding the fetish of reading and writing—writing that is inseparable from the very sensuousness and its materiality (the sound of the sense, the sonorous and resonating quality of the sign)—would end up, when this avoiding (that often assumes the form of critique of German idealism) is pushed to the limit, in being a fetishism itself (Hamacher 1998: 69). The Book that claims to say everything, substitutes itself by saying nothing; the Book that seeks to present itself in its self-presence, substitutes itself by absenting itself; the Book that seeks to realize its possibility by employing its power of the negative, only murmurs its own impossibility: the end of the Book, and its indefinite opening for the future of reading and writing that prepares to say a certain 'Yes'! With the exhaustion of the Book's realization, and the historical transformation of Being that labour effectuates, there occurs—without occurrence—silently, the infinite fatigue of writing, its patience of time's absence that exceeds the work of the Book, exceeds the sense, or, points towards the outside of sense. Not belonging to the totality of the Book's sense, nor to the outside of the Book's Book, the worklessness of writing slowly demises the labour of the negative, and ruins sense. Disaster: the endlessness of writing, its effacing of itself that cannot be recuperated by memory, a dying that refuses the name of the 'event' and 'instant', a dying without sense or concept. Such is disaster: the impossibility itself—of the Book, of death and of the name; disaster that cannot be totalized because it refuses the concept or even sense, outside of death's possibility because it is not a lived experience, and hence cannot present itself as sense, outside absolute knowledge because it is sheer passivity and is worklessness itself, the absence of time's presence (Blanchot 1995a: 50-51).

Writing of the disaster

In his *Logic*, Hegel states his notion of the "limit" in the following words,

> In Being-there-and-then, the negation is still directly one with the Being, and this negation is what we call a limit. A thing is what it is, only in and by reason of its limit. We cannot therefore regard the limit as only external to being what is then and there. It rather goes through and through the whole of such existence ...man, if he wishes to be actual, must be-there-and-then, and to this end he set a limit to himself (Hegel 1975a: 136).

What happens to this "limit"—this limit as negation (or, negation as limit) which, being one with Being in its immanence ("we cannot regard the limit as only external to being what is then and there", says Hegel in the above quoted lines), man posits so as to actualize himself—when writing or dying, not being able to be actualized (because it refuses to be inscribed as a localizable, datable, determinable "event" or "instant"), exceeds the work of death?: writing and dying without name, without possibility, without concept and without sense, and not limited by this "limit" (Hegelian limit), does not have this "limit" for its limit. To think disaster would be to think limit without (Hegelian) "limit": "I call disaster that which does not have the ultimate for a limit: it bears the ultimate away in disaster" (Blanchot 1995a: 28). If writing has an essential relationship with disaster; or, better, if writing is writing of disaster, it is because "it bears the ultimate away", that exceeds the "limit" and is excess itself. It is towards this excess of writing, the measureless interruption of "limit", or, the measureless interruption of "presence" (because for Hegel,"limit" means nothing but this absolute presence)—the writing of the Other or writing towards the Other (the measureless effacing of writing of its own presence!)- That Blanchot's writing and thinking of disaster points towards. If writing does not have "limit" as its limit ("limit" as negation: the Hegelian "limit"), then writing cannot be determined as negation; or, that would not have determination as negation (that would not have negation as determination). Writing then calls forth something exterior to itself, something excess of negativity. But this excess (or, responding to the exterior to itself) is nothing but writing's own disaster: its infinite dying, its patient effacing of itself that would not be death's possibility. The writing of the disaster, thus, refers to something beyond absolute knowledge, beyond the closure of the onto-theo-logical realization of the Book; writing opens the Book towards that exterior, the other of all presence-absence, the other of the negative-negating subject-object. If the onto-theo-logical Book seeks to actualize itself through setting the "limit" as negation, then writing or dying that "bears the ultimate away" and that does not have negation as its "limit", infinitely remains outside the Book like a remnant still to be 'negated'; at each and every moment of sense, this remnant inhabits and persists, forever deferring the closure of the Book: this infinite deferral, which is dying, this nothing does not bear the form of "negativity" or "negation" that makes Concept possible. Would this infinite deferral of the Book that philosophy assumes as

History, would the death of poetry itself be deferred infinitely: Or, this would death of poetry itself be this deferral, this infinite dying itself without name and without concept? How would we understand here Hegel's famous announcement of the death of poetry?

Perhaps Hegel was not wrong to announce the disappearance of poetry! Or, perhaps it is not a matter of being right or wrong at all? But there rings something false in this dialectic. The question that I like to pose here is this: how the very passage in Hegelian dialectic takes place—the passage from the death of poetry to its sublation into the philosophical concept? As we will come soon, it is bound up with the question of writing and sense in relation to the problematic of negativity. I suspect that there something rings false in Hegel's recounting this very passage itself, something that halts the very movement of the dialectical processing of sensible becoming sense; and it is essentially the problematic of writing that seems to halt this process's becoming. Here I would like to show that this halt—inasmuch it is problematic of writing and dying—would infinitely defer every moment, from the very moment Hegel announces the death of poetry (not in his book on aesthetics but in his Book), of the philosophical realization of the concept. What inhabits and hence defers every moment of philosophical realization of the concept is nothing but death of poetry itself, and thereby—and this is important—rendering philosophy itself an infinite dying: measureless disaster of its work and labour, and the ruin of name (which Adam gives to everything), and the demise of sense.

We are asking, then: what happens of the *passage*, of that temporal becoming in the very processing of the dialectical movement itself when the death of poetry opens itself to the philosophical realization of the concept? Does poetry and its language (or writing) *necessarily* passes into (hence sublated into) philosophical language of concept, without *remainder*, poetry that would be totally transformed into the philosophical language of negativity? We also ask, in the same gesture, whether the relationship of the writing of literature with the language of the negative (of philosophy's concept) is one of unity, simultaneity and continuity, because *only inasmuch as* these languages are contemporary with each other which would make them continuous, simultaneous and unified, the unity of the world and knowledge is achieved, the Book would be realized and history be accomplished. Thus it is a matter of *two languages*: the language of literature, of unworking and neuter, writing of the time's absence, writing of disaster and its impossibility of dying on the one hand; on the other hand, the language of the negative, of labour and concept, language that transforms the 'thing' into the concept, the temporal language of presence in the name of sense. The problem is now this: if the onto-theo-logical Book is to be realized, it is *only* inasmuch as there is *Aufhebung* of the language of poetry into the philosophical realization of the concept. Since *Aufhebung* is a matter of death and negativity, the onto-theo-logical realization of the Book is essentially a matter of death of poetry: the language of poetry must inevitably pass itself into the concept, disappearing into the language of speculative without remnant, without trace. Hence, there is Hegel's pronouncement of death of poetry in sight of this *Aufhebung*, for the sake of the possibility of the Book.

But something *else* happens (without happening!) in this very disappearing of poetry. Writing and dying—that refuses the death's possibility, which makes concept possible—refuses to disappear once and for all, but keeps disappearing and never stops disappearing. While philosophical language, through the power of the negativity, seeks to transform the world by makings things disappear without remainder, by destroying the things to make them appear as sense; literature and its infinite dying, disappearing all the time and dying all the time, refuses to disappear without remainder. What remains to disappear, this incessant remainder, is nothing but *disappearing* itself: the sheer nothingness of writing other than negativity, other than death's possibility, the impossibility itself! Writing, dying does not occur in any 'here' and 'now', in any self-presence of the 'event' and 'instant'; it prolongs infinitely towards infinity, disappearing infinitely, and therefore deferring the possibility of the philosophical realization of the concept to that of indefinite future. That means: the passage from the one language to another, from the writing that is dying to writing that is death, from the language of worklessness to the language of labour does not occur in any immanence of self-presence. While the language of negation and death annihilates (rather seeks to annihilate) the thing without any trace or *remnant*; writing, in its impossibility of dying, makes this nothingness itself and this dying itself *remains* present in the very materiality of the word: nothingness made word!

Literature is, then, this remnant of dying (that refuses to die, therefore refuses death's possibility, persists in its very inability to persist or to maintain its being) that remains outside 'possibility'. This passage halts, or, interrupts the whole movement of the realization of the sense, by emptying out this *passage* from its possibility and self-presence: the result is the incessant interruption of time, the time of dialectical presence, incessant deferral and disaster, and halt of the dialectical movement itself. While the language of negativity seeks to destroy the thing without remnant in order to sublate itself into sense; writing of literature, invisibly, which is nothingness made word, incessantly retains the elemental depth of the thing in the very materiality of the word: the perfume of the flower, the rustling of the leaves in the wind, the haunting humming of the distant sea! "In verse", says Blanchot, "words become "elements" again, and the word *nuit*, despite its brilliance, becomes night's intimacy" (Blanchot 1989: 40).

It is in his "Literature and the Right to Death" that Maurice Blanchot decisively addresses this question of language in its relation to work and negativity, while pointing towards another language of dying and worklessness at the limit of the former, showing thereby that the limit that calls philosophy and literature in their *non-dialectical* responses towards each other, cannot itself be sublated into the dialectical language of negativity. This is because this limit itself would not have the characteristic feature of negation. What remains as this limit is difference between the two languages that Blanchot refers as common language and literary language. While the common language recuperates the thing, which it annihilates in the sense or idea, literary language makes this non-existence of the thing into word. Supposing the thing to be 'cat', the difference of the two languages would be:

> The first accepts that once the non-existence of the cat has passed into word, the cat itself comes to life once again fully and certainly in the form of its idea (its being) and its meaning: on the level of being (idea), the word restores to the cat all the certainty it had on the level of existence. And in fact that certainty is even much greater: things can change if they have to, sometimes they stop being what they are—they remain hostile, unavailable, inaccessible; but the being of these things, their idea, does not change: the idea is definitive, it is sure, we even call it eternal... But the literary language is made

> of uneasiness; it is also made of contradictions. Its position is not very stable or secure. On the one hand, its only interest in a thing is in the meaning of the thing, its absence, and it would like to attain this absence absolutely in itself and for itself, to grasp in its entirety the infinite movement of comprehension. What is more, it observes that word "cat' is not only the nonexistence of the cat but a nonexistence made *word*... (Blanchot 1995b: 325).

What happens with the Book that would be realized through the work of death and negation? Something, however, is remained to be negated and would not be negated once more: nothingness that persists, dying that never stops dying (Ibid: 328). The Book remains to be closed, the closure of the Book being never achieved; dying, writing that refuses to be contemporary with the language of death and negation, forever makes the Book non-co-incidence with itself, non-present in its self-presence. It is as if the Book, with all its power of death and negative, operating so as to transform absolute non-being of the night into the Day, that can convert even absence into self-presence of the present, discovers something that is stronger than it, which exceeds all its possibility: the agony of dying beyond measure and beyond the strength of preservation and elevation, incessant dying without sense!

> There is in death, it would seem, something stronger than death: it is dying itself—the intensity of dying, the push of the impossible, the pressure of the undesirable even in the most desired. Death is power and even strength –limited, therefore. It sets a finale date; it adjourns in the sense that it assigns to a given day [*jour*] –both random and necessary –at the same time that defers till an undesignated day. But dying is an un-power. It wrests from the present, it is always a step over the edge, it rules out every conclusion and all ends, it does not free nor does it shelter. In death, one can find an illusory refuge: the grave is as far as gravity can pull, it marks the end of the fall; the mortuary is the loophole in the impasse. But dying flees and pulls indefinitely, impossibly and intensively in the flight (Blanchot 1995a: 47-48).

If the onto-theo-logical possibility of the Book has been conceived negating–negatively in speculative language of Hegel, and if with this possibility, Hegel sought the utmost realization of the metaphysics of presence by discovering its origin in presence (in which case limit would be conceived only in sight of this presence), there is also another language that would, likewise, search its origin that makes this search itself disappear itself in this origin, effacing itself in its very presenting, attracting and fascinating itself towards itself, to its source and centre which is nothing but abyss. Such is the ambiguity which literature retains that exceeds every dialectical attempt to totalize it in the name of self-present origin and self-present telos, throwing itself outside any origin of presence. Yet literature, at the same gesture, seeks nothing but its own origin, and is nothing but this incessant search of an inaccessible and unavailable origin that always already effaces itself; and yet, as if it is yet to arrive, arriving too late or too early for absolute knowledge, arriving too late or too early for any presence to occur. In other words: literature—this nonexistence becoming language, this dying without possibility—attracts itself towards its own origin, the abyssal grounding or the groundlessness of origin, the abyss itself that makes literature itself disappear by itself, destroying itself. If speculative language makes concept possible by employing death, dying is the impossibility of the passage which empties out time's presence, thereby delivering concept to its forgetting: such is the passivity of the language, the language of dying and disaster that persists even beyond death (Ibid: 40-41). If philosophy seeks to ground human community, of human discourse and its meaning on the basis of a foundational, ontological structure of sense (and this structure is sought in language by making language itself the annihilating power of negativity), literature, on the other hand, delivers language to its origin that is never present, that does not work, that effaces itself, and thereby brings untold torment of rupture in the very ontological structure of community, as if opening an open wound onto that ontological structure of sense, a wound that only murmurs its own impossibility. Literature—this "nonexistence made word"—reveals, without any phenomenological revelation, the ground (which philosophy seeks) itself to be the abyss that constantly ungrounds itself: an abyss without sense and without origin, without truth and without knowledge. Disaster would be the name of this abyss.

Negativity

Both in his *The Step Not Beyond* and *The Writing of the Disaster*,

Blanchot repetitively affirms the exigency of at least two languages: language that assumes time's labour and employs the sovereign death by making death itself possibility of effectuating history (language that *tarries with the negative* by looking death in its face); there is, however, another language, that of dying that exceeds death's realization, the writing of sheer disaster and demise of the unity of knowledge, the torment of literary language in which things disappear to appear in their elemental depth, affirmation of a solitude that persists even in the anonymous and impersonal language of history:

> ...There must always be at least two languages, or two requirements: one dialectical, the other not; one where negativity is the task, the other where the neutral remains apart, cut off both from being and from not-being. In the same way each of us ought both to be a free and speaking subject, and to disappear as passive, patient—the patient whom dying traverses and who does not show himself (Ibid: 20).

To write is, perhaps, to response to the double requirements, the double tasks—to the language of the negative and also to the language that turns away (Ibid: 34-35) from this work of negative, defers any possibility of negation. "Write", writes Blanchot, "in order that the negative and the neutral in their always concealed proximities—might recall to each other their respective specificity, the one working, the other unworking" (Ibid: 37). While in the former, language constitutes the Book, the totality of significations wherein all particularities disappear and that reduces singularity of the sensible to mere moments of the cold, anonymous, impersonal Book by means of the tyranny of the negative, by means of a violence that destroys the singularity of the elemental and silences it to the nameless, faceless impersonality; the latter language, by affirming the elemental depth of the singularity ('nonexistence made word', as says Blanchot), opens the Book of violence once again, infinite times, to the affirmation of the Other, the exteriority of the Other that puts into question this violence. It is necessary to question this Book of violence or the violence of the Book, with its language of negativity and work so that an opening towards the infinite Other, to the language of the Other or other of language be affirmed who is dying infinitely and towards whom the Book must respond, each time, all the time in its inability or impossibility of close into itself, in its impossibility of achieving its closure. It is necessary—if it is necessary that the violence and tyranny of the Book be questioned and judged—to affirm the limit of the Book, in the Book's inability of closure, so that another language be opened up for the future to come, or future to be opened so that another language can be affirmed. Hence, the necessary for the two languages to be affirmed is essentially an ethical exigency—the language of the closure of the Book and the language of the opening of the Book—to affirm the other that exceeds the closure of all sense and all measure, of the concept and its tyranny. Therefore the two languages must be understood here as one of limit—but not of speculative-dialectical "limit", not the limit as negation which is immanent of being-there-and-then (as Hegel says)—in which case limit is to be understood as one of exteriority that exceeds any measurement of either Being or Nothing, limit that calls both the languages in their *non-dialectical* responses towards each other, limit that would be neither that of transcendental synthetic judgment or that immanent speculative judgment but that of excess beyond judgment, beyond synthesis, beyond memory .

To write is to respond to what excludes all possibility of response, to respond to the aporetic demands of the double tasks that exclude any medium of common measure, in which case the two languages can only be that of *discontinuity*, in constant *displacement*, deferring and differing the other. If to write is essentially an ethical exigency, a demand to respond, it is with the same gesture, to enter into a space that excludes any possibility of itself but rather one of impossibility of any space or any location that defers and differs infinitely. The ethical exigency of writing demands that one responds to the impossible demand of writing, to enter the space where death is prohibited but wherein infinite dying, in its impossibility, makes disappear the one who writes so that the Other, in his singularity, be affirmed, so that violence of the language of negative is interrupted and limited. In the very language of death and its violence, there as if occurs—without occurring in any present—writing that refuses to be enclosed in the Book, dying that refuses to die in history as history; writing that never stops writing outside the Book, dying that never stops dying outside history which itself cannot be violated and negated once more. Writing outside the Book, dying outside history: this is what Blanchot calls 'disaster', the affirmation of the outside (of the Book, of history), response to the Other (other than Being or Subject), refusal of Hegelian onto-theo-logical telos of *Aufhebung*. Blanchot's thinking of disaster that falls outside history can be understood, thus, as an ethical demand. Thus Blanchot writes,

> "Already" or "always already "marks the disaster, which is outside history, but historically so: before undergoing it, we (who is not included in this we) will undergo it. It is a trance, motionless transgression, the passiveness of the passive beyond. The disaster is the improperness of its name and the disappearance of the proper (Derrida); it is neither noun nor verb, but a remainder which would bar with invisibility and illegibility all that shows and is said –a remainder which is neither a result (as in subtraction), nor a quantity left over (as in division). Patience again –the passive. The *Aufhebung* turns inoperable, ceases. Hegel: " innocence alone is nonaction (the absence of operation) (Ibid: 40).

To write is not merely to make the world appear and concept realize but to respond to the Other, outside presence and being: "otherwise than Being", as Lévinas would say. In every discourse wherein is sought the realization of presence through which Being speaks its sovereign mastery, there also occurs in this discourse a refusal of this discourse, a refusal of Being's audacity to take upon itself its legitimacy, a refusal of its violence upon the Other. Every time there is the requirement to found community ontologically so as to effectuate freedom, and to realize history and its reason (which is the requirement of philosophy itself!), we must also respond to the other demand, the other requirement—to respond to the Other beyond history and reason, beyond freedom and sense, Other beyond the Book so that freedom and its sense would not violate the freedom of the Other, and would not destroy in its power of anonymity the face of the Other. If writing means exceeding the Book, it means nothing but responding to the ethical demand of the Other, and yet, the necessity for us so as to effectuate freedom and sense. But in that case it would no longer be considered as "my" freedom in the name of the Subject but in the name of the Other. Rather than the ethics of self-consciousness grounded on the negativity of presence where Being as universal is achieved, reading and writing points towards the ethics of the Other by opening itself to the 'otherwise than Being'. If ethics here assumes a kind of communication, it is to the extent that the communication through/in reading puts into question or effaces the closure of all kind (of the Book, of the authorial voice and of the reader's presence, etc.). Writing, reading: the infinite movement of communication whose infinity would be nothing but the infinite movement of erasure. As such, communication takes place without the Subject (the author or reader) assuming the right or prerogatives to communicate. If there is something like an *ethics* of communication here, it is rather because it is inseparable from the eternal torment of dying, the anguish of writing and the innocence joy of reading. Exceeding the closure of death, communication opens the Book to the infinity of Other, to the future of writing and reading and to a dying that has not yet taken place and that is yet to take place. In this way, the Book is judged by this movement of communication so that the closure of the Book may not assume the tyranny of the negative, so that the power and Right of the Book gives itself over to the affirmation of the impossible Other. This movement—the infinity of communication—would be the very unsublatable *passage*, which halts the dialectical process of negative. Literature is this *passage* where silently, away from the light of the negative, a *Yes* is prepared through reading and writing, unrecognized by the dialectic's owl of Minerva taking flight after the dusk. The non- relationship between the reader and author here no longer is the relationship of master and slave, engaged in the life and death struggle in their desire for recognition, but is rather that where one effaces himself, erases any possibilities of saying 'I' so that the infinite movement of communication take place. The ethics of communication, of reading and writing—and not the dialectic and dialogic communication wherein both parties mutually recognize each other—is, thus, not ethics based on self-conscious desire on each' part to recognize the other's desire for recognition, but an ethics where the Other is not reduced to a mere moment of 'my' reading. Blanchot's thinking of writing, his thinking of disaster and dying, incessantly seeks to respond to this ethical demand at the limit of the Book, at the limit of philosophy itself. Or better, writing, dying, disaster—in other word, 'literature'—is affirmation of this limit, limit that would forever exceed any dialectical appropriation of the same. It is because it is without its property and propriety. Non-proper of dying: *the writing of disaster.*

Conclusion (Beyond "Closure")

> The "basis of communication" is not necessarily speech, or even the silence that is its foundation, but exposure to death, no longer my exposure, but someone else's, whose living and closest presence is already the eternal and unbearable absence, an absence that the travail of the deepest mourning does not diminish. And it is in life itself that the absence of someone else has to be met. It is with that absence—its uncanny presence, always under the prior threat of disappearing –that friendship is brought into play and lost at each moment, a relation without relation, or without relation other than the incommensurable.
>
> —Maurice Blanchot (1988: 25)

> Community does not weave a superior, immortal or transmortal life between subjects (no more than it is itself woven of the interior bonds of a consubstantiality of blood or of an association of needs), but it is constitutively, to the extent that it is a matter of a "constitution" here, calibrated on the death of those whom we call, perhaps wrongly, its "members" (inasmuch as it is not a question of an organism). But it does not make a work of this calibration. Community no more makes a work out of death than it is itself a work... Community is calibrated on death as on that of which it is precisely impossible to *make a work* (other than a work of death, as soon as one tried to make a work of it). Community occurs in order to acknowledge this impossibility or more exactly—for there is neither function nor finality here—the impossibility of making a work out of death is inscribed and acknowledged as community".
>
> —Jean-Luc Nancy (1991: 14-15)

Instead of its customary manner of gathering into its self-presence the result of the research that has been achieved, and reaching the *telos* of predetermined, calculated research project which will finally deliver itself the closure of self-satisfaction and pleasure, this work at its conclusion rather hopes to point towards a thought that exceeds any sense of "closure" or "closure" of sense; it thereby hopes to call up the exigency of thought to affirm another time of research, to take up another time beyond the time of this work and beyond its space and its possibilities: in such a case, the "conclusion", being a convenient way of putting this work in front of the examiners and for the future readers to come (if there would be any), can be seen only as a point of departure, a new beginning that must begin incessantly and which must incessantly interrupt any desire for the closure of thought and thus calling forth, all the time and for the time to come and each time anew, the exigency to take infinite new beginnings, and to assume the task of thinking in all its patience and sufferings. In a certain way, this work attempts to open towards nothing other than the following: the opening of thought to the measureless patience of time that should be irreducible and irrecuparable to any closure of Being. If thereby thought puts itself into question (since it exceeds itself, exceeds its own measure and desire), and if we call this measureless patience of thought as 'the end of philosophy' (following Heidegger but also opening to beyond the 'Heideggerian deconstruction'), it does not at all mean end of thought; rather it means the ever new beginning of thought. Hence is the exigency to take up the task of thinking anew, all the time and for the time to come, so that thinking learns to affirm the time *to come*, the time of promise of the future, the messianic time of thinking. Thinking, the time of thinking, has this relationship with future, has this messianic sense: that in its measureless patience, its affirms the incessant interruption, or, discontinuity, a promise of renewing time itself through its displacement of all possible closures. If closure has been sought in the metaphysical tradition by thinking thought, or, community on the basis of death—and here Hegelian onto-theo-logical constitution of metaphysics is the example here (where death itself is put into work to achieve the interiority or its innermost identity of self-presence of the Subject)—the idea of the messianic, on the other hand, in the space of dying which is impossibility of work: it displaces the closure of community based on death's work, and renews itself by infinitely by interrupting the mythic foundation of community. Thinking community in this sense—" community to come"—has this relationship with dying: dying without name and without Concept, dying without being "event" and irreducible to its work, dying that does not present itself to any phenomenological consciousness, a dying that exceeds itself and brings its own disaster. If Nietzsche calls this community "tragic community", it does not mean thereby that such a community is based upon the celebration of death and sublation of this death into the universality of signification where all particulars would be subsumed/sublated into the universality of impersonal Reason; it is rather the affirmation of the differential singularity of each one of us, irreducible to the particular moments of universal significations, whether this universality of significations assume the institutional form of the state or any other juridical-religious form of institutions. Dying of the Other that calls forth the infinite responsibility of from "us", responsibility that affirms this singularity of the Other that would not be sublated into the immanence of my self-presence: mourning, beyond any desire for the profit of meaning, and beyond the work of death's effective realization in history; mourning that exceeds any self-grasping of absolute knowledge! Such a tragic community, "a community to come", that I would call a *community of mourning*, in which case it is neither a question of the effective realization of ontological freedom through rational institutions, nor is it to think a community on the basis of self-consciousness reached through mutual recognition of each other's right after a life-death struggle (self-consciousness that sublates its disparate, disconnected existence through death into universality of Reason). Mourning for the Other's dying is neither the production of my thought, nor is it an essence to be effectuated through the negativity of action; community, hence, does not have the essential ontological structure immanent in its possibility. If there takes place any communication with the Other—the Other whose ceaseless dying calls forth our infinite response, the Other to whom 'I' responds with an infinite mourning—this communication exceeds (such is the measureless mourning over the other's dying!) any mythic foundation of the Subject! Community, where communication takes places only as this measureless mourning, marks the very limit of time; and marking this limit, it exposes itself to its own disaster and unworking; not being able to constitute its 'interiority' as self-enclosed Subject, it exists only as this *ex-sistence*: exceeding any persistence and insistence. Therefore, community cannot be effectuated or produced (as the metaphysics of subjectivity seeks to produce itself in the onto-theo-logical figure of the worker); community cannot be work, or, even be the work of death. Not being able to produce itself on the modality of the onto-theo-logical production of metaphysical Subject, community exceeds the closure of History: it exceeds the closure of signification. If community takes the form of reading and writing and if this communication of reading and writing is inseparable from a certain experience of dying (we discussed this point in our last chapter) and mourning, this communication of the community would not be thought within the Book of signification. Mourning—mourning in reading and mourning in writing—in its essential relationship with thinking and communicating, exceeds sense because it is not sublatable in the death's possibility of work, in the work's possibility of signification. Mourning does not work; it is rather the pure passivity of the time's patience, the distressed time of god's absence.

It is towards this question of community that both Maurice Blanchot and Jean-Luc Nancy's thought of community indicates. Not a community whose foundational ontological structure would be assured through the work of negativity by the metaphysical Subject. Thus, Jean-Luc Nancy ceaselessly reminds us that the thought of community would already be closed when the metaphysics of subjectivity assumes the right to produce a community with the power of its negative; it is, therefore, the thought of community that is absent from the metaphysics of the subjectivity:

> The question of community is so markedly absent from the metaphysics of the subject, that is to say, from the metaphysics of the absolute for-itself—be it in the form of the individual or the total state—which means also that the metaphysics of absolute in general, of being as ab-solute, as perfectly detached, distinct and closed: being without relation. This absolute can appear in the form of the Idea, History, the Individual, the State, Science, the work of Art …(Ibid: 4).

Thus community cannot be the work of death and its effective realization, but rather, to borrow a word from Blanchot, its *unworking*: its ceaseless renewal through its interminable interruption/disruption of itself, community that exceeds its own measure and that would not be recuperated to its immanent interiority. As such, mourning would not be the constitutive possibility of the community but delivering community to its unworking, to the suspension of its law. Nancy would give a name to it as 'inoperative' community, and while Blanchot calls it 'unavowable': community irreducible to work and operation, community that does not promise its self-same ground.

I would have liked and I would like to think these questions further: thinking community and experience of mourning, to develop further the thought of a *mourning community*, community beyond the onto-theo-logical closure of subjectivity as work and as its product, and to think further how such a *community to come* has this relationship with a certain irreducible experience of dying. I would like to take these questioning further, which means that I need to take up another time of research beyond this dissertation, of the *time to come*, itself time of promise. These questions would be taken as points of departure, a new beginning of another research—of reading, of thinking, of writing through which a *community to come* would be thought anew, beyond this conclusion, which by no means a "closure" of thought in any sense. If there is a sense of ethics implied here—this very process of writing, reading, thinking and what one might refer to as pursuing research—it is because this very thinking demands another thinking of community, another philosophical exegesis, another language of time.

Bibliography

Bataille, Georges, *Bataille Reader*, ed. Fred Botting and Scott Wilson (Oxford: Blackwell, 1997).

Bataille, Georges, *The Theory of Religion*, tr. Robert Hurley (New York: Zone Books, 1992).

Bataille, Georges, *Visions of Excess: Selected Writings, 1927-1939*, ed. Allan Stoekl (Manchester: Manchester University Press, 1985).

Bataille, Georges, *Inner Experience*, tr. Leslie Ann Boldt (New York: Suny Press, 1988).

Blanchot, Maurice, *The Instance of My Death* with Jacques Derrida's *Demure: Fiction and Testimony*, tr. Elizabeth Rottenberg (Stanford, California: Stanford, 2000).

Blanchot, Maurice, *The Writing of the Disaster*, tr. Ann Smock (Lincoln: University of Nebraska Press, 1995a).

Blanchot, Maurice, *The Work of Fire*, tr. Charlott Mandell (Stanford: Stanford University Press, 1995b).

Blanchot, Maurice, *The Infinite Conversation*, tr. Susan Hanson (Minneapolis: University of Minnesota Press, 1993).

Blanchot, Maurice, *The Step Not Beyond*, tr. Lycette Nelson (Albany: State University of New York Press, 1992).

Blanchot, Maurice, *The Space of Literature*, tr. Ann Smock (London: University of Nebraska Press, 1989).

Blanchot, Maurice, *The Unavowable Community*, tr. Pierre Joris (Barrytown: NY Station Hill, 1988).

Deleuze, Gilles, *Nietzsche and Philosophy*, tr. Hugh Tomlinson (New York: Columbia University Press, 1983).

Derrida, Jacques, *Margins of Philosophy*, tr. Alan Bass (Chicago: University of Chicago Press, 1982).

Derrida, Jacques, "Economimesis" in *Diacritics* 11, no. 2 (1981): 3-25.

Foucault, Michel, *The Archaeology of Knowledge and the Discourse of Knowledge*, tr. A.M. Sheridan Smith (New York: Pantheon Books, 1972).

Girard, Rene, *Violence and the Sacred,* tr, Patrick Gregory (Baltimore: The John Hopkins University Press, 1977).

Hamacher, Werner, *Pleroma – A Reading of Hegel*, tr. Nicholas Walker and Simon Jarvis (London: The Athlone Press, 1998).

Hegel, G.W.F., *Phenomenology of Spirit*, tr. A.V. Miller (Delhi: Motilal Benarasidass, 1998).

Hegel, G.W.F., *The Jena System, 1804-05: Logic and Metaphysics,* tr. John W. Burbridge and George Di Giovanni (Montreal: McGill-Queen's University Press, 1986).

Hegel, G.W.F., *Hegel's Logic*, tr. William Wallace (Oxford: Clarendon Press, 1975a).

Hegel, G.W.F., *Aesthetics*, tr. T.M. Knox (Oxford: Clarendon Press, 1975b).

Hegel, G.W.F., *Hegel's Philosophy of Mind*, tr. A.V. Miller (Oxford: Clarendon Press, 1971).

Hegel, G.W.F., *Philosophy of Nature*, tr. A.V. Miller (Oxford: Clarendon Press, 1970).

Heidegger, Martin, *Nietzsche,* ed. David Farrell Krell (San Francisco: Harper and Row, 1991).

Heidegger, Martin, *Ontology: The Hermeneutic of Facticity*, tr. John Von Buren (Bloomington: Indiana University Press, 1999).

Heidegger, Martin, *Pathmarks*, tr. William McNeill (Cambridge: Cambridge University Press, 1998).

Heidegger, Martin, *Basic Writings*, ed. David Farrell Krell (London and Henley: Routledge and Kegan Paul, 1978).

Heidegger, Martin, *Poetry, Language, Thought*, tr. Albert Hofstadter (New York: Harper and Row, 1975a).

Heidegger, Martin, *The End of Philosophy*, tr. Joan Stambaugh (London: Souvenir Press Ltd, 1975b).

Heidegger, Martin, *Early Greek Thinking*, tr. David Farell Krell and Frank Capuzzi (New York: Harper and Row: 1975c).

Heidegger, Martin, *Identity and Difference*, tr. Joan Stambaugh (New York: Harper and Row, 1969).

Heidegger, Martin, *The Question of Being*, tr. Jean T. Wilde (London: Vision, 1959).

Hume, David, *A Treatise of Human Nature*, ed. L.A. Selby-Bigge (Oxford: Clarendon Press, 1978).

Husserl, Edmund, "The Phenomenology of Internal Time Consciousness" in *Husserl: Shorter Works*, ed. Peter McCormick and Frederick A. Elliston (Indiana: University of Notre Dame Press and The Harvester Press, 1981), pp. 277-293.

Hyppolite, Jean, *Logic and Existence*, tr. Leonard Lawlor and Amit Sen (Albany: State University of New York Press, 1997).

Klossowski, Pierre, *Nietzsche and the Vicious Circle*, tr. Daniel W. Smith (London: The Athlone Press, 1997).

Lacoue-Labarthe, Philippe, *Typography: Mimesis, Philosophy, Politics*, tr. Stanford: Stanford University Press, 1998).

Lacoue-Labarthe, Philippe, *The Subject of Philosophy*, tr. T. Trezise et al (Minneapolis: Minnesota University Press, 1993).

Lévinas, Emmanuel, *Is It Righteous To Be? Interviews with Emmanuel Lévinas*, ed. Jill Robbins (Stanford, California: Stanford University Press, 2001).

Lévinas, Emmanuel, *God, Death and Time*, tr. Bettina Bergo (Stanford: Stanford University Press, 2000).

Lévinas, Emmanuel, *Otherwise Than Being or Beyond Essence*, tr. A. Lingis (Dordrecht: Kluwer Academic, 1991).

Lévinas, Emmanuel, "Trace of the Other" in *Deconstruction in Context*, ed. Mark Taylor (Chicago and London: University of Chicago Press, 1986) pp. 345-354.

Lévinas, Emmanuel, *Totality and Infinity: An Essay on Exteriority*, tr. Alphonso Lingis (Pittsburgh, Pennsylvania: Duquesne University Press, 1969).

Nancy, Jean-Luc, *Birth to Presence*, tr. Brian Holmes & Others (Stanford: Stanford University Press, 1993).

Nancy, Jean-Luc, *The Inoperative Community*, tr. Peter Connor et al (Minneapolis: University of Minnesota Press, 1991).

Nietzsche, Friedrich, *Thus Spoke Zarathustra*, tr. Walter Kaufmann (New York: The Modern Library, 1995).

Nietzsche, Friedrich, *Human, All too Human*, tr. Marion Faber and Stephen Lehmann (London: Penguin Books, 1994).

Nietzsche, Friedrich, *On the Genealogy of Morals* and *Ecce Homo*, tr. Walter Kaufmann (New York: Vintage Books, 1989).

Nietzsche, Friedrich, *Beyond Good and Evil*, tr. Walter Kaufmann (New York: Vintage Books, 1989).

Nietzsche, Friedrich, *Daybreak*, tr. R.J. Hollingdale (Cambridge: Cambridge University Press, 1982).

Nietzsche, Friedrich, *Ecce Homo*, tr. R.J. Hollingdale (London: Penguin Books, 1979).

Nietzsche, Friedrich, *The Gay Science*, tr. Walter Kaufmann (New York: Vintage Books, 1974).

Nietzsche, Friedrich, *Selected Letters of Friedrich Nietzsche*, tr. Christopher Middleton (Chicago and London: University of Chicago Press, 1969).

Nietzsche, Friedrich, *Twilight of the Idols and The Anti-Christ*, tr. R.J. Hollingdale (Harmondsworth: Penguin Books, 1968a).

Nietzsche, Friedrich, *The Will to Power*, tr. Walter Kaufmann and R.J. Hollingdale (New York: Vintage Books, 1968b).

Nietzsche, Friedrich, *Schopenhauer as Educator*, tr. James W. Hillesheim and Malcolm R. Simpson (Chicago: Gateway Editions, 1965).

Plato, *Selected Dialogues*, tr. Benjamin Jowett (New York: Modern Library, 2001).